ENVIRONMENTAL EDUCATION
Problems and Prospects

ENVIRONMENTAL EDUCATION
PROBLEMS AND PROSPECTS

Editors

Prof. Ramesh Ghanta,

Principal, Institution of Advanced Study in Education
Dean Faculty of Education, Kakatiya University,
Warangal- 506010, Andhra Pradesh.

Dr. Bhaskara Rao Digumarti

R.V.R. College of Education
Guntur-522 006
Andhra Pradesh.

Discovery Publishing House

New Delhi-1100 02

First Published – 1998

Reprinted – 2017

ISBN: 978-81-7141-423-9

Environmental Education
Problems and Prospects

Published by:

DISCOVERY PUBLISHING HOUSE PVT. LTD.
4383/4B, Ansari Road Darya Ganj
New Delhi - 110 002 (India)
Phone: +91-11-23279245, 43596064-65
Fax: +91-11-23253475
E-mail: discoverypublishinghouse@gmail.com
sales@discoverypublishinggroup.com
web: www.discoverypublishinggroup.com

Printed at:
Infinity Imaging Systems
Delhi

PREFACE

Man, as a part and parcel of the environment, has to recognise the role and importance of environment in order to protect it and to get protection from it, for this, he needs environmental education as 'the environmental education is the process of recognising values and classifying facts in order to develop skills and attitudes necessary to understand and appreciate the inter- relatedness of man, his culture and his biophysical surrounding', and as it also 'entails practice in decision making and self formulation of a code of behaviour about issues concerning to environmental quality'.

Recognising the importance of environmental education, we have included the articles on various issues concerned to environment and environmental education which will make the readers aware of the need of the protection of nature and its resources in order to save the mankind from the natural and man-made disasters. The diversified views, discussions, strategies and information on environmental education will make the readers respond to the environmental issues. This book will be of great use to teachers, students, scientists, researchers and social service activists.

Prof. G. Ramesh
Dr. D. Bhaskara Rao
5th June 1998
The World Environment Day

CONTENTS

CONTRIBUTORS

1. **Prof. Anjaneyulu, Y.**
Head, Centre for Environment
I. P. G. S. R.
J.N.T. University
Hyderabad- 500 028

2. **Prof. Appa Rao, B. V.**
Department of Chemistry
Regional Engineering College
Warangal- 506 004

3. **Dr. Aruna, G.**
Reader in Education
St. Joseph's College of Education for Women
Guntur- 522 001

4. **Dr. Bhaskara Rao D.**
R. V. R. College of Education
Nagarjuna University
Guntur- 522006

5. **Dr. Bimal Charan Swain**
Reader in Education
J. N. Government College
Parighat
Arunachal Pradesh

6. **Dr. Chauhan, C. P. S.**
Reader in Education
Aligarh Muslim University
Aligarh

7. **Mrs. Deepika**
Lecturer
Fatima College of Education
Kazipet, Warangal- 506 009

8. **Mr. Dutt, B. S. V.**
A. P. S. W. Residential College/ School
Thriruvuru, Krishna District, A.P.

9. **Prof. J. S. Grewal**
Regional Institute of Education
Shyamala Hills
Bhopal-462 013

10. **Dr. Kaiser Jamil**
Head, Biology Division
I. I. C. T.
Hyderabad-500 007

11. **Dr. Lakhman, N**
Madras

12. Prof. Marlow Ediger
Division of Education
Trumann State University
Route 2, Box 38
Kirksville, Missouri
USA

13. **Dr. Mrunalini, T.**
Lecturer in Education
Osmania University,
Hyderabad- 500007

14. **Prof. P. Mohan Rao**
Principal
Institution of Advanced Study in Education
Andhra University
Visakhapatnam

15. **Dr. Prameela Devi, Y.**
Reader
Environmental Biology Research Laboratory
Department of Zoology
Kakatiya University
Warangal -506 009

16. **Mrs. Rajalakshmi Das**
Lecturer in Education
J. N. Government College
Pasighat, Arunachal Pradesh.

17. **Dr. Rama Krishna, A.**
Lecturer in Education
Institution of Advanced Study in Education
Osmania University
Hyderabad- 500 007

18. **Prof. Ramesh, G.**
Dean, Faculty of Education
Kakatiya University
Warangal-506 009

19. **Dr. Ramnath Kishan, N.**
Reader in Education
Institution, of Advanced Study in Education
Kakatiya University
Warangal -506 009

20. **Dr. Ranga Rao, R.**
Lecturer in Telugu Education
A. J. College of Education
Machilipatnam- 521 001
Krishna Dt, A.P.

21. **Dr. Sambasiva Rao, K. R. S.**
Department of Zoology
Nagarjuna University
Nagarjuna Nagar- 522 510
Guntur District

22. **Prof. Satyavathi, A.**
Institution of Advanced Study in Education
S. P. Mahila University
Tirupati -517 502

23. **Dr. Seetha Rama Raju, P. V.**
Lecturer in Social Studies
D. N. R. College of Education
Bhimavaram- 534 202

24. **Dr. Sharma, K**
New Delhi

25. **Mr. N. Siva Ram Prasad**
Department of Zoology
Junior College
Inkollu Post
Paruchur Mandal,
Prakasam Dist., A. P.

26. **Prof. Sarma, V. B. B.**
Head, Department of Education
Osmani University
Hyderabad-500 007

27. **Mrs. Sridevi, Y.**
Research Scholar
Department of Zoology
Nagarjuna University
Nagarjuna Nagar- 522 510
Guntur Dist.

28. **Dr. Swamy, A. V. V. S.**
Reader
Nagarjuna University
Nagarjuna Nagar- 522 510
Guntur, Dist.

29. **Dr. Vijaya Lakshmi, G.**
Reader
Institution of Advanced Study in Education
S. P. Mahila University
Tirupati- 517502

30. **Dr. Vijaya Lakshmi, R.**
Reader
Institution of Advanced Study in Education
S. P. Mahila University
Tirupati- 517 502

31. **Dr. Vikram Reddy, M.**
Reader in Zoology
Kakatiya University
Warangal -506 009

32. **Dr. Viveka Vardhani, V.**
Reader in Zoology
Nagarjuna University
Nagarjuna Nagar-522 510
Guntur Dist.
Andhra Pradesh.

1

ENVIRONMENTAL EDUCATION THE NEED AND THE CHALLENGE

Prof. G. Ramesh
Dean. Faculty of Education
Kakatiya University.
Warangal, A.P.

Today man is living in a world of crises. The social, economic, political and value crises are some of the threats which the humanity faces and these threats are quite alarming. Added to this, in the recent decades, the environmental crisis has become another important factor which has made everyone in the world to think of its gravity. Though the environmental dimenson has its own history, it has gained prominence in the recent past due to several reasons such as urbanisation, industrialisation, automation and population explosion, along with pollution, acidrains, gas leaks, nuclear disasters which have made man a helpless victim. In this background several international organisations including some Non-Governmental organistions have started working on the sustainability of environment and ecological balance. In this direction a large number of workshops, seminars and meetings have been conducted. Among these intellectual experiences we may cite a few like the workshop held in Belgrade on environmental education in 1975, the first inter governmental conference on environment education held in Tibilisi, former USSR, 1977, Tibilisi plus ten conference (1987) held in Moscow and more particularly the Earth Summit which took place in Rio de Janeiro in 1992 which was attended by about 120 heads of state and government together with delegates from over 170 countries. Several important documents were signed at the summit, representing the beginning of a long process of interpretating, responding to and implementing recommendations and agreements designed to change the future of this planet. The centre piece of the Rio agreement is known as Agenda 21, a major action programme setting out what nations should do to achieve sustainable development in the 21st century. There are implications for environmental education throughout this document, but of particular significance, the chapter 36 aims at promoting education, public awareness and training. One of the key outcomes of the Rio conference for educators is the recommendation that environmental and development education should be incorporated as an essential part of learning, within both formal and non-formal education streams. A proposal is made that Governments should strive to update or prepare strategies aimed at integrating environment and development as a cross cutting issue into education at all levels within the next three years.

The European Community has also been active in the environmental education debate. The 1988 meeting of the Council of the European Community agreed on the need to take concrete steps for the promotion of environmental education, so that this can be intensified in a comprehensive way throughout the community. A resolution on environmental education was adopted with the following objective.

"The objective of environmental education is to increase the public awareness of the problems in this field as well as possible solutions and to lay the foundation for a fully informed and active participation of the individual in the protection of the environment and the prudent and rational use of natural resources."

Further, it was resolved that member states would make every effort to implement certain measures including the promotion of environmental education in all sectors of education..giving consideration to the basic aims of environmental education when drawing up curricula...taking appropriate measures to develop teacher knowledge of environmental matters in the context of their initial and in-service training.

Good environmental education, like any good education, must lead students out and on from their immediate perceptions and experience to a wider understanding. It must develop their capacity. None of that happens by chance. A number of subjects and aspects of the school curriculum deal with matters to do with the interplay between man and his environment. Pupils must first learn about natural phenomena in order to understand complex environmental matters. The importance of environmental education is that it sensitises us to the causes and effects of problems, of which for long, we have been only dimly aware. The enviornment involves our children's future and many already know that we must encourage them to think positively about it.

As a result of international initiatives a broad consensus has emerged on the principles and objectives of environmental education. They are:

—To foster clear awarness of and concern about economic, social, political and ecological interdependence in urban and rural areas.

—To provide every person with opportunities to acquire the knowledge values, attitudes, commitment and skills needed to protect and improve the environment.

To create new patterns of behaviour of individuals, groups and society as a whole towards the environment.

Environmental education should provide experience of problem solving, decision making and participation, with consideration based on ecological, political, economic, social, acsthetic and ethical aspects. It is also about promoting chages in behaviour that will help solve existing problems relating to the environment and to avoid the creation of new ones.

The ultimate aim of Environmental Education is to formulate a responsible attitude towards the sustainable development of planet earth, an appreciation of its beauty and an asumption of an environmental ethic. To fulfill this aim every school needs adequate arrangements for planning and implementing successful programmes of work and teaching and learning tasks.

Planning for the inclusion of environmental education in the curriculum needs to take into account of the three inter-linked components which comprise the theme:

- education about environment

- education for the environment

- education in or through environment

In our coutnry too, people, concious of the future survival of the society, initiated number of activities to highlight the importance of ecological balance for the sustainable development of the human race. In addition to the several measures initiated by the state in this direction,there has been impressive participation of non-governmental organisations with commendable activism and involvement. The most noteworthy movements like the Chipko and the Narmada Bachao.. have entered the consciousness of the people in general radically affecting their attitude towards environment.

This is what the Chainese say about the need to educate: " If you plan for a year plant rice, if you plan for the years, plant trees, but if you plan for a century educate the people. With this, we can say that educate the people about environment to protect the human reace and the planet Earth.

2

ENVIRONMENTAL EDUCATION

Prof. P. Mohan Rao
Department of Education,
Andhra University,
Visakhapatnam.

Environmental conservation is the axis for the economic well-being and the peaceful existance of humanity on the surface of the Earth. Hither to the need and importance of environment have not been realised by the people. But the fast development of science and technology which resulted in the establishment of a good number of variety of industries, and the quest of humanity for sophisticated living are contributing significantly for the degradation of the environment. it is not out of place to quote G. Hardin, who said " so long as a commons remains unmanaged in a world of ever increasing demands, intelligence is almost irrelevant, over consumption and over pollution are inevitable". The intelligence is not at any rate commensurate with the ever increasing demands of the people. Destruction of environment has unforunately become an inseparable part of human development. Before going to study the importance of Environment Education, it is essential to know, what is environment at the outset.

According to Oxford dictionary the environment is the surrounding objects, circumstances of life of person or society. So environment consists of land, atmoshphere and the water. it can be further said that the total Eco-system, i.e., the dependence of Biotic and Abiotic constitutes the environment. Having understood what is environment in its general sense, let us understand how it is defined. According to prof. M.V.V. Rao the environment is the sum of all; physical, Chemical, Biological and Sociological factors which compose the surroundings of Man. The broadly classified components of environment are the Atmosphere, Hydrosphere, Lithosphere and Biosphere.

These environmental components can be considered a resource to be exploited to fulfil and long range goals for glamorous and superficial immediate needs. But wisdom demands self imposed restraints, to avert the environmental crisis and the threat to Man's existence itself. The environmental crisis and its far reaching adverse consequences on the very existence of humanity have been identified throughout the world. So precautionary measures must be taken to conserve the environment at an early date. Since it is a universal problem, the UNO conducted a world summit in Rio de Janeiro at Brezil, which is popularly known as "Rio summit" in 1992. This summit generated Global consciousness on the problem and suggested remedial measures.

Hence, people from all walks of life must contribute for the protection of the environment. So the target population of Environment Education should be according to Johnson, three categories i.e., (1) the general public (in both formal and non-formal systems), (2) special social and professional groups, (3) Technicians, scientists and specialists. By and large it can be said that the protection and conservation of environment is the responsibility of all the people. No single individual nor the factor can foster remedial measures for its proper protection. So it can be suggested that three areas i.e., individual, the society at large and the system of education in all its forms should contribute for the protection of the environment. it is rather an " Umbrella concept" to protect the Environment.

The main purpose of this paper is to discuss about the feasibility of the third area i.e. education for introducting Environment as subject at different levels. As far as the two areas i.e., the individual and the society are concerned they must contribute their share in protecting the environment. The individual must be educated and enlightened on the subject with an objective of "think Globally and Act locally". So also, at the societal level, the tradition and customs must be followed. The Government should decide the share of the village, taluk and the district for the protection of the environment. Even it can be included in the curriculum grade-wise.

Coming to the contribution of Education, Environment Education has acquired popularity throughout the world from about 1972. Following the indian Education Commission Report (1964-66) the NCERT prepared curriculum for ten-year schooling in 1975.Text books and teacher guides were also prepared. But the distribution of the subject at different levels was not definite and clean; paricularly at the primary stage. In other stages, the NCERT, prepared text-books in science and social sciences with good coverage of environment oriented topics. Teaching aids, films and slides have also been produced. Non-formal models of Education like, health, enviornmental studies, literacy, vocation, social awareness and numeracy were also developed. Since the subject of Environment Education is comprehensive, inter-disciplinary approach is inevitable to solve the environment problems. inter-dependency and inter-relation of the subject is inseparable. It is not out of place to quote Vidant, who has developed a detailed theory of Environment Education. He distinguishes between the broad view of Environment Education which is infact "a pretext for working out a grand theory of Education embracing all the philosophical, social and educatinal ideas that converse to form the ' New Education' and the narrow thenarrow sense of the term which is rather ' a pragmatic response to the defacement of the Environment both in affluent societies where pollution results from wealth' and in the thrid world countries, where "pollution results from poverty". He further said that Environment Education should align itself with the broader, open-ended, democratic and life-long models of education.

So a new Education is essential to understand and tackle the Environment problems. In the light of the above, it is suggested that :

(1) Curriculum must be constructed with definite subject, taking into account, the class and age of students both in the formal and non-formal system. The content at the primary stage must be easily accessible to young minds.

(2) Inter-disciplinary approach must be adopted at the higher level of education, creating awareness and orientation at the primary and secondary levels.

(3) Case-study must be constructed at identified areas as disertation and field work reports to confirm the Environment problem and Research must be conducted thereafter. Research can also be conducted on academic and social areas.

(4) In research, generally educational innovation tends to flow from the above, where downward flow is the sole model of innovation diffusion. But in the case of Environment Education it has to start from the lower level i.e., from the teacher; this is particularly an impor-

tant area where the grass root reacher is the innovator and developer who can use the Environment as a basic resources for his study. For the researchers and scientists, the teacher will work as a catalyst for the successful completion of the work.

So, on the whole, for the proper protection and management of Environment, the 'Umbrella concepts' of Education, covering all the related disciplines, spreading of curriculum adeouately,using the services of all people and conducting case studies and research will to some extent serve the prupose of Environment protection. Apart from this, the government should take it as a priority area, like, the family planning programme and total literacy campaign for proper management of Environment.

3

ENVIRONMENTAL EDUCATION: THE NEED OF THE HOUR

B.S.V, Dutt,
A.P.S.W.R. School
Tiruvuru, Krishna District,
Andhra Pradesh.

The study of the interactions between the man, the natural and social environment is called Environmental Education. Environment is generally taken to consist of two main aspects natural and human i.e. man made or social. In recent years the word' Environmental Education has gained much popularity and the importance of the subject has been realised by researchers, scientists, Environmentalists and Educationists. The scope of environment is so wide that covers various aspects of Nature-Ecological, cultural, technologies, economical, legal, educational and communal.

COMMUNITY AND INTERDEPENDENCE

Every human being forms a part of the environment; lives along with other members of the community. The different members of the community take part in a wide variety of activities. Some raise fodder crops to raise animals; others manufacture machines of various kind; still others engage in a wide variety of business and professional pursuits. Each individual plays a particular role in the total life of the community and whatever he does affects every other individual directly or indirectly. Community is also made up of animals and plants dwelling in the same locality. There is a strong relationship that exists among all the plants, animals and men that live together in the community, one is dependent on the other directly or indirectly.

In animal and plant communities, all the members, large or small, active or anchored, ferocious or passive, play a definite role. Directly or indirectly animals and Man depend on plants for food. They together form the so called 'Eco-system'.

The green plants convert the energy of sunlight in many stage operations, into sugars and other substances, and these products are the source of all the energy used by themselves and the other members of the community. There are animals that feed upon these plants, and other animals that prey upon the plant-eaters in their turn. Certain small parasites fasten upon the bodies of larger animals and feast upon the living fresh of their victims. Animal scavengers feed upon carcasses; plant scavengers, upon animals and plants and organic wastes. Human beings too feast upon plants and animals. Plants in turn depend on Man for their portection, better nutrition and multiplication of their species. Thus plants, animals and Man form a most intimate bond between themselves in the community.

HOW TO IMPART ENVIRONMENTAL EDUCATION TO CHILDREN?

Every human being is a part of nature and whatever action he does will have its own consequences. the children should be given a chance to understand, love and care 'nature' even from their childhood. The teacher is the best person to induce and inculcate a sense of responsibility among children about the environment, the hazards of pollution, the interdependence of plants and animals, the care to be taken to protect the environment etc. issues, since, children spend considerable time in school. Every place and area in and around our community is fit to explore eventhough they are familiar to children. The following activities can be taken up by the teacher.

A visit to a nearby city or township can give information about the pollution caused by various vehicles by releasing smoke, the poisonous gases released by the factories, the poisonous gases like Carbondixide, Carbonmonoxide, oxides of Nitrogen etc. and the ill-effects of these gases can be explained to children. The measures to check it up can also be explained. By planting more and more trees in cities, by asking automobile drivers to check up their engines, and by not allowing the people to burn the garbage dumps, pollution can be reduced.

Occasional visits to nearby canals, rivers can be planned by the teacher to explain how water gets polluted by man made errors and careless methods adopted by him. Human beings take a dip in rivers to clean themselves, wash clothes and clean their cattle. All these pollute rivers and indirectly the drinking water. besides this, the factory owners indiscriminately and carelessly leave the chemicals into the nearby streams and nearby paddy fields. These destroy the flora and fauna living in canals and rivers.

Along with, the importance of social environment should also be taught to children. How have people changed their ways of life in course of time, the aspects of socio-economic environment, various professionals and people at work, the dignity of labour, realtionship(spatial) between man and his environment, relationship between man's past and present and to hold past in proper perspective, the importance of our culture and tradition and several other issues can be explained.

A group of geographical skills, observation faculties, love for environment, are developed in children if the above said issues and carefully explored. The children can therefore become worthy and useful citizens of the society.

MAN AND THE BALANCE OF NATURE

Man has been disturbing the orderly balance of Nature. Alone of all the creatures, he has sought to make over nature. He has destroyed selfishly forests, killed animals and birds just for his own pleasure and drained swamps in order to make room for his crops. he has threatned the normal soil building cycle by repeated cultivation of a single crop. His reckless methods of planting have exposed the soil to wind and water. By adding greatly to the numbers of the animals and plants that are useful to him, man has provided insects and vermin of all kinds with an endless variety and therefore they have increased and multiplied.

As if this weren't enough he has started industries, invented vehicles and neglected to utilise them with proper care. The result is that they create alarming health problems to the creatures on the globe and to man himself. Air pollution, water pollution have become a constant source of worry to human beings. Besides these, recently sound pollution has also become a major problem. Sound pollution is mainly caused by sounds made by motor vehicles, fire crackers during festivals and marriage functions, use of loud speakers during festivals etc. Many people damage their ears and even buildings are damaged by sound pollutions, especially in cities like Delhi, Mumbai, Chennai and Hyderabad. A sense of responsibility and civic sense on the part of people can only minmise the effect of sound pollution.

Nothing can be imagined now about the hazards of pollution, we will encouter in funture. To add to these circumstances, man has brought nuclear radiation of the worst type that destroys the living creatures without discrimination and produced indescribable havoc. The examples of Hiroshima and Nagaski, the recent Gulf War are typical examples of how the world is going to be tomorrow if a war breaks out again.

WHAT CAN BE DONE?

In this ever changing world of science and civilisation and when man habituated himself to lead a comfortable life it is a "million dollar " question that can man sacrifice his comfort and demands to protect environment? Man is the most intelligent, useful and thoughtful animal on earth and he knows how to strike a balance between the growing demands of the population without disturbing the order in nature. it is almost impossible to completely lead a pollution free life in this age but man-made erors can be cut down. Only at the cast of "eternal vigilance" can Man protect nature and try to re-establish the balance of nature. He can educate the masses, by waging relentless war against persons who cause serious problems to the environment, by conserving and adding to forest resources, by maintaining a fair balance among animal life. He should also realise that he is a part of nature and should not destroy himself in his greed to dominate nature itself. Somehow or the other, he has to make peace with animal and plant communities for his own survival. Otherwise, he has to pay a heavy penality just like the 'Dinosaur' for its inability to adjust to its environment.

EDUCATION AS AN INSTRUMENT TO PROTECT ENVIRONMENT

As already mentioned inculcating an awareness of environment among children is the responsibility of the teachers and to carry out this noble task, Education is the perfect instrument. if right attitudes are induced in children, these attitudes will be transmitted to later generations also by them. But school level educators and teachers have insufficient time to spend some time to the issues relating to environment. More success might be achieved if the school, curriculum includes and produces the desirable personal and moral attitudes in children such as 'I ought to consider the indirect consequences of my actions ? Not only so, the teachers and parents should make children feel and realise that every creature, whether tiny or gigantic, has a purpose and work to perform on this earth and they have equal right to share and enjoy the life along with man. Man doesn't have any moral right to disturb their way of life.

Secondly, by presenting planned instructional material with specific learning goals and by producing entertainment material which create an awareness of relationship between Man and Environment. An album on 'Nature' can be prepared by the teacher with the help of students, which emphasizes the beauty, grandeur and wonders of nature. Environmental Education should be made a compulsory subject at primary level and Environmental studies part 1 (Social Studies0 and environmental studies part II(science) should be viewed integratively as the product of the interaction between man, the natural and social environment.

Education for environment can't succeed if it is directed to school children alone and every person should think of the consequences of his actions that disturb the order of Nature. As these children alone are not in a position to make many of the decisions needed to preserve environmental recources, it will taste success only when it is deliberately attended by the public on a larger scale.

4

ENVIRONMENTAL EDUCATION THE NEED OF THE DAY

Dr. A.V.V.S. Swamy,
Nagarjuna University,
Nagarjuna Nagar-522510

Environmental conciousness is not a new concept for Indians, which is evident from the accounts of rulers, historians, visitors, rock and pillar edicts, etc. In Kautilya's Arthasastra it was stated that'the stability of an empire is dependent upon the stability of its environment'. Environment is a broad term which means 'the surroundings that influence the development and growth of mankind: This environment covers all important facets of our life, viz, the physical, chemical, biological, social and economic. Educating our populace on this important aspect is the prime requirement of the day. Institutionalisation of education has restricted one to get enlightened in very narrow discipline. The advent of degree-based education, vocational education etc. has further restricted the scope of education. The present education system imparts social, political and economic education besides biological and physical sciences. These subjects taught nowadays are mere conceptual and theoretical rather than realistic and need-based.

Population, poverty and pollution are the three major problems now facing the country. These three are interlinked with each other thus forming a problem-web. During the post independence era, there have been separatae policy programmes to deal with poverty and population only very recently for environmental protection.

Environmental education, unlike any other programme, to be imported to each and every citizen. Most of the people including the urban elite are under the misconception that environmental education means creating awareness among the people about pollution and to check it.

But the fact is otherwise. To meet the needs of the growing population, we need industries and these industries are bound to release their wastes in the form of effluents which are ultimately responsible for the pollution. Thus, pollution is very much an invited evil into òur life style, and we are badly in need of certain industries knowing pretty well their hazardous input materials for the production of certain fertilizers and chemicals. Similarly, for achieving the self-reliance and self-sufficiency in the agricultural sector, the intensive agricultural practices and high yielding varieties have been introduced which in turn requiré very high quantities of fertilizers and pesticides. These pesticides and fertilizers used in excess enter the water dobies in dissolved state or remain in the soil thereby polluting the aquatic bodies and soil. This is a sensitive aspect where we cannot minimise the use of fertilizers but can minimise the pollution only through the judicious use of those fertilizers and pesticides. Another example is the automobile pollution. Particularly in the cities where one has to travel longer distances to attend to one's duties, one ought to use a vehicle for his own conveyance, which obviously enhances the air pollution. These are certain aspects which cannot be avoided totally, but judicious and concious efforts ony will minimise the pollution levels. Besides pollution, over exploitation of natural resources also distrubs the recharging capacity of the natural system thereby minimising the protective cover. Our developmental activitis should be aimed at 'Sustainable Development' i.e. development without destruction. All these things are to be dealt in the curricula of the environmental education for the various target groups, where the participation of each and every citizen is essential with a responsibility of keeping our environment clean and inherit a safer environment to our next generations.

Environmental education thus to be extended to all the workers (of both organised and unorganised sectors), industrialists, teachers, students, housewives, policy makers and planners. The focal theme of the environmental education should be the health of man and how to make this planet more congenial to live in; the philosophy shold be 'a healthy planet only can harbour healthy people.' Who defines health as " Health is not merely the absence of any disease, but the physical, physiological and psychological well being of the individual". This holistic concept of health can be realised only when the 'surroundings' (environment) are kept clean. To cover all the sections of the populace, it need to be implemented in various stages with various strategies, each covering a particular target group. For example, the curriculum for industrial worker should be different from that of agricultural labour. Though both these target groups need to be imparted occupational health education, the curriculum varies depending upon their working conditions. Similarly, curriculum differs for industrial workers and the residents of industrial areas.

Environmental education is to be taken up as a 'Movement' involving all the groups of the population. The literates of the country have a more responsible role to play in developing the curricula and imparting the environmental education, because much of the population consisted of illiterates and neoliterates. And also the most important as pects of implementation is that environmental education to be taken up linking with local problems thereby creating interest among the populace in mass participation.

Already efforts were on in this direction and there were some sucess stories like-'Chipko' movement in Uttar Pradesh and Appiko movement of Karnataka where in the local people participated with dedication and could save their forests. The realistion from the part of government is evident from banning of the silent valley project of Kerala. These success stories tell us the strength of mass movements and participation.

The government of India also has taken up programmes for imparting Environmental education through Centre for Environmental Education (CEE), Central Board for Workers Education (CBWE), Indian Institute of Ecology and Management(IIEM), etc. But these few institutes cannot meet the requirement. many voluntary organisations have also been working on these lines and are actively conducting the environntal awareness campaigns. The voluntary organisations or Non-governmental Organisations(NGOs) have been mainly dealing with the local and regional problems. Several women organisations have also been coming forward to take up environmental awareness compaigns.

Students, the most active group of the society, have much considerable role to play. They not only can involve themselves in the service activities but also be instrumental in involving others. The student community can be trained through N.C.C.,N.S.S.,and can establish activist societies like "Environmental clubs (En-Clubs)" for creating awareness and imparting environmental education thus gicing thrust to the already initiated 'Environmental Education' campaing, shaping it as a 'MOVEMENT'.

5

ENVIRONMENTAL EDUCATION
Concept of Environment and Ecosystem in Relation to Man

Dr. M. Vikram Reddy
Environmental Biology, Research Unit
Department of Zoology, Kakatiya University
Warangal 506 009 - A.P.

The international Union for Conservation of Nature and natural Resources (IUCN) Commission of Education,in the international working meeting on Environmental Education in the school curriculum held under the auspices of UNESCO in paris in 1970 has defined " Environmental Education' as "the process of recognising values and classifying concepts in order to develop skills and attitudes necessary to understand and appreciate the interrelatedness of man, his culture and his biophysical surrounding. Environmental Edcation also entails paractices in issues concerning environmental quality". This definition has since then influenced the thinking of many countries concerned with forming policies on environmental education.

The philosophy of Environmental Education asserts that MAN is an integral and inseparable component of the Environment and Ecosystem. He interacts with biotic and abiotic environment. An understanding of the biotic and abiotic environment i.e. ecosystem is necessary in order to keep his living sustainable. Such an understanding could be made possible only through an education system which clearly explains the structure and function of ecosystem and the ecosystem management.

Therefore, Environmental Education should aim at:

1) Providing factual information to the students. Which will lead to

the understanding of intricate inter relationship between biotic and abiotic environment maintaining the ecological balance in relation to the position of man in it.

ii) By developing concern and respect for environment, and

iii) Informing them how man can play an effective role in protecting the environment.

WHAT IS ENVIRONMENT?

The word "Environment" is derived from the French environner which means to encircle or surround. Environment can be defined as:

1. The circumstances or conditions that surround an organism or group of organisms, or

2. The complex of social or cultural conditions that affect an individual or community.

THE UNITED NATIONS ENVIRONMENT PROGRAMME (UNEP) HAS DEFINED

Environment as the outer biophysical system in which people and organisms exist. In a broad sense, the word environment can be used to refer to anything, living or non-living, that surrounds and influences living organisms. The environment really represents the interconnections, the dynamic relationships between organisms and their physical and biological surroundings. Environment begins with an exploration of the basic ecological principles that govern the natural world and consider the many ways in which human beings affect the environment.

ANTHROPOCENTRIC ECOSYSTEM

Ecosystem is a biological community together with its physical environment, Biological community consists of all the populations of different species that live and interact within an area.A population consists of all the members of a species living in a given area. Thus , an ecosystem includes not only all the interactions among the living organisms of a biotic community (in which man is also included), but also the interactions among the organisms and their physical environment.

In 1964, George Perkins Marsh, in one of his essays, analysed the cause of the decline of ancient civilization in which he has mentioned about ecosystemic view of man and nature. The term ecosystem was first proposed by british Scientist, Arthur George Tansely in 1935 for the fundamental ecological unit.

Ecosystem has an underlying holistic concept. To understand the meaning of the word ecosystem and to appreciate the role this word plays in communicating men's increasing concern about his environment, one has to consider the holistic concept that underlies the word. Holism, in this connotation is based on the theory that living components (organisms including man) and non-living components (the physical environment) function together as a whole, according to well defined physical and biological laws. An anthropocentric or human centered definition of ecosystem could be : a life supporting system composed of air, water, soil, plant, animals-including men, and micro organisms all of which function together and maintain the whole.

In this connectiion, holism (holos= whole) is based on the theory that biotic components and abiotic components function together as a whole. According to the theory of integrative levels. When the components are considered together, it creates larger functional units and gives a holistic view in which a unit is evaluated without specifying the internal contents. Such an ecosystem concept is entirely different from merological view (meros=part) of the ecosystem, in which parts of the system are discoursed, and trial is made to build up the whole from parts. For example, when hydrogen is combined with oxygen in a certain manner, water is formed which is distinct from both of its components, similarly, when some friends get together, the function of entire unit differs from the single one. Therefore, to understand fully water or a unit of friends, a knowledge about the functional wholes as well as the parts is required.

An ecosystem can be of any size: there is no size limit implied in the definition of an ecosystem. it may be a square kilometer of a jungle or square meter of desert or a pond or a closed container of small organisms (for example : an aquarium). The largest ecosystem is the biosphere.

Although the idea of ecosystem was accepted from a long time before 1960's , it was not in any way applied to man's affairs till this time. There was forest management, agroecosystem management, water management and wild life management etc., but there was no real planning and management of whole environmental complex i.e. man had not yet practiced true ecosystem management. Only recently on 4th December, 1995 the ecological Society of America has brought out a scientific report entitled "The Scientific Basis for Ecosystem management". The authors (Ann Bartuska and Jerry Franklin) discussed the key elements of ecosystem management, and addressed some of the implementation aspects of the ecosystem management approach.

THE COMPONENTS OF THE ECOSYSTEM

An ecosystem has two major components that are usually practically separated in space and time.

i. An autotrophic or self-nourishing component which constitutes mainly green plants, and in which light energy is used to build-up complex organic substances from simple inorganic ones.

ii. A heterotrophic or other nourishing component, in which the complex organic substances are utilised, rearranged and ultimately decomposed.

From the structural and functional point of view, the ecosystem comprises of six structural and six functional components.

A. STRUCTURAL COMPONENTS:

i. Inorganic substances (C.N.Co2 H2O etc.) involving in material cycles.

ii. Organic compounds (proteins, carbohydrates, lipids, humic substances etc.) that link biotic and abiotic compondents.

iii. Climatic regime (rainfall, temperature etc)

iv. Autotrophs or producers, largely green plants able to maufacture food from simple sustances.

v. Phagotrophs (Phago = to eat) or macro-consumers, heterotrophic organisms largely animals which ingest otehr organisms of particulate organic matter. They are also known as consumers- primary and secondary consumers.

vi. Saprotrophs (Sapro = to decompose) or micro-consumers (also called Osmotrophs), heterotrophic organism, chiefly, bacteria. fungi, some protozoa, nematodes arathropods and earthworms that breakdown complex compounds with release of products that are recycled by plants or that affect other biotic components.

B. FUNCTIONAL COMPONENTS:

i. Energy flow circuits.

ii. Food-chains (trophic relationships).

iii. Diversity patterns in time and space.

iv. Nutrient (biogeochemical) cycle.

v. Development and evolution.

vi. Control (cybernetics).

These components are operationally inseparable from the holistic point of view. There are some key principles which are relevant to human ecology. A few of these principles are:

- The available energy declines with each step in the food chain. So that a system can support more herbivores than carnivores. On the other hand, materials often become concentrated with each step in the food chain. Biomagnification of pollutants such as non-biodegradable agrochemicals (e.g.. DDT) occur causing serious problems in man's enviornment.

- Man must be aware that he will have to pay the costs of added antithermal maintenance, or " disorder pumpout" as H.T. Odum (1970) calls it. It is dangerous strategy to try to force too much productivity or yield from the landscape, because very serious " ecological backlashes" can occur. These may result from: (1) pollution caused by heavy use of fertilizers and pesticides, and (ii) the consumptions of fossil fuels.

- From the evolutionary history, it is evident that the ecosystem process, production has slightly exceeded decomposition, so that a highly oxygenic atmosphere has replaced the original atmosphere of the earth. Man is tending to reverse this trend by increasing decomposition (burning fossil fuels etc.) at the expense of production. The most immediate problem is created by the increase in atmospheric Co2 leading to the large effects on the heat budget of the earth.

- Ecological investigations indicate that the diversity is directly correlated with stability and perhaps inversely correlated with productivity in the most of the situations. Preservation of diversity in the ecosystem is important for man.

- Recycling pathways in nature are of great interest to human society. There are atleast four major ones which vary in importance in different kinds of ecosystem.

(a) Recycling of detritus via biological decomposition.

(b) Recycling via animal excretion.

(c) Direct recycle from plant back to plant via symbiotic micro-organisms such as mycorrhizae associated with root system particularly of food plant in tropics, and

(d) Autolysis or chemical cycle with no organism ivolved.

ENVIRONMENTAL LITERACY

There should be enviornmental literacy in wich every citizen should be fluent in the principles of ecology and should have a "working knowledge of environmental wisdom".Environmental literacy, according to william K Reilly (the former Administrator of Environmental protection Agency (EPA), U.S.A.) can help create a sense of duty to care for and manage wisely our natural endowment and our productive natural resources for the long haul. " environmental Education". boils down to one profoundly important imperative: preparing ourselves for life in the next century.

It requires that every discipline include an environmental component in each major course. Environmental literacy is not the responsibility of a single discipline or a few disciplines but of all disciplines. To accomplish this, substantial faculty retaining is necessary.

SUGGESTED READING

Brewer; R. The Science of Ecology, 2nd ed, Saunder College publishing, philadelphia, 1994.

Odum; H.T. Environment, power and society, John wiley and sons, New York, 1970.

Odum, H.T.

Reddy; M.V. Soil Organisms and Litter Decomposition in the Tropics, westview press, Boulder, San Francisco, Oxford, 1995.

6

ENVIRONMENTAL EDUCATION AND WOMEN

Dr. G. Vijaya Lakshmi
Reader in Education,
S.P. Mahila Visva vidyalayad
Tirupati - 517502

God has created so many living and non-living beings. But the living beings, particularly human beings, intentionally are more responsible for environmental destruction than any other species. Importance was given in almost all cultures for environmental protection. So it is very much necessary to safeguard the environment as far as possible and it is our responsibility to handover safe environment to our future generations.

WOMEN AND NATURE

Woman is part and parcel of environment. Woman contributes a lot in so many ways for the enviornmental protection. Women revolutions in developed countries are helping so much to protect the environment. The women, particularly from hilly region or rural areas, are the victims due to the age-old traditional blind beliefs. So it is needless to say that these women should be educated to bring them out from these orthodoxical clutches. The should be provided with proper training to create suitable awareness and insight into the new demands in the physical and social environment.

When compared to men, women have more direct relation ship with their immediate environment. Regularly they collect their own life requirements like fuel, water, food like leaves, roots, fruits, fish etc. Their activities are also confined to these. Women tend to rear the cattle. They grow or collect grass for their domestic animals, particularly milk animals and birds. So, women have closer vicinity with the animals as well as flora and fauna of that region by living with them.

Even in the past primitive society also women had relationship with the nature. Only men used to hunt and kill the animals for food whereas women used to collect forest resources to meet their life requirements. Men also cut trees for preparing coal or for construction purposes by seeing from the business point of view.

WOMEN AND WATER

Women act as suppliers and consumers of water. Women have more knowledge about the existence and quality of water available in the local environment. They carry water so many times in a day and it requires so much time and energy. As a result they feel responsible for using the waterin an economic manner. Usually women and girls are engaged in carrying water needed for their families. So consumption of water at family level is more associated with the female folk in their daily life. Moreover, women are involved in preparing the food and related items. The water required in cooking, cleaning etc. is the concern of women. Water resources like river, lake, pond, well or tap are the look out of women and the maintenance of these resources are part and parcel of their routine work. So it is necessary to provide knowledge relating to preservation of water, storing water, use of water etc. to women folk.

WOMEN AND MATERIALS

Women use widely the forest resources. They buy articles made out of wood, wool, rock, shells, thorns or ivory etc. Just for fashion either on their clothing or jewellery. Decorative pieces prepared out of some species like snakes, rabbits, squirels, iguana etc. Due to this, these may disappear from the environment. The awareness to avoid the capture and killing of these species for the sake of entertainment or luxury should be provided to women. Otherwise they will be out of sight or become extinct. Unless women deny the use of these things it is not possible to protect these species.

Even in modern society the use of some varieties of sanitary napkins, towels, cosmetics, creams and powders containing some poisonous mercury and hydroquinines should be abandoned. Even the milk powder for infant's use is really threatening one leading to diarrhoea due to improper water use of boiling during the process of preparation. Mothers need to be educated about all these negative consequences leading to health hazards.

WOMEN AND WORK

Majority of women work as labourers either in the agricultural farms, industries or mines even for less wages. They need training in sparing their time and materials in these fields. The economic return they receive for the amount of work they turned out.

WOMEN AND SOCIETY

Recently women are entering into the gainful employment. That means they are looking after their job requirments besides fulfilling their familial responsibilities. Moreover, they are contributing to their family income. The roles played traditionally by women are disintegrating and modifications are taking place. As a result the nature of work attended by women has changed drastically. The reasons for this are migration of men, green revolution, publicity of high yielding crops, mechanisation, urbanisation including industrialisation leading to pollution, lessening the cultivable land and other natural resources etc.From this point of view also they need to be orineted towards these changing times.

WOMEN AND TECHNICAL KNOWLEDGE

Women are involved in collection of firewood, water, materials and engaged in cooking and meeting the requirements of family members for hours together in addition to their traditional responsibilities like rearing, caring and bearing children. Besides this they have to work in their workplace for longer durations. They get very little time in due to several difficulties. They need to be exposed to the several gadgets available to save time and to spend their time in an effective manner to get more benefits. Several petty things take away the time of a housewife. These traditional means of cooking, water collection, grinding, firewood collection etc., need to be replaced by modern technological devices and non-conventional energy resources for their optimum use to improve their living and health conditions. For all these purposes technical knowledge is required which need to be provided for information, use and repair of these devices.

WOMEN AND POPULATION

Women can control population explosion through family welfare education. Standard of life can be improved only by limiting the children. Even today the status of women is decided on the number of male children they possess. The menstrual cycle, child birth, early marriages, economical and social factors are responsible for population growth. Women need to be exposed to the various evil consequences of population growth and the need for small family by adopting various methods to control the birth of children as it is considered the main reason for environmental destruction as well as pollution.

Due to illiteracy among women and resources are being exploited from women. There is an immediate need to plan programmes to create awareness among women to move further without causing environmental destruction and to work for environmental construction which was already affected, to develop literacy socially, culturally, economically and industrially. They should be given knowledge about the resources, their management, selection of materials, implementation, control and evaluation of different procedures and appropirate environmental technology should reach the ordinary women through various women's organisations for environmental protection.

7

ENVIRONMENTAL POLLUTION

Mrs. Y. Sridevi
Dr. V.V. Vardhani
Department of Zoology,
Nagarjuna University,
Nagarjuna nagar- 522510
Guntur, A.P.

Pollution means the direct or indirect changes in the environment which are harmful and undesirable to organisms and man. There are several kinds of pollution and the causes are also many. Due to a rapid rate of increasein the human polulation the space on earth available to each man is getting smaller. The needs of modern man are also increasing both in quantity and complexity whereas the storehouse of natural resources is limited. In the process of the manufacture of certain goods some materials are invariably thrown out as wastes. The amount of wastes that are dumped in soil, water and air have reached such proportions that due to limitation of space the waste dumping space of one section of population is the living space of another. Thus, in almost all countries, environmental pollution is on the increase and is due to the industrialisation and technology. The components of the environment air and water are much more affected by the toxicants.

WATER POLLUTION

Water bodies such as ponds, lakes or rivers have been used as dumps for the wastes of villages, towns and cities. There are different kinds of pollutants such as sewage, oganic chemicals like detergents and pesticides, inorganic chemicals, harmful micro organisms and sediments. In the sea radioactive materials are also being dumped. Certain chemical processing industries discharge mercury components; these compounds in the form of chemical effluents get into the water and then to the aquatic environment, the effluents enter the bodies of animals and also human beings. Both the aquatic and marine environment be effected by the chemical toxicants. Mercury compounds which enter into the bodies of human beings leads to mercury poisoning-it results to the impairment of vision and muscles. Ultimately the patient suffers from convulsions, madness, paralysis, coma and death.

Usually mercury compounds enter the body system of fish and shell fish. There are no well defined 'safe limits' for different toxins or elements in humans, animals and or their eating food stuffs. The response of the defence system of a human body to different toxins varies differently. The pollution in water can be detected by analytical measures of human or animal tissues. The concentrations of the common elements in water, air, food stuffs and on the surface of the earth can be investigated and an experimental data can be prepared. Food and agricultural organisations and/or World health Organisation usually make enquiries and collect data for different elements in food stuffs except fish and shell fish. The abnormal amounts of certain elements in animal or human tissue indicate the encironmental pollution.

Pesticides, especially DDT, used in the control of mosquitoes and pests of agriculture have become the most serious pollutant of water. Many of such pesticides are chlorinated hydrocarbons. Chlorinated hudrocarbons are universal poisons i.e. they are not very selective. Many other inorganic chemical and fertilizers washed down to lakes and rivers from crop fields in watershed areas act as nutrients to aquatic plants. Overcrowding by algal blooms or macrophytes reduces the utility of lakes and rivers.

Polluted waters are turbid, not pleasant for drinking, sometimes smell bad, and are not suitable for bathing or washing. They are generally hamful and diseases like typhoid, dysentry and cholera are spread through polluted waters. Still other sources of pollution in water are the modern washing powders called detergents. These act as nutrients for organisms in water and hasten the process of eutrophication. Aquatic weeds are also regarded as pollutants. They reduce the utility of ponds and lakes and shorten their life. Sodium, copper, chromium and cadmium are some of the more common effluent pollutants discharged from various kinds of factories. Metallic pollutants are very harmful for human health and therefore such affected waters need purification before supply by water works.

AIR POLLUTION

Pollutants in the atmosphere contaminate the air leading to air pollution. Atmospheric pollution is principally caused by man. Carbon monoxide, sulphur hexaflouride, ammonia, hydrocarbons and ethylene which is present in automobile exhausts are the common air pollutants.

Large quantities of particles enter into the atmosphere through technol ofical activities. Hydrocarbons are emitted in huge quantity by the burning of petrol in the automobiles. Tetraethyl lead is commonly used as an additive to gasoline- it is balmed for causing atmospheric pollution and respiratory diseases in human beings. Another toxic pollutant is Peroxy acetyl nitrate, which is a bye product of automobile exhausts, is reported to supress photosynthesis.

Particulate pollutants reflect too much of light and reduce visibility. it is found that cement dust around cement factories settles on tree leaves and reduces the chlorophyll content and leaf sizes in many trees, thus reducing the overall primary production. There are many kind of biological materials in the air like bacteria, fungal spores, pollen grains etc., which quite often cause allergy and bronchial troubles like asthma. Besides reducing visibility and causing diseases the particulate pollutants adversely affect plant life in a number of ways such as photosynthesis, necrosis in leaves and diseases.

Air pollution has creted a considerable interest and a global effort is being made to control it. Air pollution has very bad effects on human health. Not only this but also it is responsible for corrosion of metals.

SOIL POLLUTION

Arsenic, chromium and nickel are suspected to be increasing in quantity in the soil environment. Unrestricted use of fertilisers, pesticides and other chemicals add to the pollution. Effluents from fertilisers reduce both the quantity and quality of agricultural crops and the soil properties are also adversely affected. Consequently, many of the chemical elements find their way into the human body primarily through the food chain.

SOLID WASTE POLLUTION

Most of our daily needs are obtained from the market in nicely packed containers made up of thin polythene, plastics, glass etc. After the use of contents the packing material is usually thrown out as garbage. Many of the old used up things like automobile spares, machines, cycle parts etc. are thrown out. Some of them are degradable by the activity of micro-organisms in nature and the materials are recycled but some are not easily degraded like metals, plastics, nylons and polythenses. Solid wastes are assuming alarming proprotions in affluent countries like those of America and Europe, where labour charges of waste collection are high. In India however all old junks are puchased by professional hawkers from house to house.

RADIOACTIVE POLLUTION

Nuclear war materials and test explosions are principal sources of radioactive wastes in the atmosphere, soil and water. Already two thousand nuclear detonations must have been done in underground, underocean and in atmosphere and the cumulative radiocativity level is rising particularly in oceans. Ionizing radiations cause mutations, abnormality and lethality in many organisms, including man. Cancer is commonly caused even under low level exposures. Radiation effects persist for a very long period in the environment. Therefore, an utmost caution and complete foolproof of technology is needed in handling such scientific activities to prevent radioactive pollutions.

NOISE POLLUTION

Sound is produced in many kinds of work and we use and enjoy sound in talk and music. Only when sound is not liked or is unwanted we call it as noise. When the loudness of the sound is irritating or unbearable we regard it as noise pollution. Loudness of sound can be measured in terms of energy, decibels. Scooters, trucks and buses create about 90dB. Uncomfortable noise inside factories usually exceeds 100dB and jet planes while taking off create noise in the range of 150dB and rocket engines about 180dB. Sounds beyond 80dB can be safely regarded as pollution for it harms our hearing ability. Beyond 100dB the sound becomes very uncmofortable and beyond 120 it is painful. Noise interferes with communication, causes loss of hearing and disturbas mental peace.

Persons living in the humdrum of cities and industrial townships become hard of hearing at yound age. Noise also causes mental stress, increase in the rate of heart beat and sometimes damages eye sight, brain and liver functioning.

In addition to these, some of the agricultural, animal, agroindustrial and community wastes available in rural and adjoining areas are at present either not utilised in an uneconomic manner. Due to these wastes, unhygienic conditions prevail in the society of living. Ultimately this creates environmental pollution. If the wastes from different sources are utilised properly it will be a positive step to control pollution. For example paddy husk can be used as fuel. Activated carbon can be manufactured from paddy husk; carbon can be useful for decolourisation of vegetable oils, sugar solutions etc. Rice bran is a rich souce of oil which can be used for edible and industrial purposes. Similarly wheat bran can be utilised for the manufacture of amylase, amyloglucosidase and pectinolytic enzymes for food industry and fugal acid protease for leather industry.

Coconut and coir can be used as raw mataerials. Recently coconut pith is used in the joint fillers of road and buildings. Moreover, cement coconut pith concrete is used in thermal insulation. Many other by-products of agriculture can be used as useful products through proper processing.

8

ENVIRONMENTAL POLLUTION

Dr. B.V. Appa Rao
Professor of Chemistry,
Regional Engineering College,
Warangal-506 004- A.P.

The magnificent mountains, the lushy green forests, the great rivers, the deep oceans and seas, the blue lagoons and lakes, marvelous reservoir of underground wealth ... water and minerals, the bewildering carieties of animals, the beautiful brids with all their musical tones, several insects, pests, tiny and invisible micro organisms...... all these constitute our planet Earth. As the knowledge goes till date, the Earth alone of the solar system supports life. Interactions between matter and energy and among carious living species decide the composition of this planet and also the ecological balance at a point of time.

Ancient man identified himself as part of Nature, lived as one among the various living species, competed, with other animals only for food and shelter. But because of his superior mental faculties, he started dominating all other living species and used several of them for his comfors, for his betterment. In this pursuit, man slowly alienated himself from Nature. In order to overpower stronger animals he discovered the metal iron (though accidentally). The discovery of making iron from its ore was an important break-through in human civilization. Discovery of petroleum and its various constituents revolutionized the civilisation further. Thus man explored all the possible mineral sources stored beneath the earth and started extracting metals from them and then making several new alloys from metals. In his quest for more and more comforts, luxuries, wealth and power, man could, just in a span of around 200 years, do many wonders in the fields of agriculture, Medicine and Industry. Several new alloys, plastics, synthetic rubber, leather products, fossil fuels, nuclear fuels,petrochemicals, fertilizers, pesticides, pharmaceuticals, thousands of various other organic and inorganic chemicals have come into civilization. The civilization is totally changed. The change has been phenomenal.

Man, simultaneously, shold have examined the consequences of his activities in terms of their possible negative impact on the environment in which he lives. But this point seems to have been long ignored until the accumulated effects of industrial civilization started threatening the very survival of mankind. It is only through post-mortam, man could realize the damage that has already been caused to the planet Earth because of non-biodegradable chemicals and other toxic constituents that were brought into atmosphere, water land and food, by himself. Technological advances with scant regard for environment, for preservation of ecological balance have seriously affected the quality of air, water and land.

If Man's intellect is responsible for all the progress of mankind, his arrogance and lack of wisdom to live in harmony with Nature are responsible for all the harmful effects on the environment, which we call 'pollution'. National Research Counicil Committee on pollution defined pollution as "an undesirable change in the physical, chemical or biological characteristics of our air, land and water that may or will harmfully affect human life or that of other desirable species,our industrial process, living conditions and cultural assets or that may or will waste or deteriorate our meterial sources".

Regarding the extent of air pollution, increase in carbon dioxide content has come about almost entirely since the industrial revolution, and mainly within the last 50 yers, as a direct result of Man's activities. The increase in concentration of carbon dioxide (Co_2) from the year 1750 to the year 1988 is shown in figure. Burning of fossil fuels is the main contributing factor for this. Deforestation in the tropical countries and changing agricultural practices, reduce the efficiency of Co_2 recycling, thus providing a secondary aggravation of the CO_2 increase. It is not only CO_2 levels that have been increasing at the rate of 1.7 percent per year since 1965. Atmospheric nitrous oxide (N_2O) concentrations are now known to be increasing slowly at 0.2% per annum. Intensive use of chemical fertilizers could lead to increased N_2O production in the biosphere. During the past 150 years, carbon dioxide is up by 25%, nitrous oxide by 19% and methane by 100%. besides, the levels of carbon monoxide and halocarbons in the atmosphere are also increasing. Increasing levels of all these gases in the atmosphere lead to a rise in the mean surface temperatures reported that the mean surface terperature might rise approximately 3°C for a doubling in CO_2 content in the atmosphere. The increase in methane by now is predicted to have increased global temperature by 0.23°C, global average temperatures are now about 0.6°C warmer than they were a century ago. At the present rate of growth, CO_2 may be double its preindustrial value by the turn of the century. As a consequence of this, a major alteration of the global environment seems possible. Man's greed for energy will have to be satisfied either by alternate sources of energy like solar energy or the human civilization has to prepare itself for major adverse climatic changes at global level. (Christopher Flavin, 1989).

Pollution of air due to oxides of sulphur and of nitrogen ultimately leads to acid-rains as witnessed in several highly industrilized parts of the world. Acid-rains will in turn pollute land and water source also — Acid-rains will cause severe atmospheric corrosion of all the exposed structures. Acid rain infact is an indicator of severe atmospheric pollution of a particular area.

Air pollution due to various gases discussed above has its adverse effect in a long time period and relates to serious global changes. There are other examples of air pollution. Which lead to immediate catastrophic effects of local environment because of the extremely high toxicity of certain pollutants. The familiar example is pollution of air due to methyl isocyanate gas which led to the terrible Bhopal tragedy in 1984. in this tragic event, 2,00.000 people were affected in all. About 5,000 died, 50,000 might have gone blind. Out of every three children born to women who were pregnant on the night of the disaster, only one was reported to have survived. 'Chernoyl nuclear disaster' (Russia) in 1986 can be quoted as an example of the pollution of the atmosphere due to nuclear radiations. More than 40,000 people died in Soviet Union because of this disaster, besides several known and unknown ill-effects on human and animal health which might be carried over from generation to generation.

Water pollution due to mercury discharged into the ocean by poly vinyl chloride manufacturing industries was indentified in 1950 in japan when a mysterious disease affected several fisherman families who were depending on fish for their food. it was then understood by the scientific community that mercury, through fish, entered the human system and was responsible for such strange illness, the symptoms of which are loss of vision, progressive weakening of muscles, numbness, paralysis, coma and death.

The effluents discharged from paper industry destroy the flora and fauna of receiving waters and also destroy the aquatic life. The effluents may also contain chemicals like methyl mercaptan, pentachlorophenol and sodium pentachloro phenate which are highly toxic to fish.

Similarly untreated waste waters from various other industries viz., fertilizer, polymer, metallurgical, electroplating, chloralkli, petrochemical and leather are responsible for water pollution of oceans, rivers, canals, lake and streams.

The solid wastes from these industries and also the domestic wastes like garbage, waste paper, packing materials and others are responsible for land pollution. land pollution also occurs when millions of tonnes of coal, oil, ores, stones, sand and other construction materials are mindelat and transported.

Environmental pollution has now become a serious global problem. Developed countries had to pay heavily for not considering the effects on the environment simultaneously at the initial stages of industrial development. Now they are spending huge amounts to clear up their river, lakes, land and atmospheric air. Developing countries like India should at least learn from the experience of the developed ones and take strict pollution control measures at the initial stages of industrialization and urbanization itself.

POLLUTION DUE TO INDUSTRIES IN INDIA

According to Central Water Pollution Control Board, New Delhi, there are 27,000 large and medium scale industries in India and 4,900 of them are causing considerable water pollution. Details regarding the types of Industries responsible for pollution are given in table 1.

Certain practical examples of industrial pollution and its effects on environment are worth mentioning here. According to a report by Jodhpur Environmental Cell of the Gandhi peace Foundation, about 1500 small scale textile units in Jodhpur, pali and Balotra discharge 15 million liters of effluents every day into open drains, river beds, reservoirs and ditches. The harmful chemicals percolate into wells, tanks and reservoirs and affect about million people who obtain water from these sources. Cattle and wildlife are also not spared. About 7000 - 10000 hectares of land also have been ruined, the report alleges.

Table 1

Some of the industries responsible for Pollution in India

S.NO.	Type of Industry	Number
1.	Sugar industries	300
2.	Distilleries	128
3.	Caustic Soda Industries	38
4.	Fertilizer Industry	65
5.	Petroleum Refineries	13
6.	man-made Fibre Industries	29
7.	Integrated Steel Mills	7
8.	Textile Mills	300
9.	Pulp and Paper Mills	150
10.	Pesticide Industries	50
11.	Petrochemical Industries	10
12.	Inorganic Chemical Industries	150
13.	Diaries	50
14.	Thermal Power Plants	150
15.	Non-ferrous Metallurgical Industries	12
16.	Dye Manufacturing and Electroplating Units and others	128

C.A. Sastry, proceedings of National Seminar on Pollution Control, Pondicherry (Central) University, 16-17 October, 1989.

The coir producing industry in Keral is destroying water quality. Coir units soak cocount huska in pits to remove the fleshy matrix from the fibre. In the process, ground water is contaminated by hydrogen sulfide and organic acids.

The River 'Ganges' is considered to be one of the most polluted rivers of the world. Most of the other rivers in India like damodar, Gomati, Jamuna, krishna, Godavari, kauveri, Tungabhadra etc., also are polluted severely millions of liters of untreated sewage and industrial effluents are being discharged into the rivers daily. In the 'Kallu' river near Kalyan town of west bengal, water is very highly acidic (PH = 1.5), River minimahi in Baroda is heavily polluted duė to petrochemical and other industrial wastes. The river Cooum flowing through Madras is also polluted severely to an extent of 900 mg of iron, 275 mg of lead, 1313 mg of nickel and 32 mg or zinc per litre of water. Kali at Meerut, Jamuna near Delhi, Ganga at kanpur, Gomati near Lucknow, Damodar between Bokaro and Panchat, Hoogly near Calcutta are heavily polluted, river waters Tungabhadra are severely polluted near Dharwad due to the effluents from a 'polyfibres' factory and a 'Rayon and Silk Manufacturing' factory near Harihar town. Almost all the villagers downstream, are forced to use the polluted water and complain of several chronic diseases.

Of the 20 well known high altitude lakes in India (near or above 2,000 m) only two are unaffected: Kodaikanal, and Mukerti in the Nilgiris, lakes of Nainital and Bheemtal in U.P.., Dal and Wular in Kashmir, Pushkara in Rajasthan, loktak in Manipur, Khichipiri in Sikkim and Ooty in Tamilnadu are polluted. Every lake near a big city is polluted. The ahmedabad lake, for example is totally eutrophied and Hyderabad's hussain Sagar is on the way. Dal lake of Kashmir is worst affected of all. if the present trend continues, Dal lake will be lost within the next 80 years. instead of Dal lake, one can see only a small area surrounded by vegetable farms and swamps.

Air pollution is severe in all the major industrial cities viz., Delhi, Calcutta, Kanpur, Madras, hyderabad, Jaipur, Ahmedabad, Nagpur, bombay and Firozabad. Air pollution in these cities is partly because of industrial and partly because of automobile emissions. national Environmental Engineering Research Institute (NEERI) has established air quality monitoring stations in Bombay, Calcutta, Delhi, Madras, Hyderabd, kanpur, jaipur, Ahmedabad and Nagpur. In a survey conducted by NEERI in 1980, it was found that Chempur-Trombay area of Bombay was having highest sulphur dioxide (SO_2) pollution while New Delhi was having highest suspended particle matter pollution. The actual values for SO_2 and suspended particulate matter in the air samples collected from all the above mentioned cities are shown in table 2.

Table 2
Air Pollution of major Industrial Cities in India

City	Mean Value of SO_2 (mg/m^3)	Suspended particulate matter (mg/m^3)
Bombay	48.1	240.8
New Delhi	44.4	601.1
Calcutta	33.9	340.7
kanpur	16.9	543.5
Ahmedabad	12.7	306.6
Madras	9.3	100.9
Nagpur	8.7	261.6
Hyderabad	6.1	140.2
Jaipur	5.2	146.1

Timmy Katyal and M. Satake, Environmental Pollution. Anmol Publications, New Delhi, 1989.

BIBLOGRAPHY

1. C.A. Sastry, Proceedings of National Seminar on Pollution Control. Pondicherry (Central) University, 16-17, october 1989.

2. Christopher Flavin, Slowing Global Warming: A worldwide Strategy, world Watch Paper 91, published by world Watch institute, Washington, USA, October 1989.

3. Dix, H.M. Environmental pollution, John Wiley and sons, new York, 1981.

4. Ghose, N.C. and sharma, C.B. Pollution of Ganga River, Ashish Publishing House, New Delhi.

5. Richard P. Wayne. Chemistry of Atmosphere, Oxford Science Publications, London, 1985.

6. S.P. Mahajan, Pollution Control in Process industries, Tata McGraw-Hill Publishing Co. ltd., New Delhi, 1985.

7. The State of India's Environment, 1984-85. The Second Citizen's Report, Published by Centre for Science and Environment, New Delhi, 1985

8. Timmy Katyal and M.Satake, Environmental Pollution, Anmol Publications, new Delhi. 1989.

9. V. P. Kudesia, Water Pollution, Pragate Prakasan, meerut, 1985

10. Warren Viessman, JR., Mark, J.Hammer, Water Supply and Pollution Control, Fourth Edition, Harper International and Row Publishers, New York, 1985.

9

MARINE POLLUTION

Dr. V. Vivek Vardhani
Mrs. Y. Sridevi
Department of Zoology,
Nagarjuna University,
Nagarjuna Nagar-522510
Guntur, A.P.

A knowledge of the various factors influencing the suitabliity of marine environment is of significance for marine operatives. Soil and water are the major components of the environment and an equilibrium is to be maintained between these two components. Water is of vital importance for the existence of life and is met from either precipitation or ground water, these two are the major sources of water. Dissolved substances are absent in pure water and that water is unable to support life. But fresh internal marine waters are enriched with various substances which come either from soil or from atmosphere. Again the amount of substances in them depends on the geological formations and on various physico-chemical factors of the environment. Heat and light are the essential requirements for the existence and growth of organisms. Solar radiation, turbidity and chemical factors are the other elements that influence the water environment. Besides these elements, the reaction of water also influences various chemical and biochemical processes of living things.

The wave of the environmental consciousness is being spread in India and all over the world. One of the major types of environmental pollution is marine pollution; it has adverse effects on human beings, on the animals that live in and around the sea and in the environment.

The common man understands pollutant as a non-living, man-made substance which accumulates in a particular area causing threat to the human activities. Marine pollution is .caused by man, directly or indirectly resultingi in harmful effects to living things and even to man.

Oceans cover 361 million Km^2 and nearly 71% of the earth's surface. A total of approximately 1.37x10^6 liters of water is lodged in oceans. The depth of all oceans vary, average being 3800m and the greatest known depth being 10,800m in the marinas Trench in the Pacific ocean. Similarly, salinity also varies with depth and geography.

Oceans remain as an abode of thousands of different kinds of plants and animals. Besides there is accumulation of valuable chemicals and minerals too. The minerals can be used as fuels or raw materials in the industry. Human beings and domestic animals harvest animals and plants as food. The requirements of ever increasing population of humans be animals and plants as food. The requirements of ever increasing population of humans be met by additional food sources. Eventually this led to the exploitation of marine enviornment.

The tremendous amount of water became seat to land in all of man's wastes. The rivers of the world join with oceans. Usually about 2.0 X10^{14} metric tones of water enter into the oceans by rivers every year. But this amount of water is much smaller than the water already there in the oceans. Rivers while joining into the oceans carry some dissolved materials. Also, pollutants from the atmosphere directly fall into the river through rain. Particularly in coastal areas where man lives, the chances of formation of pollution is more. So, pollutants are not envenly spread throughout the oceans. it is interesting to note that oceans are not exempted from pollution and being sensitized to pollutants.

Marine environment is being polluted by toxic organic and inorganic materials, acids and bases, petroleum, sediments, solid wastes, heat, radioactive materials, nutrients, and pathogens.

TOXIC ORGANIC AND INORGANIC MATERIALS

Most of the biocides like fungicides, herbicides, insecticides, rodenticides, pesticides, petroleum hydrocarbons and industrial chemicals distrub the marine enviornment. Pesticides such as DDT and kepone are more soluble in oil than in water, if once they are accumulated in various tissues of living being they stay for a long time. However, many of the toxic inorganic are quite harmless and even in larger quantities they are destructive and easily deteriorated to simpler compounds.

ACIDS AND BASES

Acids and bases are reaching the sea either from industries (accidentally) or from the damage of tankers. The ecological balance of the marine environment is distrubed due to the discharge of acids and bases. Both these elements are distrubing or decreasing the normal pH of marine water. Eventually the low level of pH has become a seat for the increase of toxins.

PETROLEUM

The sources of entry of petroleum to marine environment are many. It enters to the marine water during accidental losses, damage to tankers, losses associated with refineries etc.

SEDIMENTS

Sediments affect the growth of plants and the life of bottom dwelling organisms such as oysters. The sediments that are accumulated at the bottom block the larger portion of light and therefore effects the photosynthetic activity of sea plants.

SOLID WASTES

Now-a-days in urban areas it has become a problem to dump in the used or waste products. Due to the increase of heavy population also, most of the land is occupied for building individual houses or apartments. ultimately, the sea has become a dumping ground for the waste products. Products containing toxins cause a serious threat to small fish of coastal regions andlarger fish of oceanic environment.

HEAT

Release of hot wataer from industries directly or indirectly to the sea results inthe production of excess of heat. Many of species of fish may survive in heat environment but the reproductive capacity or the growth rate of fish are seriously effected by excess of heat. The changes of water temperature is partially unbearable by the fish immune system to get acclimatised to fluctuations of temperature may be decreased and ultimately fish may die immediately.

RADIOACTIVE MATERIALS

It is surprising to not that marine environment is also exposed to radioactivity. All the activities of nuclear power plants and the burning of coal gives out radio active materials which are then passed to the environment of the sea. There are two types radiations known as non-ionising radiations and ionising radiations. Radiations of non-ionising type have shorter wave length but cause greatest damage to micro-organisms and to higher plants and animals that live at surface. Compared to non-ionising radiations, ionising radiations are dangerous to living organisms. Some of the radiations are borne in the environment and some are made by man knowingly or unknowingly. it is interesting to note that radiations are emitted from even T.V.sets.

NUTRIENTS

Nutrients or the common fertilizers that are used by man for the growth of plants run to sea water. The use of nutrients especially in coastal areas are causing great ill health to human beings. Nutrients which are present in domestic sewage effluents and agricultural wastes have been not only run to the marine environment but also affect the general health of humans.

PATHOGENS

Different species of bacteria, virus, fungus and protozoa are found in marine water. These pathogenic forms cause disease in plants and animals which live in marine enviornment. Also, those humans who come to the marine water on any purpose may become victim when he was invaded by pathogens. By eating the marine fish or other animals (which are exposed to pathogens),man may undergo sickness. most of the pathogens are found in sewage. However, pathogens grow and reproduce whenever the conditions are favourable to them.

Marine environment is polluted mainly due to the activities of industries, electricity, sewage treatment, non-industrial -works and wastes.

Industries utilize large amounts of water. The water that is used may be heated or mixed with any chemicals/plllutants., however, whether these are harmless or not that water discharges into the oceanic environment. Similarly, the generation of electricity produce excess of heat which again creates unfavourable environment. Excess of heat is not suitable for the non-pathogenic organisms. Some marine organisms may also suffer when water gets heated abnormally .

Sewage treatment is one of the most important aspect to be taken by aquanculurists and industrialists.

A biological waste water treatment is very much needed to save the marine environment.

10

NATURAL RESOURCES AND THEIR CONSERVATION

Dr. G. Vijayalakshmi,
Reader, Dept of Education,
Sri Padmavathi Mahila Visvavidyalayam
Tirupati—517 502 -A.P.

Natural Resources which used to be available in abundance have depleted most alarmingly in some causes. Everyone having concern for environment wonders whether development can be sustained if consumption of water and energy is not requalted and if pollution of air, soil and water is not controlled. The urbrided growth of population cupled with fast changing styles of lliving based on luxurious and high energy consuming goods as led to the proliteration of industries in paper, steel, oil, sugar, pharmaceuticals, pesticides, fertilizers, power, chemicals etc.

To ensure the healthy growth and development of man and other forms of life and to conserve natural resources. There is an urgent need to avoid any conflict between development and environment.

Choices between needs and wants may come into conflict more frequently as human population grows and consumption levels rise within finite resource Imits. Many developing countries export their resources to developed countries often at low prices and poor terms of trade. The developed countries with 20% of the world's population consume 80% of the world's resources, between its extraction and its use, a ntural resource may undergo many transformations. These steps often affect the environment in a negative way.

MANAGEMENT AND CONSERVATION

Growing population, increasing consumption and poor management of existing resources are leading to a decline in natural resources. Studying and understanding resources is imperative for the proper management of the environment. Effective ways to conserve both renewable and nonrenewable resources include reducing wasteful consumption and by recycling whenever possible, sometimes it is possible to substitute one resource for another. Substitution of resources does not necessarily result in their conservation. True conservatiion of resources requires a decrease in their use. We should not exhaust our resources capital but should use our resource judiciously. Environment strategies should vary with the environment and the resources that are to be managed. For e.g. in India hill areas are entirely different from the plains and require management solutions specific to their problems. Effective conservation programmes should involve the communities adjacent to the resource are affected by resource use policy.

Multiple use management means management of a resource for the greatest possible good for the longest time with the least possible enviornmental damage. It means meeting many rather than single needs. For e.g., multi use mangement of wetland may meet needs for water storage, food production, flood control, wild life habitat and recreation. It is desirable to manage forestry agricultural or other resources so that they produce sustained yields, unimpaired by periodic harvests.

The biosphere has a limited carrying capacity based on its finite resource base. The effects of over utilization are already straining these limited resources. Therefore the resources should be used judiciously and in a sustainable quality of life to all people if resources are wisely conserved and fairly distributed. Wise management of resources requires that they be viewed from a global perspective. The quality of future generations depends on how the resources are being utilised.

Sustainable development is a process of change of which the exploitation of resources, direction of investment. Orientation of technical development and insititutional change are made consistent with future as well as present social and economic needs.

ENERGY RESOURCE

Efforts should be made to develop energy resources which are ecologically most acceptable. The decision to develop a resource must be governed by long term ecological considerations, rather than only short term economic ones. In many countries over 90% of the domestic energy is supplied by wood. Creating fuel wood plantations on maginal land is one approach to fuel wood demands.

For thousands of years people have been using the sun to dry grain, fruit and timber. But traditional open air methods are slow and food sometimes decays before its dries. Only in the present century systematic efforts have been made to harness solar energy for these uses. For e.g., simple solar dryers have been developed which speed the drying process and protect the food from pests, dust and rain.

Globally our demands for energy have increased and are continuing to increase. This is due to both, to population growth and the increase of per capita consumption, especially in industrialized countries. Fossil fuels are fossilized organic remains which over millions of years have become oil, gas and coal. Because their formation take so long, these sources are non-ronewable. Exploitation and production of oil and natural gas can have a number of adverse environmental effects.

Renewable energy sources are those which cab be replrished relatively rapidly. These include wind power, hydropower, solar energy from biological processes for e.g., recycled biomass from urban wastes However, ever some of these can be exhausted when their rate of use greatly exceeds their rate on replerishment e.g., trees used as souce of fuel wood Renewable energy sources may cause less environmental disruption that non-renewable energy sources. However, ever some of these can damage the environment like large hydro power projects.

SOLAR ENERGY

Sun provides most of the energy used by living organisms on earth. Solar energy also powers the movement of global air masses, the hydrological cycle and ocean currents. The ultimate soure of energy in most ecosystems is sunlight.

Solar energy is the energy derived from the sun. it may be used to hating, cooling and for generating electricity . However to become commercially viable, advances in technology are required for the storage of energy and its conversion to an usable form. There are many reasons for the use of solar energy , for e.g. the source is inexhaustible and its use does not cause pollution. Hence, the technology should be developed. Solar energy can be harvested indirectly through water energy, wind energy and the stored energy from plants used as duel. Harnessing of solar energy does not have adverse environmental effects like pollution or distrubance of ecosystems. In India efforts are being made to popularise the use of solar energy for domestic and commercial purposes.

WIND ENERGY

Wind energy refers to the use of wind power for creating electricity or for moving objects like water pumps, grinding stones. Wind has the potential for commercial generation of electricity.

GEOTHERMAL ENERGY

Geothermal energy is the heat from the earth which may be used to generate electricity, heat building etc. It is an effective and cheap source of energy but is limited to those places where geohermal springs occurs naturally. These waters however may contain trace minerals such as arsenic which can pollute drinking water supplies.

Wastes e.g. crop residues, animal dung are increasingly used to generate energy. Animal wastes cab be used to generate biogas. Nuclear power uses the energy released from the splitting of nuclear of atoms to generate electricity. The process requires expensive technology and is controversial because it generates radioactive wastes. Also as in the recent accident at Chernobyl, nuclear power accidents can release radioactivity into the biosphere, Fossil fuels are finite and expensive and their use can have significant environmental effects. Therefore, it is necessary to explore a mixture of energy options including nuclear energy, wind enrgy, biomass, solar energy etc., knowingly or unknowingly energy is often being wasted e.g., using in efficinent cooking methods, leaving lights on when not needed.

MINERAL RESOURCES

Mineral resources are continually being formed by geological processes, but the rate is so low that we can rely on to those deposits already in existence. The current rate of mineral use far exceeds the rate of formation. Mineral resources are thus considered non-renewable. Minerals are important in our daily life. Without the minerals from the earth the petroleum and other organic resources, modern products such as synthetic fibers drugs and slicon chips would not be possible. it is unlikely to advance into the industrial age or into the present technolgical era without extensive use of these resources. The extraction of minerals can have negative effects on the environment as waste minerals brought to the surface can cover large areas while water from abandoned mines is acidic. Moreover surface mining often leads to deforestation, dust formation reduced percolation of rain, increased run off, erosion and land slides. In humid areas it can lead to high acidity of soils and surrounding water affecting terrestrial and acquatic life. Damage caused by surface mining can be repaired some what by top soil replacement, the addition of organic fertilizers and by afforestation.

WATER RESOURCES

Water is the source of one fourth of the electricity generated in the world. Hydro power i.e. water motion converted to usable energy resources unlike fossil fuels, are widely dispensed. Asia has more than one fourth of world's potential hydropower resorces. Damage done to surface waters is harden to

Clean sustainable water supplies are today becoming increasingly rare. Growing population, agriculture and industry are increasing the demand for water. Many parts of India suffer from severe water shortage. India yet uses only one tenth of its annual rainfall. Water management practices such as collection and proper storage of rain water and afforestation of catchment areas can help to prevent such shortages. Siltation of reservoirs has shortened the life span of most hydroelectric projects in India. Siltation can be reduced by watershed management which may be easier in the case of small scale hydroelectric projects than large ones. Watershed planning involved comprehensive development and use of water, soil and other resources in a watershed, even if the area is divided by political boundaries by considering the basic needs of the people living in that area.Ground water is an important source of water for drinking, industry and irrigation. The increasing number of borewells in costal areas is leading to the growing risk of salt water intrusion. Ground water is less easily polluted than surface water because pollutants are filtered out as water passes through soil. When groundwater is becoming polluted. The pollution is more difficult to detect and treat.

Waste water treatment is the removal of pathogens (disease causing organisms) and soluble and nonsoluble materials from waste water before releasing it into the environment. Inadequate waste water treatment and lack of drainage facilities are some of the major factors in the spread of diseases such as malaria. In India, the lack of potable water in many rural areas has led to the endemic occurrence of dysentery, typhoid and other water borne diseases.

LAND RESORCES

Land use refers to the way of harnessing the potential resources in a given area. Land use profitable in the short term may not be the best use in terms of the health and ecology of the land in the long run. Good land is often wasted and degraded by stone quarrying. The effects of land use tend to be cumulative. Therefore, it is obligatory to future generations to minimise its negative effects. Wrong land use practices include deforestation, over-grazing, overcropping, excessive irrigation and unplanned urbanization. These can result in erosion, reduced ground water recharge, deterioration of soil quality, salinization, lowered crop yields, siltation of surface waters and flooding of low lying areas. Mining and quarrying activities cause significant damage to the land. However, it may be possible to reclaim such land through practices such as afforestation and replacement of top soil. Resettlement and land reforms can reduce landlessness in the short run, but only population stabilization will work in the long run. As pressure on land resorces increase, it will be necessary to use the same piece of land in a number of ways at the same time. Future land use planning will have to emphasize multiple land use. Good land use practice are those which would satisfy today's needs without compromising the ability of the land to sustain. Comprehensive information on land - its characteristics, tenure, use and legislation should be collected and constantly updated for the use of citizens and the government. Land management planning is most effective when done with the involvement of the local people and their requirement. Soil can take hundreds of years to develop. Although traditionally taken for granted as an infinite resource, soil must be consdiered a non-renewable resource and conserved accordingly. Soil conservation is vital for food production. Maintaining soil productivity is esssential to the welfare of all nations and future generations.

Legislation and education are among the measures necessary to protect them. Educating people on the importance of preserving and conserving natural resources is an integral part of management as it results in changes in people's values, attitudes and behaviour. Resources are uneven in their distribution and accessibility not only among nations, but also within them. Attitudes towards use of resources have changed throughout history. Today our conservation ethic reflects our realization that resources are finite.

Conservation requires people's recognition of their responsibility to maintain the environment and their involvement in this process. Indian tradition teaches that all forms of life human, animal and plant are sacred and so closely linked that disturbance in one gives rise to imbalance in the other. Conservation is a reiteration of this attitude.

Cultural resources in the form of historical buildings, monuments, arts, crafts and language should be preserved and maintained. Once lost those rich ties with history and the environment cannot be easily restored.

11

ENVIRONMENTAL CRISES AND CONSERVATION

Dr. N. Ramnath Kishan
Reader in Education,
Kakatiya University,
Warangal—506 009- A.P.

ENVIRONMENT

Environment comprises almost everything around us. It includes humans, plants, animals and invisible mocro-organisms. also it includes surface water, ground water, air, land, minerals and oil and other elements available from the earth.

Environment has been defined as the aggregate of all external conditions and influences affecting the life and development of an organism. Environment is both a physical and social milieu.

Eduard Suess (1875) an Australian geologist has defined biosphere as part of the world where life exists. The environment is any region surrounding or circumstances in which anything exists or everthing external to the organisation. The environment of an organisation includes the organic or abiotic milieu (geographical location) including non-living organic matter and all othe organisms, plants and animals in the region. The environment of human beings includes the abiotic factors of land, water, atmosphere, climatae, sound, odours and tastes, the biotic factors of animals, plants bacteria, virus and social factors of aesthetics. They grow out of the pressing social problems and are multi-disciplinary in nature. They include the study of man as an integral part of every problem and are conceived with human problems in relation to an environment of which man is both victim and conqueror.

ENVIRONMENTAL CONSERVATION

According to the Dictionary of Environment (Mc Millan). Environmental conservation means the planning and management of resources so as to secure their wise use and continuity of supply while maintaing and enhancing their quality, value and diversity. Resources may be man-made or natural. The action of conserving includes preservation from destructive influences, natural decay or waste.

Conservation is the careful use of land, air, water minerals and other natural resources. it is infact the planned use of the environment using all the planning foresight and cooperation that man can muster.

The function of conservation also rests on the perceptual levels of the individual. According to Whyte (1977) environmental perception is "Human awareness" and general understanding of one's environment. Behaviour in an environment is influenced by our awareness of the need to adapt to an environment which in turn triggers the behaviour of the individual.

ENVIRONMENTAL CRISES

One crisis which can has created for himself through his own action is that caused by land dereliction. Which has been taking place increasingly for man needs land for his personal use. He does not any more like to live in burrows or on trees or in caves or just on the open land like many other mammals: he lilkes to live in cottages, bungalows, flats and houses and in order to build them, he has to destroy forests, dig earth, make bricks, manufacture steel and produce concrete and cement. he has been doing this more and more as human population has been increasing. He has also been setting up industries to produce an ever increasing number of consumer goods which promise to make his life and living comfortable and has in the process been felling trees, destroying forests and despoiling pastures. In consequence, some serious problems which could have otherwise been avoided have baffled him.

The reckless destruction of forests and despoliation of pastures have distrubed some food chains found in nature and have caused extinction of some species of animals, creating thereby an ecological problem. A food chain begins with antotrophs or producers i.e. plants and goes upto carnivores. For instance, deer eats grass and lion eats deer. Their food chain would, therefore begin with grass and go upto lion. It can be represented as grass-deer-lion. Now since food contains energy, a food chain is a flow of energy. The energy flows from plants to herbivores. It gives us an idea of the dependence of one form of life on another and of man on nature and should make him realise that he should not destroy food chains recklessly because doing that would forebode his doom.

The destruction of forests has been tremendous since industrial revolution. Trees have been felled and forests cleared upto set up industries, establish villages and build towns and cities. The aftermath has been soil erosion and land dereliction, for in the absence of trees, rain water washes away the humus and the top soil making land unfit for cultivation.Besides that, the catchment area divested of trees cannot hold rain water which drains out rapidly and therefore, does not accumulate and percolate to the lakes and rivers and thus we lose a large quantity of water which could have otherwise been available for being used throughout the rest of the year.

Not only by cutting forests but also by though less disposal of industrial wastes man has created problems of water pollution for himself. The discharge of industrial wastes contaminated water and mixes it with poisonous chemicals which kill aquatic plants and animals such as fishes and crabs and disturb the eco-system. Similarly, the disposal of the sewage of big cities into the rivers promotes the growth of phytoplantons which reduce the level of oxygen in the water. This reduction in the oxygen kills many animals of the sea, chief among them being fishes, a prominent source of man's proteinous food. Thus industrial waste and sewage are dangerous sources of water pollution. A third source of water pollution is our bathing and washing in the rivers, lakes and ponds, for all the germs in the human body such as those of typhoid, cholera and hepatitis are washed into the water.

Perhaps more dangerous than water pollution is air pollution, for the same air sweeps across all the continents and all of us breathe the same air throughout the world.

The primary source of air pollution is smoke emitted by different objects, right from the hearth in a hut to the exhaust of the jet aeroplanes. We realise this everyday, no matter whether we may be in village or in cities. When in village, we find at the dusk time that smoke emitted by burning cowdung and chips of wood hangs so thickly in the air that it enters our eyes and noses. In cities too, coal burnt in power stations at homes and in factories enters the atmosphere like an eternal stream like a cloud that bursts out of the mouth of a chimney to hang around for some time and then get lost within the folds of the surrounding air, which in the process gets polluted. Similarly, smoke exhausted by automobiles, buses aeroplanes, etc, pollutes air by increasing the proportion of carbon dioxide, carbon monoxide and soot.

In addition to despoliation of land and pollution of water and air, noise pollution is also increasing day by day. An ordinary aeroplane strikes a deafening blow on our ears. The rumble of trains and the noise of the four wheelers, two wheelers plying all the time on the roads of metropolises seem to be a great nuisance. And add to all this engines of factories, sirens and a innumerable other things. One feels really disgusted with sounds, all this tells upon one's nerves and produces not only deafness but also nervous tension, blood pressure, peptic ulcers and heart trouble.

Apart from these problems of land dereliction and environmental pollution, one other problem very dangerous to mankind is that of population explosion,Population should not be allowed to explode so much as to outstrip food supply. It should rather be controlled so that the food required to feed our people may not exceed our capacity to produce it. For this he require more land hence he may be forced to encroach upon forests and mountains in his search for more cultivable and habitable land. He may also need space for grazing his cattle and finding none he may have to eat them and after that kill all wild animals for food. Thus, population explosion may aggravate the ecological crisis in which we have already placed ourselves. If we do not realise this now, it may be too late to do anything in future and we may find it very hard to fight against discomfort, over crowding and final annihilation.

The main problem before us, therefore, is that of the conservation of natural resources. Man has to afforest the despoiled lands. He has to reduce water,air and noise pollution. He has to plan for conserving soils, water, forests, wild life and for beautifying his environment. he has also to implement these plans and to evaluate them from time to time and to take remdial steps.

The conservation of water can be made possible if we are able to save as much rain water from flowing into the sea as we can. Accordingly, the first thing that we have to do is to plant as many trees as is possible in the hills and in the catchment areas. The roots of these trees and other vegetation will bind the soil and help it in holding water. A second method of retaining water is to construct dams. The dams can regulate the water supply in the rivers, prevent them from sitting on one hand and on the other can ensure a regular supply of water to the fields, the year round. Thus they can prevent floods during rainy season and drought during lean months.

Conservation of forests involves using the existing ones most prudently. It entails observing economy in lumbering, sawing the logs so as to get maximum amount of lumber, using all parts of the trees and not wasting half or two-third of it before converting it into finished products. It also implies prevention of forest fires and control of insects and diseases. Conservation of forests also means afforestation. Needless to say, forests can be grown anywhere, right from the crowded industrial cities to the slopes of the hills. They can be grown on level lands, or rocks,in swampy places, in marshy areas, on sea coasts and in mountains. Apart from growing trees in forests we may grow them in our compunds,on the avenues, and wherever we can.

The review of our experiences in environmental conservation and enrichment in India suggests the need for implementing a meaningful environment education programme to cover our students, out of school youth; the villagers, the urbanities and women particularly. The out -reach capacity of the colleges and the universities is unlimited. Meaningful learning packages could be evolved and delivered to the public, using andragogic and pedagofic principles. The face-to-face contact modalities and distance learning techniques could be utilized for sensitizing the people to resort to micro level, local conservation practices.

REFERENCES

1. Bhatia S.C., papers in Environmental Education, Published by IUACE, New Delhi, 1984.

2. Dix. H.M., Environmental Pollution, John wiley and sons, New York. 1981.

3. Mahajan S.P., Pollution control in process Industries Tata Mc Graw-Hill Publishing Co, Ltd., New Delhi, 1985.

4. Sharma, R.C., Environmental Education, Edn,2, Metropolitan Book Co, Pvt.Ltd., New Delhi, 1986.

12

BIODIVERSITY : THE CONCEPT, NEED AND IMPORTANCE

Dr. Kaiser Jamil
Head, Biology Division
I.I.C.T., Hyderabad-2

Bio-diversity is a comprehensive word for the degree of nature's variety, including.

(a) The number and frequency of ecosystems

(b) Species and genes in a given an essemblase

(c) It embraces both species richness and genetic diversity, (both of which are being threatened throughout the world)

THE THREAT

- Species extinctions and a reduction in genetic variability is taking place at rates never before witnessed.

- Natural areas are very rare in industrialized counter, although some say that they have cultural landscapes, but there are artificial.

- For the last 20,000 years humans have modified and charged the natural world, except for a few areas in the world which are not affected by civilizations and still retain climax communities.

LOSSES IN BIODIVERESITY

- there has been much speculation about the total number of specieson the earth. Some report 1.6 million, while other reports indicate 5-10 million species, However, those estimates are based on; 800.000 insect species, while there could be many more unnamed insects and arthropods.

- Recent reasearch on the number of fungal species has added to the debate abot the number of species which could be 1.6 million rather than 69,000 or so recorded earlier.

- However the rate at which species are becoming extinct as a result of exploitation, is at a level never witnesses before!

THE GROWING LOSS IN BIODIVERSITY

The cause is due to rapidly expanding world population. The symptoms can be grouped under these broad heading:

(a) Pollution disturbance and other human-made perturbations.

(b) Excessive exploitation of species and natural areas for food, collection materials, (direct extirpation of pests).

(c) Reduction and fragmentation of natural areas (habitat and ecosystem).

POLLUTION AND RELATED EFFECTS

- Plant and animals and habitats are increasingly having harmed by industrial activities and pollution.

- Excessive use of agrochemicals.

- Incidences of oil spills

- Acid rain

- Cumulative effects of DDT and other chlorinated hydrocarbons, increase in litter and debris.

- Use of non-bio degradable materials (plastics etc,). - loss of forest covers (over exploitation).

- Depleting wetlands (for concrete constructions).

(These habitants support large numbers of species, and also large number centres of endemism),

(In one hecare of Amazon's rain forests Gentry (1988) recorded 300 species of trees!)

The much publicized losses in biodiversity has been quantified with the advances in Remote Sensing techniques, Advanced remote sensing techniques, especially by way of satellites have provided much of the raw data for reliabie estimates.

- Deforestation, buring and loss of plant life, causes increase in levels of green house gases such as CO_2.

- Disruption of moisture cycling through partial deforestation may result in the steady descreation of some remaining forests.

Wetlands: A collective term for a range of inland. Coastal and marine habitats characterized by permanent water-logging.

- Wetlands comprise of saltwater, fresh water and artificial

Wetlands and these Include

Estuaries
Coasts
Marshes/mangroves
Swamps
Lakes
Peatland and
Artificial reservoirs

- Wetlands specially mangrove swamps, are areas of very high biological productivity and support high levels of species richness.

- Wetlands are important locations for fisheries agriculture, water supply, forestry, recreation and tourism, some also provide flood control and storm protection.

Reduction and Fragmentation of Habitats

- The greatest threat to wild life today is the ever increasing exploitation of land.

- In a sense, the niche of humankind is expanding at the expense of most other species.

- The ever increasing exploitation is resulting in damage, loss and gragementation of natural areas in all continuously inhabited parts of the world: it is happening in,

    1. Desert regions
    2. Temperatae regions
    3. Trophical regions

  Some reports indicate 67% of the endangered, vulnerable and rare species of vertibrates as being threatened by habitat degradation, loss and fragmentation.

- Fragmented and ioslated populations become more vulnerable to disturbance and inbreeding can occur in small isolated populations, sometimes leading to loss of genetic diversity.

- Habitat fragmentation led to population decline of musk turtles, migratory brids, and other faxa.

  (In-breeding and genetic drift, increase in population size of invasive species).

BENEFITS AND FUNCTIONS OF BIODIVERSITY

I. Ethical and moral values:

1. Intrinsic value of nature
2. Natural world has value as a human heritage

II. Enjoyment and Aesthetic Values

1. Leisure activities ranging from bird watching to walking
2. Sporting activities ranging from orienteering to diving
3. Aesthetic value by way of seeing, hearing or touching wildlife.

III. Use as a Resource for Food, Materials, Research Inspiration and Education (Utilitarian)

1. As a genetic resource for source of food
2. Souce for organisms for biological control
3. Pharmaceutical products
4. Materials for buildings, fuel for energy
5. For scientific research and educatiional value

IV. Maintenance of the Environment (Ecosystems and Climates)

1. Role in maintaining CO_2-O_2 balance
2. Role in maintaing water cycles and maintaining water catchments.
3. Role in absorbing waste materials
4. Role in determining the nature of world climates regional climates and microclimates.
5. Indicators of environmental changes
6. Protection from harmful weather conditions, wind breaks, flood barriers.

THE MEANING OF BIOLOGICAL DIVERSITY

Biodiversity may be described in terms of,
genes
species and
ecosystems
corresponding to three fundamental and hierarchially related levels of biological organisation.

Genetic Diversity

Genetic diversity is the sum of genetic information contained in the genes of individulas, of plants, animals and moiro-organisms.

Each species is the repository of an immense amount of genetic information. The number of genes range from 1000 in bacteria to 400.000 or more in many flowering plants.

Each species made up of many organisms and virtually no 2 members of the same species are genetically identified.

CONSERVATION

It seems that, in general, conservation of plants and animals is best done insites, that is in natural and semi-natural areas.

Protected areas of many kinds have a role to play in conserving the world's biodiversity in monitoring global change and in long term ecological studies.

The loss of the World's biological diversity is causing major concern world wide, this culminated in a world convention on Biological diversity at Rio de Janeiro in 1992.

Conservation of some area could also be important for sustainable developent, for e.g. BIOSPHERE RESERVES are protected areas recognised by the UNESCO Programme on Man and Biosphere (MAB) for their value in supporting sustainable development and also their value in providing scientific knowledge.

There are about 300 Biosphere Reserves in 75 countries ranging in size from 70 million hectares (North-east Greenland Reserve) to 500 ha, (North Bull Island in Ireland).

CONSERVATION

Some major organisations involved in world conservation projects include the:

i. International board for plant Genetic Resoruces (IBPGR)

ii. The world Conservation Union (IUCN)

iii. The world Resources Institute (WRI)

iv. The world Conservation Monitoring Centre (WCMC)

v. And UNESCO Programme on Man and Biosphere.

Together, these organistions formed UNEP and prepared a strategy in 1980 i.e. a milestone document which promotes these objectives.

(a) Maintence of ecological processes as life support systems.

(b) Preservation of genetic diversity conservation of wild species.

(c) Sustainable utilization of species and ecosystems.

In 1991, IUCN, WWF and UNEP Published a sequel to the world Conservation Strategy " Carrying for the Earth, A strategy for sustainability".

13

BIODIVERSITY: ITS NEED AND IMPORTANCE

Mrs. Deepika, Lecturer
Fatima College of Education
Kazipet, warangal 506 009

INTRODUCTION

Environment may be defined as the "sum of all external and internal factors- physical, chemical and biological which affect- the structure and function of a living organism or a community of the organisms, condtions of the buildings and monuments exposed to it, recreation or visual enjoyment". it includes four important components namely Atmosphere (Air), Hydrosphere (Water) Lithosphere (Land) and Biosphere. Biosphere or ecosphere is the largest and most nearly self sufficient biological system which includes all of the earths living organisms interacting with the physical environment as a whole so as to maintain a steady state system intermediate in the flow of energy between the high energy input of the sun and thermal sink of space. It is defined as a part of the lithosphere, hydrosphere and atmosphere. Biosphere includes the bio-diversity.

The decline in environmental quality has been evidenced by increasing pollution, loss if vegetational cover and biological diversity, excessive concentration of harmful chemicals in the ambient environment, in the food chain, growing risk of environmental accidents and the threat to the life support systems.

BIO-DIVERSITY- DEFINITION ANDMEANING

Bio-diversity means the variability among living organisms from all sorces including terrestrial, marine and other aquatic ecosystems and the ecological complexes of which they are part, this includes diversity within, sepcies, between species and of ecosystems. Ecosystem is a dynamic complex of plant, animal and micro-organism communities and their non-living environment interacting as a functional unit.

Bio-diversity indicates variations and abundance of species and their living environment. Species diversity is represented by morphological, physiological and genetic features. The relative percentages of species of different life forms in a given area indicates biological spectrum.

The process of species diversification started soon after the origin of life on the planet. it is a gradual process, influenced by various geo-physical and climatic factors, resulting in the emergence of new strains and subspecies. Bioolgical diversity is species richness (number of species in a community of living systems). Bio-diversity can be discussed under four levels:

a) Individuals

b) Population (interbreeding between individuals of a species and a sexual reproduction of individuals in some species).

c) Communitics (combination of population of different species occupying the same habitat) and

d) Ecosystems (interacting group of communities in a climatic region which is self-sustaining and self-regulating).

Genetic diversity is heritable diversity within and between the species of a genus. The diversity of biological resoruces is the result of three cardinal processes which are responsible for organic evolution. The three cardinal processes are (1) mutations, 92) Recombination, (3) Natural selection.

MUTATION

Any sudden, inheritable change in genotype that is not a result of recombination and which does not exist previously in the parents. If somatic cells undergo genetic change, it may result in abnormalities of growth. Such changes are somatic mutations and are not inherited. Mutations may be gene mutations i.e., alteration of a single gene or chromosomal mutations that involve large number of genes present on a segment of chromosome. Latter include delection, duplication, inversion and translocation. Frequency of spontaneous mutations is extremely low and differs with different gene loci. gene mutations soemtimes gives rise to diversification.

RECOMBINATION

It results in genetic material DNA (De-Oxy Ribo Nucleic Acid) in which crossing over or chromosome reassortment has occurred naturally. At present genetic material with novel sequence is formed by techniques of genetic engineering (recombinant DNA technology).

NATURAL SELECTION

It is the action of nature in organisms allowing the survival and reproduction of only those organisms in a population which are best adopted to the conditions of their habitat. The action is the basis of Darwinian evolution and it results in diversification, speciation and evolution.

On this planet 5-10 million species of biota (all the organisms of all species living in an area or region) are the result of 3 billion years of evolution. At present 1.5 million species are known to inhabit the earth (humans are just one of them), an estimated one fourth to one third is likely to become extinct within the next few decades.

BIO-DIVERSITY IN INDIA

India's biological diversity comprising living components of three different realms, namely palearactic, indomalayan and Ethiopian is one of the most significant in the world, because of its unique biogeographical composition. The country has about 5 percent of living resoruces, one third of which are land bound with just two percent of landmass. Therefore it has been designated as one of the 12 mega-diversity states in the world.

The country has more than 17 percent of land under forest cover and more than 54,000 sq.km. of wetland under protection. Its living resources include 60,000 species of insects, 5,000 species of mammals, 1230 species of birds, 400 species of reptiles, 150 species of lizards, 30 species of turtiles, 3 species of crocodiles, 142 species of amphibians, 105 genera of fresh water fishes. Besides this, the Indian fauna has been enriched by migration of birds from siberia, Europe and other animals from anepal, Malasia, Bangladesh, Burma and Bhutan. india has 45,000 species of wild plants which includes more than 75 pecent of the 425 families of flowering plants found all over the world.

In India, ther is an equally impressive range of domesticated bio-diversity. At least 166 species of crops and 320 species of wild relatives of crops are known to have origniated here. Within each of these species, the variety is astounding. For instance 50,000 to 60,000 varieties of rice were grown in India. Similarly significant in the indigenous livestock diversity, with 27 breeds of cattle, 40 sheep and 22 goats.

NEED AND IMPORTANCE OF BIO-DIVERSITY

Biological diversity plays a prominent role in the Nature. It porvides major clues regading the orgigin and the evolution and the speciation process of species to the scientists. Species diversification is influenced by various factors and bio-diversity acts as a major tool for assessing the impact of various factors in the process of species diversification. The health of a particular habitat and its potential to sustain life is indicated by its bio-diversity.

Bio-diversity plays a significant role in Ecology, by enriching the soil (by adding sufficient organic matter and increasing soil fertility), maintaing water and clilmate cycle, humidity, precipitation and recycling and conversion of waste material into nutrients. Ecological diversity is of great significance to human society. Food, medicine and raw material for industry and household purposes are obtained from various living resources. Its need is felt in four specific areas:

1. Preservation and restoration of ecological balance;

2. Preservation of National Heritagae of the country;

3. Meeting the basic needs of the people;

4. Meeting the intrinsic relationship between forests, tribals and other people.

The scientific explanation to know the need and importance of bio-diversity includes:

1. All forms of life-human, animals and plants are closely inter-linked and istrubance in one form gives rise to imbalance in the other. Each species has its own place, duty and special utility. All life forms on planet are interdependent and man is only a strand in the delicate web of relationship. Every time a species becomes extinct, a strand is broken and man himself moves closer to his doom.

2. Each species in ecosystem is vital to maintain a unique ecological status. Earth consists of ecosystem and ecosystems are important for existence of man. Change in composition of species in ecosystem will change human environment and affect the human life which sometimes is not noticed.

3. Man should know the evolutionary process and biology in an ecosystem. All animals including man are subject to evolutionary process. Knowledge of bio-diversity helps man in understanding his own evolution and biology. Thus it is essential for evolution and for maintaining life sustaing systems of the biosphere.

4. The livestock and crops are hybrids, the rusult of cropbreeding. Probability for the creation of new superior varieties depend upon the richness of genetic diversity in the nature. The breeding potentiality, existence of hybrid and selected one will be endangered without wild ancestors.

5. The physical conditions of environment (Atmosphere, lithosphere and hydrosphere) are improved and maintained properly by bio-diversity functioning in the nature.

6. Certain animals, small organisms and creatures are indicators of change in environment. Any change in quality of water, land and air will be known by variation of population or change in behaviour of certain living organisms. Change in ecosystem community structure and function give early warning of expected danger to the health.

7. Bio-diversity is directly related to 'quality of life'.

8. In addition to the above scientific information, bio-diversity is very valuable from cultural, recreational, aesthetic and economic points of views.

9. Conservation and sustainable use of biological diversity will strengthen friendly relations among countries and contribute to peace for human kind.

10. Conservation and sustainable use of bio-diversity is essential for the benefit of present and future generations.

11. Biological diversity results in broad range of environmental economic and social benefits.

CONCLUSION:

Through out the World, Bio-diversity has come under tremendous pressure. Biological extinction which led to the disappearance of one species in several hundred years has now been replaced by accelerated rate of extinction of species. The giant Dinosaurs and other large mammals and birds in the past, who had once ruled over the animal kingdom has become extinct. At present the world has realised the importance of bio-diversity. Several conventions and agreements on conservation and protection of various organisms have been drawn up since 1970, when UNESCO heald the first Man and Biosphere convention. Some other major ones are CITES (Conventions on International Trade in Endangered Species, 1973), and the Convention Bio-diversity conservation. According to convention on Bio-diversity both Ex-Situ and In-Situ conservation of bio-diversity should be adopted, and sustainable use of biological diversity is of critical importance for meeting the food, health and needs of the growing world population, for which purpose access to and sharing of both genetic resources and technologies are esential.

14

ENVIRONMENTAL MANAGEMENT AND PROTECTION

Dr. Y. Prameela Devi,
Environmental Biology
Research Laboratory
Department of Zoology,
Kakatiya University
Warangal—506 009 -A.P.

Environment is the physical chemical and biotic conditions surrounding an organism or the sum total of all conditions and influences the development and life of organisms. The system resulting from the integration of all the living and non-living factors of the environment is simply known as ecosystem where interactions of various life forms of nature are seen. Biosphere is the life zone of the earth and in an important and unique realm of our natural environment which consists smaller ecosystems like terrestrial (soil) ecosystems such as forest desert, grass land and aquatic (water) ecosystems such as fresh water, marine etc. of different sizes.

As a result of propulation growth, rapid industrial and technological development, urbanisation, unjudicious planning without due regard to sustainable development, a variety of changes in the environment took place. Human activites induce such changes in the form of pollution and perturbation that cause wide spread damage to the living organisms in the biosphere which resulted in the desruption of ecological balance and threat to entire life support system which cause extinction of wild species.

In order to assess the changes caused by different reasons as above, effective and reliable monitoring systems are required to recongise and predict hazardous effects. Environmental Impact Statement Report based on detailed studies through monitoring periodically that describes the environmental consquences of a course of action and this is useful as an aid to decision making. In many countries, Industrial and other Organisations planning new projects are required by law to conduct wuch studies and to produce an Environmental Impact Statement which can then be examined critically.

The integrated relationship between environment and development have given shape to the emerging discipline of Environmental Management. In the coming years it will get too priority in National Policies all over the world. The central theme of envioronmental managaement is "the reduction or minimisation of the impact of human activites on the environment, thus an endeavour to avoid the over use, misuse and abuse or environmental resources. In the name of the development and civilisation we have plundered this earth and now facing its ill effects and imminent danger of human environment. The reasons for environmental degradation are many like population explosion, industrialisation, unplanned urbanisation, depletion of natural resources, deforestation, sewage, liquid and solid waste materials, technological advancement etc. All these resulted into environmental pollution, ecological imbalance thereby causing ill effects on human health, plant and animal life and upset the biosphere by causing global environmental problems like global warming, acid rains, ozone layer depletion, desertification etc. Hence,conservation and preservation of environmental quality is the cry of the day.

The following poem by kenneth Boulding with the heating " A conservationist"

" The World is finite, resources are scare
things are bad and will be worse,
Coal is burned and gas exploded,
Wells are dry and air polluted,
Dust is blowing, trees, uprooted,
oil is going, ores depleted,
Drains receive what is excreated,
Land is sinking, seas are raising,
Man is far too enterpising,
Fire will rage with man to fan it,
Soon will have a plundered planet".

Reveals the state of the global environment. A half century back poets used to describe the nature in its beauty, but now there is no beauty in the nature and even poets are able to see the degraded nature.

Environmental degradation is a global concern and people every where should accepts that the maintence of ecological balance is a responsibility of all. The Human Development Report 1991 of the United Nations observed:

"It is ironic that significant environmental degradation is usually caused by poverty in the south countries and affluence in the North Countries...There quarters of the poor people in the south live in ecologically fragile zones, and around 14 million have become environmental regugees driven from their homes by ecological degradation".

THE WORLD HEALTH ORGANISATION (WHO) REPORT SAYS

"One hospital bed out of four in the world is occupied by a patient who is ill because of polluted water. Provisions of a safe and convenient water supply is the single most important activity that could be undertaken to improve the health of people living in rural areas of the developing world". The Burgen Ministerial Declaration on sustainable development in the region has pointed out: "Today destruction of the biosphere and its ecosystems, environmental degradation, population pressures, depletion of resources and extinction of species threaened the quality of human life as well as human health and many of the earth's biological systems. Unsustainable patterns of production and consumption particularly in industrial countries are at the root of numerous environmental problems notably foreclosing options for future operations by depletion of the resoruce base".

Justic Krishna Iyer's opinion "The unconscionable industrialisation, the unpardonable deforestation and the inhuman extermination of living species betray an exploitative brutality and anti-social appetite for profit and pleasure incompatible with humanism. Today a bath in Yamuna and Ganga is a sin against bodily health, not a salvation of the soul-so polluted and noxious are there holy waters now".

Bondi D. Ogolla is of the opinion that "Environmental law has an important role to play in the development process. The creation of Institutional and normative structures for environmental management, ensures first, the utilisation and development of natural resources proceeds on ecologically acceptable lines and second the environment considerations are incorporated in development planning".

THE STATE OF GLOBAL ENVIRONMENT

1. Population explosion: World population doubled in last 40 years (1950-90) and the natural resorces utilisation increased enormously.

2. Water pollution: The water utiliisation for agricultural purpose (60%), industry (23%), domestic usage (8%) increased enormously and the water get polluted during the course of utilisation and release the polluted waters into the natural environment. Besides these poverty, famine are also polluting the natural waters there by degrading the aquatic habitats, decreasing the quality and quantity of marine food, decline in oxygen depletion producting dead zones.

3. Air pollution: Atmospheric changes due to primary pollutants like, sulphur oxides, nitrous oxides,carbon monoxide, carbon dioxide, suspended particulate matter from industries and automobiles and there by changing into another chemical forms in the air creating secondary pollutants like acids, PAN, Photochemical smog etc. All these are causing the global environmental problems like acid rains, ozone depletion etc.

4. Soil pollution: Besides the pollutants and their effects on the soil structure and biota, due to human interference in the natural environment 77% land is eroded (47% dry lands, the worst victims of soil erosion, 4% crop lands affected by erosion) due to loss or extinction of plant species, deforestation etc.

5. Biodiversity" Species are at risk due to deforestation for food, fuel and raw materials, forest bioresources are directly in use by industrial countries to develop and improve crops, medicines and chemicals.

6. Industrial Growth: Due to this energy is utilized much and waste is thrown into the natural environment, 37% of world's energy is utilized for industries and 50% Co2, 90% SOx are emitted into the

atompshere thereby causing ozone depletion, water and air pollution.

7. Waste Materials: Both solid and liquid wastes are discharge from industrial and domestic sources. It is estimated that the United States of America, with its affluence and industrial might, reported that each year Americans throw away 16 billion disposable diapers, 1.6 million pens, 2 billion razors and blades, 220 million tyres much more wast plastic which cause solid waste problems.

All these conditions cause the global environmental problems.

ENVIRONMENTAL CHALLENGES IN INDIA

Population, poverty and environment are interrelated. The major environmental problems in India are water pollution, deforestation, urbanisation and species extinction. For agricultural growth the forests are converted to crop lands which results in soil health problems, nutrition deficiency, lack of organic matter soil salinity increase, damage to physical structure of soil which all these lead to soil degradation Enviromental problems in India can be classified into two broad categories.

1. Those arising from conditions of poverty and under development.

2. Those arising as negative effects of the very process of development.

The first category has to do with the impact on the health and integrity of our natural resources such as soil, land, water, forest, wild life etc. as a result of poverty and the inadequate availability, for a large section of our population, of the means to fuflil basic human needs, food, fuel, shelter, employment etc. The second category has to do with the unintended side effects of efforts to achieve rapid economic growth and development. So the environmental management in India must be in all three lines and any development programmes must be environmentally sound and sutainable without any constraints to quality of life.

In the Indian context the following are the environmental problems where priority action is needed.

1. Population stabilization
2. integrated land use planning
3. health crop land and grassland
4. Woodland and revegetation of marginal lands
5. Conseration of biological diversity
6. Control of water and air pollution
7. Development of non-polluting renewable energy system
8. Recycling of wastes and residues
9. Human settlements
10. Environmental Education and awareness
11. Updating environmental law
12. New dimensions to national security

A goal ultimately is an environmentally sound and sustainable development.

NEED FOR PROTECTION

To safe guard the natural environment from the above constrains, as we cannot stop development, protection measures are very much necessary. Protection is that part of the resorce management that is concerned with the discharge into the environment of substances that might be harmful or with harmful physical effects and with safeguaring beneficial uses, Environmental pollution is said to be the gift of modern technological development, rapid growth of industrialisation and urbanisation. The environmental damage is now assuming a dangerous portion throughout the world and a growing awareness is discernible to maintain ecological balance for the future generations. Thoughout the last quarter of this century a global concern to protect environment is witnesses to pressure our right to life. Though the subject is science the environment problems are really social problems. They begin with people as the cause and end with the people as victims. Though the protection of environment is not new to the Indian culture, as the environmental degradation in its grwoth, fast measures to be taken to protect the environment is rapid. For this the Indian Government enacted several laws from the last one century.

List of Acts for protection of Indian environment since 1897:

1847 Indian fisheries Act.
1905 Bengal smoke Nuisance Act.
1912 Bombay smoke Nuisance Act.
1917 Mysore Destruction by Insects and Pests Act
1919 The poison Act
1919 Andhra Pradash Agricultural, Pest and Discare Act
1923 The Indian Biolers Act
1927 the Indian Forest Act
1946 Bihar wastchands Act
(Reclamation Cucltivation and Improvement)
1947 Mines and Minerals Act
(Regulation and Development)
1948 The Factories Act
(Pollution and Pesticides)
1949 Andhra Pradesh Imporvements Scheme Act
(Land Utilisation)
1951 Industries Act
(Development and Regulation)
1953 Orissa River pollution and Prevention Act
1954 Assam agricultural pests and disease Act
1954 Prevention of Food Adulteration Act.
1955 Acquisition of land for Flood Control and prevention of Erosion Act
1956 River Boards Act
1958 Ancient Monuments and Archeological sites and Remains Act
1958 Kerala Agricultural pests and Disease Act
1962 Atomic Energy Act (Radiation Protection Rules 1971)
1963 Gujarat Smoke Nuisance Act
1968 The Insecticides Act

1969 Maharastra Prevention of Water Pollution Act
1970 Merchant Shipping (Amendment) Act
(Harbaour and Coastal Water Dumping of Oil etc)
1972 Wild life protection Act.
1974 Water Act (Prevention and Control of Pollution)
1976 Urban Land Act (Ceiling and Regulation)
1977 Water less Act (Prevention and Control of Pollution)
1980 Forest Conservation Act
1981 Air Pollution Prevention and Control Act
1986 Environment (Protection) Act
1992 Policy Statement for Abatement of pollution by Ministry of Environment and Forests.

To be able to preserve and imporve our environment, we have to move towards certain broad goals such as:

(a) Identification of stable and healthy environment,

(b) Protection of such environment from adverse natural or man-made perturbations and

(c) Optional sustained utilisation of natural resources for the management and protection of the following broad categories should be considered.

1. Collection of relevent data and information from existing lierature or through scientific research and systematic investigation and the processing of these date through analytical techniques and statistical methods.

2. identification of specific environmental problems and using processed date to make recommendations to solve or aleaviate the problems.

3. Activities associated with the implementation of recommendations based on the efforts under the first two categories and evaluation of such implementations with a view to enumeration of further steps which may be necessary. To the extent we preserve the environment and imporve it and make it more congenial and satisfying. To that extent we ensure our health and our survival.

Hence, the ecologists, environmentalists, engineers, scientists, administrators felt that there is a need to tackle the global problems in common. If is felt that most natural resoruces are international, an isolated ecomanagement of a single country is senseless. Therefore, international cooperation is necessary in the case of a shared natural resources. This lead to holding two big International Conferences on the environmental problems. The first one is stockholm Conference in human environment in 1972. After 20 years the second big International Conference is United Nations Conference on Environment and Development (UNCED), an International Earth Summit on Environment protection at Rio do Jeneirio at Brazil in June 1992.

THE EARTH SUMMIT

Heads of 150 nations assembled for the earth summit, the second United Nations Conference on Environment and Development (UNCED) at Rio de Janerio on June 3-14, 1992. This was attended by 40,000 delegates including 150 heads of states, 7,000 media persons, 1200 women, a large delegations from industries, thousands of officials and 200 (non-governement Organisations) NGO representaives.

The impact of science and Technology on environment in the post-industrial revolution period has been assessed over the last two decades. Environment has recently become a major foreign policy issue. No longer can the earth's ecological ills be treated as separate. The developed and developing countries were divided on the issue who should pay for cleaning up the ecological mess that the earth finds itself in.

The nations realigned themselves into North-South environmental blocks, China, India and third world nations united under the group of 77 or the organisation of Economic cooperative and Development (OECD). The Chinese representative expressed the feeling of the wouth block. " The developed countires are the major polluters and they must accept moral responsibility and pay for it. The logic of the south block is clear. The north has been able to achieve a higher GNP (Gross National Product) largely by abresing non-renewable natural resources to sustain an extravagant life sytle. While they may have only 16% of world population they consume 60% of world's food, 7% of global energy resources and 80% of industrial wood. The North block is of opinion that poverty and pollution explosion in the south are the major causes for the earth's degradation. The richest tropical forests of the south today would soon be destroyed to feed their rapdily growing population.

The widening gulf between the two blocks arise from different perceptions about who is to blame for the present ecological mess. Earth summhit looked like a moderate 'earth war' with sharp division between the North and South blocks. The year long preparation for the summit with committee meetings around the globe appeared to be a kind of negotiation never attempted before on such a massive scale. But it did not yield the desired result, namely signing of two treaties at the summit.

1. curtailment of green house gas emission by 20 percent by 2000 and

2. Conservation and management of biodiversity.

The second treaty on biodiversity evoked bitter controversy and could not be signed. However the biodiversity treaty was finally signed with some amendments in December 1993 following two Biodiversity conventions after the Earth Summit. This treaty meant an agreement to preserve the living natural resource, plants animals, microbes with options to use the resource for human welfare through the frontiers of biotechnology. The generich countries (South Bloc) in the tropics are poor but willing to share their enormous biodiversity and want a share of biotechnology. But the technology-rich countries (North) particularly USA, are not willing to share their biotechnology.

The UNCED Secretariat was keen for implementation of an action plan to tackle all the major environmental and development problems confronting the south estimating the cost at over $625 billion. The North has set up the Global Environment Facility (GEP) with an initial corpus fund of $ 1 billion to tackle urgent environmental problems like global warming, ozone depletion and conserving forests. The fund would be administered through the world Bank and the United Nations Development programme.

ACTION PLAN FOR INDIA

1. Shift from coat fired thermal stations to more efficient gas-fired ones. Serious efforts should be made to harness wind and solar energy which are pollution free.

2. Reduce live stock population of 460 million which generates methane (green house gas).

3. Impose heavy penalties for motor vehicles exceeding emission levels in metropolitan cities.

4. Introduce CFL substitutes in all air-conditioner units and refrigerators from 1998 onwards.

5. Population growth rate must be reduced by at least 30% in the next five years.

ENVIRONMENTAL EDUCATION

Most people recognise the urgent need for environmental education, but only some have clear ideas about what needs to be done, and very few have either the actual experience or the knowledge about the courses that need to be taught. The chief objective of environmental education is that individual and social groups should acquire awareness and knowledge, develop attitudes, skills and abilities and participate in solving real life environmental problems. The perspective should be integrated, inter-disciplinary and holistic in character. The lay public in rural, tribal, slum and urban areas, women and students and teachers in schools, colleges and universities as well as planners and decision and policy makers, programme implementors and R & D workers need to be educated about environment.

A Chinese perception about environmental education is worth mentioning here. "If you plan for one year plant rice, if you plan for ten year plant trees, if you plan for hundred years educate people."

The goals of Environmental Education are to develop concern and awareness among world population about the total environment and its associated problems and commitment to work individually and collectively towards solution of current problems and the prevention (UNESCO 1975).

The Goals of Environmental Education

1. To improve the quality of environment.

2. To crete an awareness among the people on environmental problems and conservation.

3. To create an atmosphere so that people participate in decision making and develop the capabilities to evaluate the developmental programmes.

The objectives of the Environmental Education are:

Awareness to acquire an awareness about the status of environment and to develop sensitivity to the total environment.

Knowledge to gain a variety of experiences so as to have a basic understanding of the environment and its associated problems.

Attitude to develop values and feelings of concern for the environment and for active participation in improving the environmental quality and protection.

Skill helps in dentifying the environmental problems and gives knowledge in solving the Environmental problems.

Evaluation ability guides in evaluating environmental measures and education programmes in terms of ecological, economic, social, aesthetic and educational factors.

Participation helps in providing an opportunity to actively participate at all levels in working towards the resolution of environmental problems.

The Guidng Principles of Environmental Education are:

1. Considering the environment in its totality that is natural, artificial, technological, social, economic, political, moral, cultural, historial and asetetic.

2. To consider Environmental Education continusously from pre-school to all higher levels both in formal and non-formal education.

3. It should be interdisciplinary in approach.

4. Emphasising active participation in prevention and solution to environmental problems.

5. Examining major environmental issues from local, national, regional and international point of view.

6. Focussing on current, potential environmental situations.

7. Considering environmental aspects in plans for growth and development.

8. Emphasising the complexity of environmental problems and need to develop initial thinking and problem solving skills.

9. Promoting the values and necessity of local, national and international cooperation in the prevention and solution of environmental problems.

10. Utilising diverse learning about environment and different approaches to teaching and learning about environment.

11. Helping learners to discover the symptoms and the real causes of environmental problems.

12. Relating environmental sensitivity, knowledge, problem solving and values clarification at every grade level.

13. To enable learners to have a role in planning their learning experiences and provide an opportunity for making decisions and accepting their consequences.

The knowledge to be covered under Environmental Education Programmes

1. **Environmental studies** concerned with the environmental disturbance and minimisation of their impacts through changes in the society.

2. **Environmental Science** includes the study of the processes in water, air, soil and organisms which lead to pollution or environmental damage and to know a environmental damages and to know a sceintific basis for establishing a standard which can be considered acceptably clean, safe and healthy for human and the natural ecosystem.

3. **Environmental Engineering** includes the study of the technical processes which are used to minimise the pollution and the assessemt of impact of these on environment.

The above knowledge can be implemented through formal and non-formal education system.

Formal Education

At primary school stage, lower secondary school stage, higher secondary school stage, college stage, university education should be implemented. The syllabus should be framed in such a way so as to reach their level of understanding at various levels in schools and colleges. There are also some institutes, centres assisted by Development of Environment which provide formal education, training in Environmental areas. Some of them are Centre for Environment Education (CEE), Ahemedabad, Indian Institute of Forest Academy, Dehradun, Indian Institute of Ecology and Environment (IIEE), New Delhi etc.

NON-FORMAL EDUCATION

It should be designed to participate in social, economic cultural development of the community of all the people arranging club activities, exhibitions, public lectures, meetings, environmental compaigns. It can also be through adult education programmes, Tribal awareness programmes, children activities, ecological development programmes such as afforestation programmes. Also through government, non-government organisations by conducting Training programmes, Foundation courses through teaching aids.

15

ENVIRONMENTAL DEGRADATION - HEALTH IMPLICATIONS

Dr. Vijayalakshmi Ramamohan
Prof. A. Satyavati
S.P.M. University
Tirupati - 517502 (A.P.)

INTRODUCTION

The very concept of growth and development has undergone a radical change over the past decade. In the eighties those who swore by national development indulged in indiscriminate burning of fossil fuel, unabashedly released harmful chemicals, gaseous material from industrial establishments and dumped untreated, often toxic affluents into the atmosphere particularly the oceans, river, lakes, forests were ravaged and exploited to the hilt. Consequently the planet earth had to face the problem of global warming, acid rains, greenhouse effect and gradual depletion of ozone layer and a host of other environmental threats. The natural flora and fauna were faced with near extinction.

However, the Riode Janeriro meet in 1992 aimed at identifying environmental and economic link and replacing the concept of growth at all costs with the concept of sustainable development.

The fallout of environmental degradations and pollution have primarily affected women, because women are pivotal characters around whom the family life evolves. The woman is viewed as a care provider, family manager, resource person and presently even as an economic provider. The reflections of environmental degradation on family health is what this paper focuses on. The various family needs include energy in the form of fuel/firewood, water, clean air (breathing space), food and adequate shelter for protection against natural calamities and elements of nature.

ENERGY CHOICES

As Dr. Reddy (1992) has very rightly stated the present Growth Oriented Supply sided Consumption directed (GROSSCON) Paradigm has to be replaced by Development-Focussed End Use Oriented Service directed paradigm (DEFENDUS). The grosscon depends heavily on energy sources which are non renewable or sources which are getting depleted at a more rapid rate when comparaed to the rate of replacement. The availability of energy sources is also linked to another problem i.e. Wherever energy sources are available, industrial establishments are coming up. This leads to problems of dislocation of communites. Displacement of communities causes human unrest, leading to the victims of development opposing these development projects. The economic aspect of the problem is that every unit of energy is becoming more expensive than the previous one. Thus families have to pay more for fuel/walk greater distances for collection of firewood, thus the already limited resources available to the women are placed under greater stress. Moreover fuel emissions such as gases cause respiratory problems for women who spend hours of cooking. The DEFENDUS paradigm offers an alternative wherein conventional energy sources such as coal oil, nuclear and major hydroelectric plants could be mixed with a supply of energy from wind, solar and biomass; such a mix of energy supply sources would result in a shift from energy consumption to provision of energy services.

FORESTS

Deforestation is depriving millions of poor households from subsistence: satellite imagery revealed that the country was losing on average 1.3. million hectares of forests per year and the quantity of top soil lost due to degradation and destruction of forest land was equivalent to the loss of 30.50 million tones of foodgrains/year. As a spin of deforestation the dams are silting at a much faster rate. Thus the ecological functions of the forests are being harmed to a large extent. Women are now forced to walk greater distances to collect firewood. They are also forced to look for substitute foods/medicinal cures for their ailments because forests are being denuded at a rapid pace. The alternative would be to have wood production on a commercial scale on lands which are unfit for cultivation. Decentralised and 'participatory' forest management has been considered to be the long term solution to problems of deforestation and environmental degradation. The joint forest management includes negotiating partnership for sharing forest protection responsibilities in exchange for a share of the income from forest products. This partnership operates between local institutions (LIS) of forest users and State Forest Departments (FDs), West Bengal has the largest JIM programme and has yielded fairly good results. However patriarchal gender relations operating at all levels of society have excluded women from active participation at the community level. This has resulted in women having to travel longer distances to fetch firewood and also switching over to poorer quality cooking fire such as dung droppings and weeds.

WATER

Around seventy percent of all the available water in India is polluted. The advent of technology and scientific advancements have accelerated the production of toxic effluents. For instance major industries release their wastes into nearby water sources. While doing so, they are expected to treat the waste and cure it of the toxic effect before release. How well this is being done is anybody's guess. An example of the leather industry is narrated here. The raw hides have to be preserved and transported to tanning centres. This involves treating the skin with common salt. At the tannery, the sodium chloride is washed out-leading to the salty water causing soil erosion and salination of the land. Also large amonts of water are used for this process. All industries there are thus at some stage drawing on previous water sources and releasing effluents into the atmosphere. The point here is that water is most precious commodity more so because there is no substitute for water.Hence, water pollution is a major problem which calls for innovative and alternate methods which would cut down on the quantity of water used and also minimize the pollution levels of surface and ground water deposits. Inadequate monitoring and control of industrial pollution of water is due to little or no involvement of community at various levels because the Government is presently charged with this responsibility. As and when local communities come into the picture, there is bound to be a more strigent enforcement of pollution control measures.

FOOD

According to the Centre for Science and Environment, "the poor live within a biomass-based subsistence economy, all their fundamental needs (food, fodder, fuel, firewood, cowdung, crop wastes, fertilizers, dung manure, leaf litter, building material, timber, thatch and herbal medicines are collected (often freely) from the immediate environment". Water though not directly a biomass by itself is also crucial for survival. This being so the act of deforestation has resulted in destruction of vegetation, increased drought and water scarcity and has increased the water requirement of the cultivable soil. Local production of food grains is affected, leading to escalated cost of food purchase. Similarly, vast rural populations depend on livestock. The shrinking of flazing lands has reduced the fodder availability and production resulting in low yields and low income. The green revolution has pulled out more soil nutrients than adding to the soil nutriture, this aggravating the probem of food availability at a reasonable cost. India is the largest producer and consumer of pesticides in South Asia. The pesticide residue in food chain, in vegetables, fruits, milk, egg, fish, meat, edible oil is becoming a common feature, pesticide poisioning is killing both humans and livestock, Further the marine foods which were hitherto available to the fishing communities along the coastlines have also been affected due to release of untreated effluents into the sea and due to oil rigs being errected in the seas, disturbing the sea life. To compound the issue of food availability, we have the overwhelming problem of unprecedented pollution growth, thus already scared natural resources are placed under greater stress. Despite huge public expediture on primary health and education, the vast population growth continues unabated and illiteracy reigns.

Health Implications Source	Health Hazards
1. (a) Fuel - Biomass (cowdung/ charcoal wood and cooking	Foecal/oral/infections—skin infections, Co/Smoke poisioning Burns/traima/cataract Conjunct-ivitis, Respiratory and Pulmonary infections.
(b) Fuel Collection	Allergics/Fungus infections Bites from poisionous/venomous reptiles/insects, Muscle fatigue body aches and pains Infant and childcare affected.
2. (a) Water-infected Drinking water Drinking water sources	Diarrhea, Dysentery water borne infections.

(b) Stagnant pools of water/poor drainage	Viral microbial and insect borne diseases.
(c) Nitrates in drinking water	Gastric cancer, blue baby syndrome.
3. (a) Food	Over use of pesticides poisonous residues on all food items, toxic discharges in soil, water leading to serious environmental conse quences.
(b) Application of fungicides pesticides, herbicides	The personnel involved in the application are ignorant of the toxic nature of the chemicals involved. Poor handling inhala-tion of the posion in the form of fine drople and penetration through skin has led to deaths.

The health implications of an environment threatened on all sides spell doom for human life unless suitable and timely remdial measures are taken to arrest environmental degradation and pollution before it is too late. Therefore, it is gratifying to note that this vital issue of environment and education has been taken up for debate and discusssion at the university level. The bottom line in this particular paper is that the health implications from environmental threats are very real and the environmental warning need to be headed in order to save the environment and human kind.

SELECTED READINGS

1. The Hindu : Survey of the Environment Madras, 1995

2. The Hindu : Survey of the Environment Madras, 1992

16

ENVIRONMENT AND HEALTH

Dr. G. Vijayalakshmi,
Reader Department of Education,
S.P. Mahila Visvavidyalayam,
TIRUPATI 517 502- A.P.

The relationship between the environment and the human health is an established fact. Clean air, water and soil are the vital ingredients for a happy life. Their abundance or paucity have a direct bearing on the quality of life of the community. And yet despite these well established norms, environmental degradition is progressing at a frightening pace. Human being has become the prime victim of this environmental degradation. Considering the high stakes-the difference between life and death-urgent steps are required to bring back to life of our dying air, water and soil to make leaves green, the water blue, the air pure to breathe and the humanity to live and lead healthy life.

To all pervasive nature of the environment cannot be stressed adequately. The quality of water being consumed for drinking or for personal and household tasks, the soil in which our food is grown and on which waste material is being disposed the animals and plants around us, the air that is being breathed and the rural and urban setting in which we dwell or work determines to a large extent the levels of our physical, mental and social well being. Over the ages, man has been altering his environment by accident or by design as illustrated below.

Environmental degradation undermines development and damages human health. Ill health on the other hand affects the work force, hinders development and leads to environmental degradation. Environment, development and health are thus closely interlinked with proper development improving the environment, sustaining development and increasing community health, making possible sustainable development. The role of each and every individual in the maintenance of a clean and healthy environment is therefore indispendable.

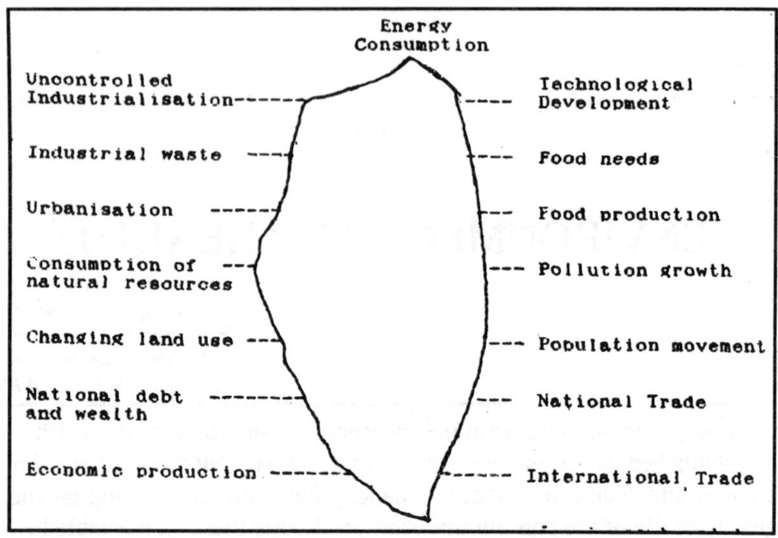

URBANIZATION AND INDUSTRIALIZATION

Urbanization and industrialization and the resultant influx of population has resulted in serverely stretching the existing facilities such as housing, water supply and waste disposal, roads and transport system and basic services.

The domestic wastes and garbade in the congested settlements cause unsanitary conditions, as well as insect and rodent problems giving rise to many illnesses and deaths. Indiscriminate spraying of insecticides, rodenticides and pesticides often result in health risks. Unsatisfactory housing, overcrowding, inadequate excreta disposal, buring of wood, coal and cowdung cakes for cooking lead to severe health disorders. Industrial emissions and inappropriate disposal of these wastes create additional health problems.

Every one has a right to enjoy a reasonably clean, safe and healthy environment to live and work. Development activites must therefore be controlled and well planned and steps ensured to see that waste products are removed safely without causing any damage either to the natural resources or to the human beings.

PLANNING OF URBAN DEVELOPMENT

Rapid urbanization is reaching serious proportions in the developing world leading to problems like unhealthy living conditions, overcrowding, psycho social stresses and violence. Unplanned, hastly planned settlements or squatter settlements are invariably deficient in housing and essential services for healthy living. Towns and cities must be therefore developed in a planned manner segregating residential areas from those meant for commerce and industry.

HOUSING AND SHELTER

Shelter is one of the essential requirements for human life. Uncontrolled migration from rural to urban areas makes housing a major problem. Poor housing has been shown to be associated with tuberculosis, Streoptococal infections,rheumatic fever and rheumatic heart diseasses. Housing must be so designed and constructed as to allow adequate air and sun light to enter and at the same time, protect its dwellers from the elements. Where firewood, coal or cowdung cakes are used for cooking, houses must be provided with smokeless 'chulahs' and proper ventilation to let out the smoke from the buring fire, thereby keeping the indoor air clean. Residents should have access to safe drinking water, waste disposal sites and sanitary latrines.

WATER SUPPLY AND SANITATION

In most countires the supply of drinking water has not kept pace with population growth. Waste collection and disposal facilities are often lacking. Contamination of sources of water supply often occurs as a result of unsanitary disposal of solid and liquid domestic wastes including human excreta.

It is not uncommon for whole settlements drawing water from public taps or open wells or community hand pumps forcing people either to draw insufficient quantities of water or to go to polluted water sources. Lack of adequate water for washing and cleaning coupled with poor sanitation lead to infection and reinfection through the oral faecal route. The provision of safe water supply and satisfactory disposal of wastes is therefore imperative for a clean envionment and healthy living.

DISPOSAL OF SOLID WASTES

large volumes of refuse are produced by the committees. Until the turn of the 20th century, the generally accepted way of disposal of domestic refuse was either to dump it into the court yard of the house where it accumulated and decomposed till it was finally carted away to farms or other disposal sites, or throwing it out into the streets where it dispersed. This however, encouraged the breeding of flies, i sects and rodents which inturn, transmit many diseases.

Yet, the more new industries and expant industries explain, the more the environment gets affected. Although environment issues have become matters of great concern, the speed at which new technologies are introduced is rarely with measure to protect the environment and the people.

On the other hand, hazardous substances produced are being handled by the public without being fully aware of their dangerous side effects, Pesticides, for instance are the most important and most widely used hazardous chemicals in the rural region. Their improper application leads to thousands of deaths every year.

Albert Einstein once stated, "Concern for man himself and his fate must always from the chief interest of all technical endevour". If he was alive today he would certainly realise that concern for man and his fate would become meaningless without conçern for the environment.

In the case of industries it would mean careful consideration of a number of issues of far reaching consequence.

1. POLICIES AND PLANNING

Again it will be politicians, policy and decision makers and planners who will have to take the first step and formulate proper policies and develop realistic plans for establishing and expanding industries.

2. LEGISLATION

Although some form of legislation mostly exists it is usually inadequate or in need of improvement or for strengthening procedures for enforcement. It should typically include the setting of standards and maximum allowable concentrations as well as drawing up of regualtions covering the repoduction, conveyance, disposal and accidental discharge of dangerous substances.

3. INTRODUCTION OF NEW TECHNOLOGIES

New technologies and industrial innovations are being introduced all the time often without due regards to safety. Legislaion should promote safe production technologies as well as the recycling or proper disposal of waste.

4. SITE SELECTION

The selection of a proper site for an industry vis-a-vis well serviced housing is extremely important. If carefully located, as industry will not only present a minimum risk but will also mean reduced distances for employees to travel to work.

5. HEALTH OF THE WORKERS

In the case of an industry the working environment is atleast as important as its surroundings, workers have to be properly proteced against harmful factors (toxic fumes, dust, noise, radiation etc). The provision of first aid equipment and protective devices is not enough. Safety will have to start at the source through hazard control.

6. PUBLIC INFORMATION

There is a general lack of awareness on the part of both? The public information programmes should, include safety aspects of handling and disposal of hazardous substances and of industrial accidents.

CONCLUSION

Never before in history have three been cities as large as today's, dubling their size every 10 to 15 years. Never before have goods been produced in such quantity and variety and never before have our energy requirements been of such proportions. In view of the fact that our numbers and our demands are still increasing. So there is need to consider future steps carefully and remember Einstein's words and act accordingly.

17

URBANIZATION, ENVIRONMENT AND EDUCATION

Dr. C. P. S. Chauhan,
Department of Education,
Aligarh Muslim University,
Aligarh

The population of India has increased at a faster rate during the post-Indpendecne period than during the preindependence period. In 1901 we were only about 238 million and increased steadily to 361 million in 1951 excluding the population of Pakistan which was created in 1947. Since 1951,our number has grown rapidly to 439 million in 1991. In view of 2.0% annual growth in our population,we are over 920 million now (1996). As far as population is concerned we are the largest democracy in the world. The total population of the world at present may be estimated to be about 5700 million (manorama Year Book 1995).

So, we are a vast country covering about 329 million hectares of land area supporting 16% of the world's population on only 2.4% of land and 2% of the total world's income (Chauhan, 1990). Being predominantly a rural society, over 70% of us live in about 5.80 lakh rural habitations. As a conservative estimate 25% of us live under poverty line. We are essentially the land of youth and children becausee 65% of our population is below the age of 30 years. In addition to multiplicity in numbers and poverty, there is large scale illiteracy, with over 330 (324 million in 1991) million illiterates aged 7 years and above. The iliiteracy among women and socially disadvantagaed groups and minorities is challengingly high. In view the increasing number of children to educate and increasing months to feed, the problems of education and socioeconomic development are compounding.

URBANISATION

Due to accelerated pace of development of economy as a result of strategy of planned development and industrialization, there has been a massive migration of rural population to urban clusters. Urbanization is both a cause and effect of rapid industrialization. Industrialization increased job opportunities in urban areas by creating new means of livelihood as opposed to under-development of rural sector. The majority of migrants from rural areas were attracted to cities by these new job opportunities. Urbanization, therefore, is an integral part of scientific, technological and socioeconomic development and a booster of the process of modernization.

In 1901, the number of cities in India was 1834 which reached 2844 in 1951, 3245 in 1981 and 4689 in 1991. In 1901 only 10.84% of the total population inhabited the cities while this increased to 17.34% in 1951, 23.73% in 1981 and 25.70% in 1991. At present the urban population may be estimated around 28%. The number of big cities recorded a record growth rate to increase from only 12 in 1981 to 23 in 1991 (Kukreti, 1993). By 2001 the urban population in India would be around 350 million forming about 35% of the total population. This projection inclucates that the country is entering the accelerating stage of urbanization process (Singh, 1990).

TABLE *

DEMOGRAPHIC CHARACTERISTICS OF INDIA'S POPULATION (1901-1991)

Year	Total Population (millions)	Literacy Rate (Percentage) Male	Female	Total	Urbanization (Percentage)
1901	238.40	9.83	0.60	5.35	10.84
1911	252.09	10.56	1.05	5.92	10.29
1921	251.32	12.21	1.81	7.16	11.18
1931	278.98	15.59	2.93	9.50	11.99
1941	318.66	24.90	7.30	16.10	13.86

1951	361.09	24.95	7.93	16.67	17.34
1961	439.23	34.44	12.95	24.02	17.98
1971	548.16	39.45	18.69	29.45	19.91
1981	685.18	46.74	24.88	36.17	23.73
1991	843.93	63.86	39.42	52.11	25.70

*Compiled from different sources.

The growth of urbanization caused by massive movement of people from rural areas to towns and cities has raised certain issues. There is a popular misconception that urbanization is incompatible with environment and development. The truth is that urbanization by itself is not the enemy of environment and development (Alexander, 1994), but unplanned urbanization can be. In fact urbanization has become unavoidable and irreversible process because of the compulsions of social and economic changes.

Therefore, it is imperative to devise appropriate policies and programmes to cope with this situation by judicious planning.

Given the natural concomitants and modernizing influences of urbanization such as faster communication network, much better facilities in the fields of health, education and recreation, greater availability of electricity and safe drinking water and more employment opportunities a lower level of urbanization necessarily denotes the denial of these opprotunities and facilities to a very large part of the population. The deprived people remain deeply rooted in the backward economic and social structure of a traditional rural society, thus blocking the onward march towards modernity. The increasing concentration of growing urban population in and around mega cities has a serious fall out (Puri, 1993). The major problems relate to the provision of housing facilities, drinking wataer, electricity, health, infrastructure, sanitation, roads and transport facilities. Roughly half the population in Delhi, Bombay and Culcutta live in slums and this figure is growing very fast. Deprived of the amenities of urban life, the slum populations get de-humanized and indulge in violence, breeding contempt for the established socio-political structure. The increase in the incidence of crime in mega cities is due to growth of slums.

POPULATION AND ENVIRONMENT

With increased migration from rural to urban areas, there has been corresponding growth in the density of population in mega cities. According to 1991 census the density of population in India is 267 persons per sq.km. The population density was only 117 in 1951 which increased to 142 in 1961, 170 in 1971, 221 in 1981 and 267 in 1991. The population density in Delhi and Chandigarh is respectively 6319 and 5620.

Urbanization coupled with rapid industrialization is aggravating the problem of envirnomental pollution. A multitude of environmental problems such as deforestation, desertification, soil erosion, silting of rivers, imporishment of important flora and loss of biodiversity, depletion of non-renewable sources of energy, global warming and pollution of air, water and land, has been generated by population growth alongwith urbanization. The emission of carbondioxide has incresed to about 6.8. billion tonnes in 1985 from 2.4. billion tonnes in 1950. Urbanization factor is contributing significantly to environmental degradation not only in India but also in many third world countries because of the growing demands for fuel, fodder and timber, According to one estimate, one percent increase in population is associated with an increase of 0.5% of deforestation in the third world. The deforestation rate in third world countires is estimataed to be around 1 to 1.5 percent per annum.

Urbanization in India has creataed acute shortage of water in mega cities and whatever water is available is contaminated by pollutants causing serious health hazards. The air of cities is being increasingly polluted by poisonous gases and harmful gases discharged by vehicles, chimneys of industries, burining of fire-woods, garbage and whole range of human activities generated by the explosive growth of cities. The major source of pollution is transportation and its brown black fumes. Due to all these reasons human beings breathe sulphurdioxide, nitrogenoxide, fluorides and carbon mono-oxide gas.

It has been rightly argued that pollution is a by-product of energy and a necessary evil of the society. The conventional sources of energy such as coal. diesel,petrol, Kerosene oil provide a major part of energy required for industry and other functions, while non-conventional sources of energy such as solar energy, hydro-energy, wind energy, biogas, nuclear energy and biomass are used in a very small proportion. In india, about 66% of the total energy consumption in agriculture, industry, transportation and other sectors is supplied by conventional energy sources (Kukreti, 1993). The major part of this energy is supplied by firewood, coal and kerosene oil to fulfill the household requirements which leads to deforestation, on the one hand and, discharge smoke which adds to environmental pollution.

EDUCATIONAL IMPLICATIONS

The discussion in the previous section indicates that unless some deliberate attempt is made to create environmental awareness among the people,especially, those living in urban areas, there will be serious problems in future. In the mega cities the fast development and growth of slums are going to pose very threatening challenge. The migrants who come to cities for employment, without having adequate level of training and education, will create law and order problems and spoil the social atmosphere by indulging in crimes and other antisocial activities. These slum area are generally inhabited by poor and uneducated people who require proper education for gainful employment on the one hand,and for safe and happy life on the other.

The formal type of education cannot serve the purpose of education the slum dwellers and other working and poor people. It is here that the non-formal approach may be used very effectively. There is a need to set up more and more NFE centres and organize functional literacy programmes in these areas. Voluntary agencies can play a very important and constructive role. The government, both central and state should provide increased funds to voluntary organizations to runNFE centres and TLC campaigns.

The curriculum of these classes should be given proper bais in favour of environmental education by building the awareness component in the literacy programmes. A large majority of slum dwellers constitute the industrial workers. The industrial sector should take initiative to organize literacy programmes for workir :, people. The government may finance such efforts by providing partial grants.

People in general should be educated to economize the consumption of fuel to save fuel on the one hand and to protect the environment on the other. Health education is another component of environmental education that must receive proper attention. In fact a National Policy on Environmental Education is called for. The government should take immediate steps in this direction.

REFERENCES

1. Alexander, P.C. Population-Development-Environment nexus, University News, Sept. 5 1994

2. Kurkreti. B.R.Environmental Education- A Blue Print. University News Aug. 16. 1993

3. Singh, Shamsher, Indian Urbanization at cross roads. The Hindustan Times, May 31 1990

4. Puri. R.K. Mega Cities- Bane of Urbanization. The Hindustan Times oct.11. 1993.

5. Manorama Year Book, Thirtieth Publication, Malayala Manorama Publishers, 1995.

18

ENVIRONMENTAL IMPACT ASSESSMENT

Prof. Y. Anjaneyulu
Head, Centre for Environment
I.P.G.S.R., JNT University
Hyderabad 500 028

1. INTRODUCTION

Environment impact Assessment is a study of the probable changes in Socio-economic and Biophysical characteristics of the Environment that may result from a proposed action.

EIA can be considered to be a planning tool which assists planner in anticipating potential future impact of different development activities, both beneficial and adverse, with a view to select the 'optimal' alternative, which maximises beneficial effects and mitigates adverse impact on the environment. EIA can be not only for major projects such as dams, highways, power stations, but also for development activities, which involve plans, programmes and policies. it is generally recognised that ETA, if carried out properly, can identify major areas of environmental damage due to developmental activities in a systematic and comprehensive manner.

Recognising the urgent need to incorporate consideration into developmental planning process, pollution plans, programmes and projects, as well as the need to envolve strategies and approaches towards this objective, ministry of Environment and Forests, Government of India has formulated a general legality and Environmental impact Assessment (EIA) for practical application in India.

It may be during this process,"now" alternatives are generated which achieve desired objectives at less cost to the environment.

The EIA scientific process scheme is as follows:

Description of the project Description of environment	Material balance
Description of the project (Prediction of environment)	Air Environment Water Environment Noise Environment Land Environment Ecosystem, Socio-economic Environment Ecology
Evaluation	Environmental pollution Aesthetics Human interest Construction phase Post Construction phase Post project monitoring Management strategy plan
	Damage criteria Safety precautions (chemicals) on site and off site emergency plan

II. ENVIRONMENTAL IMPACT STATEMENT

(1) Project Description:

(a) Purpose of the action-Goals and objectives.

(b) Description of the Action- Summarise the activities:

(Magnitude of the Action Area Extent, Equipment, Manpower, and Material Requirements)

(c) Environmental Statement:

- Environment as it exists prior to the proposed action.

- Information may be taken from either existing data sources or acquired data sources.

III. LAND USE RELATIONSHIPS

(a) Conformity or conflict with other land use plants and poilcies and controls.

(b) When in conflict- Extent of Recommendations Reasons for proceeding with action.

IV. PROBABLE IMPACT OF THE PROPOSED ACTION ON THE MANAGEMENT

1. Man's health, welfare and surroundings.

2. Environment Factors (a) Air, (b) Water, (c) Land (d) Ecology, (e) Sound, (f) Socio Economics.

V. ALTERNATIVES TO BE PROPOSED ACTION

Probable Adverse environmental effects which cannot be avoided.

Water of air pollution resulting from the action

Distribution of Wild life Congestion

Threats to Health

Undersirable land use patterns etc.

VI. ENVIRONMENTAL ATTRIBUTES

ENVIRONMENTAL ATTRIBUTES REPRESENT ENVIRONMENT, SUCH THAT CHANGE IN THE ATTRIBUTES REFLETS IMPACTS

AIR

1. Diffusion Fector
2. Particulates
3. Sulfur oxides
4. Hydrogen oxide
5. Nitrogen oxide
6.Carbon monoxide
7. Photochemical Oxidants
8 Hazardous Toxicants
9. Odor

WATER

10. Aquatic safe yield
11. Flow variations
12. Oil
13. Radioactivity
14. Suspended solids
15. Thermal pollution
16. Acid and Alkali
17. Biochemical oxgen Demand (BOD)
18. Dissolved oxygen (DO)
19. Dissolved solids
20. Nutrients
21. Toxic Compounds
22. Aquatic life

LAND

23. Soli Stability
24. Natural Hazard
25. Land use patterns

ECOLOGY

26. Large animals (Wild and domestic)
27. Predatory Birds
28. small game
29. Fish, shell fish and water fowl
30. Field crops
31. Threatened species
32. Natural land vegetation
33. Aquatic plants

SOUND

34. Physiological effects
35. Psychological effects
36. Communication effects
37. Performance effects
38.Social behaviour effects

HUMAN ASPECTS

39. Life style
40. Physiological needs
41. Psychological needs
42. Community needs

ECONOMICS

43. Regional Economy Stability
44. Public sector review
45. Per capita consumption

RESOURCES

46. Fuel Resources
47. Nonfuel Resources
48. Aesthetics

VII. MEASUREMENT OF IMPACT AND COMPARISION BETWEEN ATTRIBUTES

Identifying the impact of a project on an attribute requires measurement of impact. However there are difficulties in quantitatively measuring some impacts. Also we have to have a method to compare all those environmental paramenters with one another.

EIA METHODOLOGIES

Environmental impact analysis methodology should deal with:

Impact identification
Impact measurement
Impact interpretation
Impact communication to information ursers.

The following six methods are generally used for identification of impacts

(A) ADHOC METHOD

A team of specialists will identify the broad areas that suffer impacts such as Flora & Fauna, lakes and forests. The possible nature of impacts will be recorded as no effect, short or long term impacts, reversible or irreversible impacts. No particular data or resources are required, since this approach does not suggest specific means of measuring of evaluating impacts.

(B) OVERLAYS METHOD:

A set of Transparent maps giving physical, Social, Ecological, aesthetic characteristics of the project area overlaid to produce a composite characterisation of the regional environment, the method is to perform an initial screening process to identify feasible aternative which would then be subjected to a more detailed analysis. This method is used in selection of highway routes transition lines.

(C) CHECK LIST METHOD

A comprehensive listing of environmental parameters which are related to a particular type of action is made. Four categories of check lists are in use:

i. Simple check lists
ii. Descriptive check lists
iii. Scaling - Weighing check lists

Simple check lists are a list of environmental parameters without any reference to as to how the date are to be measured and interpreted.

Descriptive checklists identify environmental parameters and give guide line on how parameters data are to be measured. But no numerical ranking is used in evaluating the level of impact. Scaling-Weighing checklists involve scaling of impacts on a relating basis from 10 to 0.

Table

AN EXAMPLE CHECKLIST FOR A PROPOSED INDUSTRY IN A STUDY AREA

ENVIRONMENTAL PARAMETER IN THE DESCENDING ORDER OF IMPORTANCE	RATING OR WEIGHT	POSSIBLE SCORE ON ENVIRONMENTAL IMPACT
1. Air pollution	High	10
	Medium	5
	Low	0
2. Water pollution	High	10
	Medium	5
	Low	0

(D) NET WORK METHOD

A project is realted to its potential impact through a cause-condition-effect network. Through this method is not necessary a full methodology it will be useful in identifying the impacts.

(E) MATRIX METHODS

Matrix methods aims relating project activities to their environmental impacts. An interdisciplinary team of specialists will assess the magnitude and importance of the interactions in terms of numerical scale varying from zero to ten, with ten representing the maximum value.

(F) COMBINATION COMPUTER-AIDED:

A combination of Matrices, Networks, and Analytical models by a computer aided systematic approach is followed for implementing major programmes.

Criteria for Choosing an EIA Methodology

In view of the large number of models and methodologies being practiced in EIA studies, one must choose between two extremes. Complete uniformity or complete uniqueness. As both these approaches have their limitations, many specialists on EIA have made there own methodologies for each one of the projects.

Finally, any EIA Methodology is expected to do:

i) Identification, ii.) Prediction and iii) Evaluation

In the process of identification, the existing environmental system has to be clearly described, the components of the project have to be clearly identified, and likely modifications in the project area have to be defined.

In the process of prediction, it is necessary to estimate the expected impacts along a time frame.

In the process of evaluation it becomes necessary to determine the costs and benefits to user groups and populations affcted by the project.

ENVIRONMENTAL IMPACT ASSESSMENT OF HAZARDOUS WASTES DISPOSAL

With increasing economic activities and technological developments, production of hazardous wastes in India has increased in recent years without knowing much about the characteristics of hazardous wastes produced, total quantities and disposal practices.

HAZARDOUS WASTES.

United States Resource Conservation and Recovery Act(RCA) defines hazardous wastes as "any waste which may cause or significantly contribute to serious illness or death or which poses a substantial threat to human or the environment, when improperly managed".

Governement of India under "Hazardous Wastes (Management and Handling) Rules, 1989 identified 18 categories of wastes with quantities as hazardous wastes.

Hazardous wastes are mostly generataed by petrochemical, chemical and allied industries, electrical equipment manufacturers and other metal related product manufacturers.

Indian chemical industry, fourth large manufacturing industry, produces 10,000 different chemicals share in gross industrial output has risen from 8% in 1970-71 to 40% today. Dye-stuffs production increased 2.5 times between 1975-89. There are 4508 water and air polluting industrial units in India of which 1642 units have potential for Hazardous Waste(HW) generation. Industries with HW generating potential are asbestos, caustic soda,inorganic chemicals, integrataed iron and steel, copper, zinc and aluminium smelter, engineering with electroplating, dye and dye intermediates, fertiisers, organic chemicals, oil refineries, pesticides, petrochemicals and pharmaceuticals.

HAZARDOUS WASTE IN MEDAK DISTRICT

There are 3284 industries in Medak district with 146 in large and medium and 3138 in small scale. Out of the above,262 are polluting industries and among the polluting industries, 111 have potential for generating Hazardous Waste (large 19, medium 30 and small scale 62). Among the potential for generating Hazardous Wastes 87%) are chemical and allied category.

The classification and distribution of industries with potential for generating hazardous waste, 33 industries are burning the waste with auxiliary fuel, 8 industries onsite land filling, 67 off site land filling and 3 reusing.

HAZARDOUS WASTAGE MANAGEMENT

The hazardous waste managaement must include the following:

i) Minimisation of hazardous wastes generation by modifying production process.

ii) Reprocessing and re-use of wastes.

iii) Transfer of wastes to another industry for their conversion to useful products.

iv) Separation of hazardous and non-hazardous wastes.

v) Transform hazardous wastes to non-hazardous by incineration, physical and chemical processes.

vi) Disposal wastes in a controlled landfill sound disposal of hazardous wastes is not cheap but in the long run it will invaribly turn out to be less expensive than inadequate disposal. The estimated cost of sound disposal at canal is less than $2 million, but after 5 years more than $36 million had been spent for the clean-up and associated expenses.

DEFICIENCIES IN THE EXISTING EIA

i) EIA, as it is practised at present is an art and not a science. EIA process has been defined in different ways in different developing countries. No two developing countries appear to have defined it in the same way.

ii) EIA reports are too academic, bureaucratic, mechnistic and voluminous. Often they do not concetrate on major environmental issues but provide lengthy deliberations on fringe issue.

iii) EIA reports contain numerous tables of collected datea without clear idea about their relevance and even necessity. Also data analysis, interpretation and their environmental implications are lacking.

iv) EIA, as it is practiced now, ends immediately after the environmental clearance of project has been received. Compliance monitoring is not carried out.

v) Poor data availability and reliability.

vi) presentation of EIA results is not understandable by non-experts.

vii) Poor public participation.

Table 1
Classification and Distribution with Potential for Generating Hazardous Wastes

Industrial	Durgs & pharma-ceutical	Organ-nic & petro-chemi-icals	Insec-ticide and Pesti cide	Paints and dye stuff	Asbes-tos	Inorg-anic chem-icals	Gen-eral Engg.	Total
Bollarm	14	2	-	-	1	1	3	21
Bonthapally & sorrounding areas*	25	4	2	-	-	4	2	37
Patancheru & surrounding areas**	16	15	1	3	11	2	15	53
Total	55	21	3	3	2	7	20	111

* Surrounding areas Gaddapotharam, Gummadidala, Domedugu, kajipally etc.
** Saurrounding areas include Insapur, Rudraram, Muthangi, Pahmylaram Chitkul etc.

CONCLUSIONS

One of the most important factors that could significantly improve EIA porcess is good education and training. Currently, very few educational and training courses exist in developing countries that properly consider various EIA methodologies available in department. Information on the legal and regulatory frame works and institutional arrangements are also necessary. Education and training processes are important, since the fundamental factors behind all EIA predictions can be given the best judgement.

Both short-time and long-term courses are necessary to develop adequate expertise. These courses however must be multi-disciplinary and the focus should be on the practical and operational spects of EIA and not on theoretical implications.

For establishing clear and unambiguous guidelines for EIA that would be useful to analysts the Technical Institutions may prepare a Handbook on good EIA case studies in the field of air, water and solid wastes. Such a book would be useful to analysts.

Table 2

Type & Quality of Waste Generataed in Medak District

Industrial Area	Solid	semi-Solid	Sol vents	ETP Sludge	Boiler Ash	Total (Excluding Boiler Ash)
Bolaram	1643	237	-	741	1589	2621
Bonthapally & Surrounding areas	6814	1822	605	1014	6490	9255
Patancheru & Surrounding areas**	2045	579	216	2288	2475	5127
Total	10502	1637	821	4043	10554	17003

Values are in Mt/Yr

* Surrounding areas Gaddapotharam, Gummadidala, Domadugu, Kajipally etc.

** Surrounding areas include Insapur, Rudraram. Muthangi, Pashymylaram Chitkul etc.

REFERENCES

Asit k.Biswas and Agarwala S.B.C. EIA for developing countries.

Associated industrial consultants (India) Private Limited (1993): Inventorisation and Management of Hazardous waste in Medak dist.

Recommendations of an International Conference on Environmental Impact Analysis for Developing Countries held in New Delhi on 28th December 1988.

Tehran N.C., Environmental aspects of hazardous wastes Disposal in India.

19

ENVIRONMENTAL EDUCATION AT THE SCHOOL LEVEL

Dr. BImal Charan Swain,
Mrs. Rajalakshmi Das,
J.N. (Govt) College
Pasighat,
Arunachal Pradesh

INTRODUCTION

Man is a part and parcel of his environment. Due to his interaction with nature on a large scale, the balance of nature have been upset and environmental decadence occurred in most parts of the world. This might be because of environmental pollution or improper and unscientific exploitation of natural resources. It has posed a great problem to the existence of man, plant and animal life on the earth planet, threatening the quality of man's life and his survival. So, there is a need to increase awareness and understanding of those environemnts and man's impact upon them and to find out effective ways to manage them. To achieve the above goal, environmental education is the need of the day.

A number of seminars, conferences and workshops have been conducted in India and abroad on environmental education. Some of them are United Nations's Conference on Human Environment (Stockholm, 1972), International Workshop on Environmental Education (Belgrade, 1975), UNEP UNESCO Conference on Environmental Education (Tibilsi, 1977), National seminar on Higher Environmental Education (New Delhi, 1979) and five day global forum on Environmental Education for Sustainable Development (New Delhi, 1993).

MEANING OF ENVIRONMENTAL EDUCATION

Environment literally meaning 'surroundings' has a wide connotation including within its purview physical, biotic and human aspects of the earth. It includes the earth surface with all its physical feataures and natural resources, the distribution of land and water, mountains and plains, minerals, plants and animals, the climates and all cosmic forces that play upon the earth and affect thelife of man. Thus, all that surrounds a designeated eco-system is called environment (Tiwari & Yadav, 1983).

The International Union for the conservation of Nature and Natural Resources has evolved the following definition of environmental education as an outcome of a conference called in Nevada in 1970:

"Environmental education is the process of recognising values and clarifying concepts on order to develop skills and attitudes necessary to understand and appreciate the inter-relatedness among man, his culture and his bio-physical surroundings. Environmental education also entails practice in decision making and self-formulation of a code of behaviour about issues concerning environmental quality."

OBJECTIVES OF ENVIRONMENTAL EDUCATION

The Mahabharata, Ramayana, Vedas, Upanishads, Gita and the Puranas contain the earliest messagaes for the preservation of environment and maintenance of ecological balance. For centuries, while worshiping to Goddess Durga, the Hindus have been saying "so long as the earth has montains, forests, trees, etc. human race will survive".

The objectives of environmental education are:

- To help social groups and individuals acquire an awareness of the total environmental and its associated problems.

- To help social groups and individuals gain experience and acquire a basic understanding of environment and its allied problems.

- To motivate social groups and individual for actively participating in environmental improvement and protection.

- To help social groups and individuals acquire skills for identifying and solving environmental problems.

- To provide opportunity to social groups and individuals to partici-pate aactively towards solution of environmental problems.

CURRICULUM OF ENVIRONMENTAL EDUCATION

Environmental Education is inter disciplinary in nature. It involves subject matter from natural sciences and the social sciences. NCERT has developed national curricula for all stages of education specially empha-sizing the aspects of population, land, resources and their uses, food and nutrition, conservation, pollution, health and hygine and man in nature of environmental education.

The environmental education at higher level in India is provided by the universities, Research Institutes, Schools of Planning and Manage-ment, Agricultural Universities, Engineering Colleges and a number of other agencies. Some of them have defined programmes of environmen-tal education and the others have included some component of environ-ment in their curricula. The introduction of environmental education programme requires the involvement and participation of teachers, stu-dents and administrators etc.

POLICY

National Policy on Education (1986) emphasizes thus: "There is a paramount need to create a consciousness of the environment. It must permeate all agaes and all sections of society beginning with the child. Environmental conscousness should inform teaching in schools and col-leges. This aspect will be integrated in the entire educational process".

The Ministry of Environment and Forests has been conducti on Na-tional Environment Awareness Campaign (NEAC) every year since 1986 with the aim of creating environmental awarencess at national leval. For the session 1993-94 the campaign has been launched by the Ministry with the theme "Animal Welfare and Waste Management". Proposals are invited from the Voluntary Organisations, Educational Institutions and State Government Departments working in the field of environment and development for conducting various activities like seminars, workshops, camps/padyatras/rallies, competions, festivals, etc. for creating environmental awareness amonngst the masses. A National Environment Council has also been set up under the Chirmanship of the Prime Minister to advise the Ministry of Environment and Forests on Environment Policy.

SUGGESTIONS

The environmental education programme in India has not made much headway due to lack of funds, inadequate infrastructure and shortage of trained personnel etc. The following suggestions are given for making the environmental education progromme successful:

- Environmental education should be closely linked with Gandhian thought.

- Environmental education should result in the development of an ecological ethics-a change in attitude of man towards man, society and nature, in realization of man as part of nature, not alien to it.

- The environmental education shold be so designed as to integrate the environmental concepts with ensuing course.

- The University Grants Commission should accord high priority in establishing courses in colleges and universities on enviornmental education.

- The instructional materials on environmental education should be produced according to the local needs. The text books and teaching aids should be developed to supplement instruction. Writing of text books on environmental education should be encouraged.

- Trained teachers should be appointed in schools.

- There should be close co-operation between different University Institutes with specific objective of training experts in environmental education.

- Adequate funds should be provided by the University Grants Commissions, Department of Science and Technology Central and State Governments for effective implementation of environmental education programme.

- Teachers, parents, public, doctors, engineers,; planners, administrators and scientists should be involved in environmental education programme.

- The inter disciplinary research projects on environmental problems should be undertaken.

- The Govt. should establish Environmental Research Centres in every state.

- A data bank and Eco-systems information base/systems should be developed so that the reaquired information are available at a central place.

- Seminars, conferences and workshops should be organised from time to time on environmental education.

- The Individual trained in environmental sciences should be given priority in recruitment at all levels.

- The gerneral public should be educated about the environmental degradtion and improvement of the environmental quality through mass media by incorporating them through regular programmes of A.I.R., T.V. and visual aids etc. Documentary films should be prepared on these themes and exhibited for the benefit of the people.

- A Committee including the students, teachers and administrators shold be appointed to establish and evaluate the environmental education prograamme.

- A fundamental re-orientation of the human conciousness, accompanied by action that is born out of inner commitment, is very much needed. To fulfil this, we should recreate basic values of religions and cultures and propagate them through national and international education programmes.

BIBLIOGRAPHY

Bandhu, D & Aulakh, G.S. (ed) Environmental Education. New Delhi: Indian Environmental Society, 1981.

Government of India. Ministry of Education, National Policy of Education(1986). New Delhi: Ministry of Education, 1986, P.23.

(1) "Ecology in the School Syllabi Necessary". (2) Gurudev.D- "The Story of City's Greening". (3) Jagmohan-"Spiritual Response to the Environment"-The Times of India-Sep.25.'93,p 7; Oct.27.'93 P.7; Oct.12,'93, P.1.

Singh, L.R.et.al.(ed.) Environmental Management. Allahabad: The Allahabad Geographical Society, 1993.

The Hindustan Times, September 24, 1993, P. 7.

Tiwari, R.C. & Yadav. H.S. "Eco system, in Environmental Management. L.R.Singh et.al., The Allahabad Geographical Society, 1983, P. 59.

20
ENVIRONMENTAL EDUCATION AND THE CURRICULUM

Prof. Marlow Ediger
Division of Education
Trumann State University
Route 2, Bose 38
Kirkasville, Missouri
United States of America

New about the environment with its diverse forms of pollution appears daily in newspapers, newsmagazines, radio, and television broadcasts. A quality environment is a must for individulas to possess good health, as well as to grow, develop, and achieve. A polluted environment and its habitat hinders optimal attainment among people as well as animal life in gereral.

PROCEDURES OF TEACHING IN ENVIRONMENTAL STUDIES

A well informed, motivated teacher may utilize several selected procedures in selecting objectives, learning activities, and evaluation techniques. In a unit on pollution in its Diverse Forms, the teacher may stimulate learners to identify relevant problems. Thus in a quality current events curriculum, the teacher might utilize a related stimulating discussion on oil spills in the news. From the ongoing dissussion, Students are stimulated to identify causes of oil spills. After the problem has been adequately delimited, students with teacher guidance, determine resources needed to secure information directly related to the problem. Textbooks, library books, video-tapes, filmstrips, slides, illustrations, video-discs,among other reference materials may provide the needed data. With adequate information, learners may develop a tentative solution or hypothesis as to causes of oil spills. The hypothesis is subject to testing. Accurate, comprehensive reference sources are needed to test the hypothesis with revisions made as needed. A problem solving philosphy might harmonize well with the students present learning style and level of achievement.

A subject centered approach may be stressed by teachers as a second philosophy in teaching environmental units. if students are studying a unit on Energy Sources in the Environment, the teacher needs to choose which general or measurably stated objectives students are to attain. The teacher then may determine that students should attain objectives pertaining to renewable and nonrenewable sources of energy. Clarifying these two sources of energy, the teacher wishes to emphasize wind, water, solar, and geothermal sources of renewable energy. Further, the teacher may decide that students should learn about coal, nuclear, petroleum, and wood as nonrenewable sources of energy. Further objectives emphasize the classification of energy into non-polluting and polluting.

A subject centered curriculum stresses idealism as a philosophy of education. Thus mental development of students becomes the ultimate objective in environmental studies. Textbooks workbooks, encyclopedias, and other sources of print discourse are the major materials of instruction. The abstract is to be preferred above the concrete and semiconcrete materials in an idea centered lesson and unit of study. Audio-visual materials are utilized in teaching to assist students in securing vital facts, concepts, and gereralizations.

A third philosophy stresses student decision making in selecting sequential tasks, be they problem solving or subject centered activities. A learning center's approach advocates students selecting ordered experiences from diverse stations in the classroom. The following are titles of different learning centers:

1. Preventing soil erosion.

2. Preserving natural resources.

3. Controlliing acid rain.

4. Supporting wild life areas.

5. Protecting endangered species.

An adequate number of centers need to be in evidence so that students may select sequential tasks which are purpose ful. Those tasks not deemed to possess perceived purpose may be omitted. The student selects which tasks to complete and which to omit. The teacher is a guide and stimulator to encourage student learning. Materials for each center, such as reading and nonreading sources, need to be ample in number to assist learners to achieve and attain.

With student decision making emphasized as a philosophy of education, worthwhile goals must be achieved. Thus in center number one above - preventing soil erosion, the student needs to attach meaning to sheet and gulley erosion, strip-cropping, use of terraces, contour farming, as well as grassed waterways. A variety of materials need to be available so that each student may choose what to pursue. The following are examples of choices at the preventing soil erosion center:

1. View a filmstrip and write a summary of the contents.

2. Read a library book and draw a picture of its contents indicating ways to minimize soil erosion.

3. Listen to a cassette and develop a related mural with two other pupils.

4. View a video-tape and write four main ideas covering this presentation.

A fourth philosophy of teaching stresses the use of an Instructional Managaement System (IMS). Prior to instruction, measurably stated objectives are written for students to attain. Each objective is precise. After instruction, learners reveal if each objective has/has not been attained. The objectives may be written in ascending order of complexity. Objectivity is involved in determining if a student has been successful in goal attainment. The goals of instruction provide the basis for objective results in the evaluation process.

Learning activities are valid when properly aligned with the objectives of instruction. Each activity should relate directly to one or more objectives. That which has no relationship to the objective should be eliminated from the learning activity. Appraisal procedures should also be aligned to the stated objectives of instruction. Appraisal results might then reveal if an objective has/has not been attained by a student.

The following are examples of mearurably states objective pertaining to studying the environment:

1. The student will list in writing three harmful and three beneficial results from the use of pesticides.

2. The student will write a fifty word paragraph on means of minimizing pollution from the use of pesticides.

In each of these two objectives, the teacher, after instruction, measures if the student has/has not attained the stated objectives.

With Instructional Management Systems, measurably stated objectives are predetermined for student attainment. Generally, student-teacher planning is not involved in selecting objectives, activities and experiences, and appraisal procedures. In the use of predetermined objectives within the IMS framework, the teacher becomes a manager of the curriculum. Thus in a unit on Our Environment, two predetermined objectives for students to attain on herbicide use might be the following:

1. The student will discuss orally how cocklebur competes with domesticated plants such as soybeans and corn for moisture, sunlight, and nutrients.

2. The student with two other learners will develop a diorama on the harmful effects of excessive use of herbicides.

Learning activities are selected by the teacher to assist students to attain each of these objectives. The teacher also evaluates if students individually have/have not achieved each objective. Thus, the teacher manages the curriculum in teaching and evaluating to notice if goal attainment on the part of the students is in evidence. A fifth instructional philosophy emphasizes a project method. Heavy student involvement is necessary in project method implementation. The learner, with teacher guidance, may wish to develop a movie set which contains a roll of paper around two dowel rods, housed inside of a cardboard or wooden box. The paper should be one foot wide. The length of the paper depends upon how many scenes are to be portrayed in the project. The flexible sequential steps involved in a project method might be the following:

1. The student wishes to develop scenes on the roll of paper for the movie set on plastic pollution in the environment. With this purpose, the student and teacher clarify these ensuing goals.

2. the students makes plans to achieve the purpose. Careful planning is necessary to develop a quality movie set showing effects of non-biodegradeable plastic and their uses. Abstract content appears underneath each illustration in the movie set.

3. the student carries out the actual plans developed. Diverse art media are needed to develop each scene. Scenes need to show how non-biodegradeable material may be recycled.

4. the student appraises the quality of the project. Here, the student, with teacher guidance, evaluates the strengths and weaknesses of the movie set. Definite criteria have been developed to utilize in the evaluation process. The criteria might include

   a. accuracy of content in the movie set.
   b. neatness and appeal of the total project.
   c. effort put forth.
   d. quality group dynamics of a committee, rather than an indvidual endeavor is in evidence.

A hands on approach is emphasized in learning when project methods of instruction are used.

IN CLOSING

Diverse methods of teaching to provide for individual differences may be utilized in teaching units on our environment. The procedures include

1. *problem solving*. Problem solving is useful in school and in society.

2. *using subject centered approaches*. Vital facts, concepts, and gen-

eralizations then need to be attained by students with teacher guidance.

3. *decision-making strategies.* A learning center philosophy here may assist students to make choices of objectives, activities, and appraisal procedures.

4. *emphasizing an Instructional Management System.* With IMS, a student may achieve at an optimal rate in attaining sequential behaviourally stated objectives.

5. *stressing project methods.* A hands-on approach in learning becomes paramount. Individual or committee endeavors might be stressed

Methods of teaching used in units on our environment should assist each student to attain optimally. Students should perceive interest, meaning, and purpose in learning. Interest, meaning, and purpose are salient concepts for the teacher of enviornmental studies within the framework of problem solving, subject centered procedures, decision making strategies, IMS, and project methods of teaching.

Saving our environment is a global problem. Thus, what transpires in one nation or region affects other areas. Each person has major responsibilities in maintaining a quality natural environment.

Relevant facts, concepts, and generalizations for students to attain must not be separated from methods of teaching. Thus content to be acquired by students in units on our environment needs to be integrated with problem solving, subject matter procures, decision-making strategies, instructional management systems, and project methods of instruction.

21

ENVIRONMENTAL EDUCATION CURRICULAR CHANGES

Prof. V B B Sarma
IASE
Osmania University,
Hyderabad - 500007

The importance of protection of environment needs no over emphasis. The concern for protection of environment in India may appear to be of recent origin. But it actually started with the framing of constitution itself. However, it will not be untrue if I say it all started from Vedic Times. The following extracts in translation prove it. [1]

THE FREE MAN ON A FINE EARTH

O Earth, pleasant by thy hills and snow-clad mountains and
Thy wood-lands.
On the Earth-brown, black, ruddy and of all colours- the firm
earth, the Earth protected by the Deity (Indra)
Upon this Earth, I- unconquered, Unslain, Unwounded have set
my foot.

(Atharva Veda, Kanda XII, Sukta 1, Mantra No, II)

EARTH'S INHABITANTS:

The earth is not for the races of men alone but for other creatures also.

Born of thee, on thee move-mortal creatures;
Thou bearest them-the biped and the quadruped;

* Paper presented at the National Seminar on: Environmental Education: Curricular Changes, held at I A S E, Kalkatiya University, Warangal, A. P. on 21st & 22nd, November, 1997.

Thine, O Earth, are the five races of men, to
Whom mortals, Surya (Sun) as he rises spreads
With his rays the light that is immortal.

(A.XII,1,15)

EARTH'S VARIETY

The earth does not belong to a single race, but to different races, speaking different languagaes.

May the Earth that bears people speaking
varied languages, with various religous rites
according to the place of abode.
Enrich me with wealth in a thousand streams,
Like a milch-cow that never fails.

(A.XII,1,45)

CONCORD WITH THE UNIVERSE:

Peace of sky, peace of mid-region, peace of earth,
Peace of Waters, peace of plants,
Peace of trees, peace of All-Gods, peace of Brahman,
Peace of the universe, peace of peace;
May that peace come to me.

(Y. 36.17 also A)

In modern India, the makers of constitution had the foresight to see the possible evils of changed life styles and the effects of industrialization and incorporated in Article 48 (A) a mandate that "the State shall endeavour to protect and improve the environment to safeguard the forest and wild life in the country". Besides, Article 51 (A) and (G) requires protection and improvement of the natural environment, including forests, lakes, rivers and wild life.

Man, with pride in his ability to invent new machines, explore and understand the mysteries of nature and produce new varieties of plants and animals, strated thinking that his intellect should enable him to control nature and the nature should dance to his tunes. But the ever increasing interference of man with natural systems and the consequent evil effects on him have; made him realize that his survival is safe and comfortable only when he lives in accordance with the dictates of nature and natural laws. The montreal protocol of 1988 of the developed countries to elimnate 90 percent of the ozone depleting substances by 2000 is only an instance to quote.

Even if we agree that man is just another creature on the earth, we must admit that he is undoubtedly a very intelligent and manoeuvring being and his doings have great influence on the enviornment. In such a situation, what is that we can do to keep the pristine condition and chastity of the nature? is our concern.

This depends on how seriously we view the threat from the polluted environment. Environmentalists are complaining that the world's air today contains 25 percent more CO_2 than it did in 1958 [3]; in the past 125 years, the earth's surface was warmest in 1990; [4] Six of the seven warmest years on record have occurred since 1980;[5] by the middle of the next century, the resulting warming could boost global mean temperature from 3 to 9^0 F.[6] This increase would cause hotter and drier summers and expanding deserts, the strinking of lakes, larger growing seasons in some areas that are now too cool for many crops and water in some currently dry regions, the partial melting of polar ice caps causing an increase in sea level from 1 to 6 ft. resultinig in a submersiion threat to Marshall Islands in the pacific, the Maldives, the Caribbean nations and one-sixth of bangladesh, etc.[7]

James Hansen, Director NASA says that though long-term data were limited, changes observed in the US were consistent with the predictions. What would such a change do in India where the weather naturally exhibits extremes-lots of rain over a few hundred hours in a year and then nothing for the rest? We do n't know; we have to wait and see. But it is suspected that some countries would also get benefitted from these changes. In Australia, some 15-20 percent increase in wheat yield has been attributed to the climate trend in the country.[8] Leading environmentalists Anil Aggarwal and Sumita Narain however caution that the trouble with atmospheric science as of now is that the early signs of climate change will be extremely complex and will be beyond the realm of the common person's understanding. In other words, we cannot be 100 percent certain that disaster has taken firm roots.[9] But then it will be too late to do anything to rectify.

In this situation what should education do? is the question. There is no doubt that all the concerned;- the common man, educationists, politicians, and environmentalists agree that education should come to the rescue of mankind. For every evil on the earth and every problem of the human being education is viewed as a panacea. Today everyone says that curriculum should *do something* to check this degradation and 'to avert the catastrophe waiting to strike on us. Even President Nixon emphasized the role of Education on several occasions. In his introduction to the First Annual Report of the Council on Environmental quality, (in August, 1970) he stataed: The basic causes of our environmental troubles are deeply embedded............... It should be obvious that we cannnot correct deep- rooted causes overnight.................. Our educational system has a key role to play in bringing about this reform. It is also vital that our entire society develop a new understanding and a new awreness of man's relation to his environment................ What might be called' environmental literacy'.[10] Our late prime Minister Mrs, Indira Gandhi stated at the United Nations Conference of Human Environment held in Stockholm in June 1972" one cannot be truly human and civilized unless one looks upon not only all fellowment but all creations with the eyes of a friend'. [11]

Now let us queastion ourselves; what does this *something* mean to us as educationists and curriculum makers?

Let us begin with a comprehensive understanding of the term Environment. Environment includes all those living organisms and non-living objects that constitute the universe and exert influence on us either directly or indirectly. Thus, environment is the universe of biotic and other physical elements as organised into dynamic systems. These systems are ecological systems or ecosystems which represent the integration of living (biotic) and non-living (abiotic) elements in the environment.

Consequently, Enviornmental Education (E E) embraces all those efforts to provide knowledge, create an awareness, develop a positive attitude to participate in and the ability to solve environmental problems with a clear understanding that the life of a human being is inextricably entagled with the nature in which he lives. A similar defination was offered by the International Working Meeting on Environmental Education in the school Curriculum, held under the auspices of UNESCO in paris in 1970. According to them: Environmental Education is the process of recognising values and clarifying concepts in order to develop skills and attitudes necessary to understand and appreciate the interrelatedness among man, his cluture and his biophysical surroundings. Environmental Education also entails practice in decision making and self-formulation of a Code of behaviour about issues concerning environmental quality."[12] When we think of curriculum for E E, we cannot but think of a content that takes into its province the three domains of learning-cognitive, Affective and Psychomotor. All these years, at all levels of education and in all subjects, unfortunately, the affective behaviour has been divorced from the cognitive behaviour. Unless a synthesis of these two behaviours is brought out, it is well high impossible to prepare individuals who have a real feeling for preservation of environment. In the absence of such a synthesis of cognitive and affective learning, one may recite how non-biodegradable substances such as plastic material cause pollution but never stops for a second to buy, use, and burn them to cause pollution. What is the practical use of such knowledge except for writing answers and passing examinations? Such people are not going to be of any use to environment protection. The proof of the pudding is in the eating.

Before we build up a curriculum that is informative and transforms a student into a nature-loving citizen, the following points have to be borne in mind.

1. state the objectives of E E you propose to achieve.

2. State the content needed to achieve the objectives this could be by way of improvement of the existing curriuclum.

3. State the values, attitudes, interests that are to be developed.

4. State the skills to be developed in relation to E E

5. Select learning experiences suitable to achieve cognitive, affective and psychomotor domains.

6. Specify the methods to be used and the media to be employed in the development of each concept,value and skillin E E

7. State the present day status of environment in and around india and specify the legal provisions available to protect the environment in

appropriate contexts.

8. Specify the role of a teacher, student, common man, Industrialists and the Government in the protection of environment.

9. Evaluate the achievement.

Let us now think a little more about these points:

1. Objectives: Taking the comprehensive nature of E, E the following objectives have been formulated at UNESCO's tbilsi conference in 1977.[13] They broadly encompass the three domains of learning:

   Awareness: The students acquire an awareness of and sensitivity to the nature of environment and its problems-pollution, degradation etc

   Knowledge: The Students acquire the required knowledge to understand and to appreciate the biodiversity and the universe and its relation with man.

   Attitudes: The students develop positive attitudes towards environment protection, moderation in the consumption of natural resorces etc.

   Skills: The students develop the needed skills to identify environmental problems (Like in pollution of water, air and soil) and apply the needed solutions.

   Participation: The students participate voluntarily and enthusiastically in environmental protection activities and in solution of environmental problems.

2. **Content**: There are at least two possiblities for providing a suitable content to E E One, by way of addition of E E. content and concepts and providing E E orientation to the existing topics. This approach may be called E E across curiculum. Two, we may make it a separate subject to teach. The first approach is preferable for at least two reasons: E E is an inter disciplinary subject and the present day

student is already over burdened. When 'learning without burden' is the slogan of educationists and the common man, increasing the learning load is not advisable.

Further, if texts have to be added, population Education, Awareness on Drug Addiction, Aids etc may also stake their claim. So, in dealing with the content of E E, if cultivation of tobacco is a topic in normal curriculum, the textbook writer and the teacher not only deal with the conditions necessary for cultivation of tobacco in terms of soil, water, and temperature but also point out that an average of 7.8 kg. of wood will be required to cure one kg. of tobacco. Increased tobacco production and curing will result in increased denudation of forests and consequent soil erosion, land degradation and threat to food production. Tobacco depletes soil nutrients much faster than many other crops and consequently more chemical fertilizers need to be applied which results in increased soil impoverishment. The occupational health risks in tobacco production also will have to be mentioned. It is observed that the hands of workers engaged in harvesting and processing tobacco get affected by the chemicals in tobacco and sickness is caused when nicotine gets absorbed into the body through skin. This causes headaches, nausea, vomiting to the extent of 86 percent in non-virginia tobacco and 53 percent in virginia tobacco.[14] In addition, all the health hazards of smaoking could be listed out so that the student realizes the gravity of problems involoved in cultivatin and using tobacco.

For providing a first-hand knowledge to the students, the teacher may plan a visit to a tobacco curing centre and a cigarette company. He can ask them to observe the workers in the factory and make a note of their health condition. He could ask them to collect information whether the managaement does anything to protect the workers from these afflictions. The teacher may ask the students to visit a colony of tobacco workers, study their problems and suggest some remedial measures or preventive steps.

Since E E involves affective learning at a higher degree the teacher plays a key role and he is the centre of the teaching-learning process. The cultivation of values related to E E directly depends on his ability to inspire students to appreciate and love environment.

3. Values, Attitudes and Interests: There are certain basic values, atti-

tudes and interests that are necessary for a student of E E. Though the list could be long and winding, some of them are mentioned here for providing the direction.

a) The student *loves nature* i.e.he memorises poems describing nature, grows plants and becomes an animal lover.
b) The student believes that all *living beings have equal right to exist* on this earth i.e. does not kill or trouble small animals, dislikes hunting and eating carnivorous food etc.
(c) The student believes that the *natural resorces are plentiful but still limited and control has to be exercised on their exploitation* i.e.does not waste wataer, oil, petrol, etc.
d) The student believes that *excessive meddling with nature can cause* imbalance in nature and result in some *devastating change in the environment* around i.e.he does not use himself and does not encourage others to use excessively items prepared from forest products, material containing chlorofluoro carbons etc.
e) The student believes *that* even the planet *Earath has a period oflife and comparaed to it our period of stay on earth is insignificant* i.e. he believes in obliging natural laws like keeping one-thrid of the earth's surface covered with plants, not polluting soil, air or water with chemical effluents and gases.
f) The student *develops interests like aversion to rampant use of non-biodegradable disposable material, love for plantation of trees and protection of wildlife and animals around him i.e.* he shuns the exceesive use of popular items like 'carry bags' adopts domestic animals as pets, informs the right authorities when somebody tries to endanger the life of some previous species by selling them for food or for game.

We should agree that a large part of the value system of an individual is not developed through teaching. He imbibes the values from the family, from teachers, peers man on the street, media etc. One has to only see on T V to develop certain inclination to the intake of vaccines for pregnant motehrs to avoid children getting polio etc.The rest is done.

4. **Skills** : As far as the skills to be developed in E E, they are not entirely different from the skills to be dveloped in normal classroom learning. They include, keen observation, conducting simple tests to assess acid-alkali level of water, contamination of water, adul-

teration of eatables like termeric etc. As a part of E E we may develop sensitivity to and the skill in identifying medicinal plants for simple ailments. Making notes of observations, presentation and preparation of herbariums should follow normal course of teaching.

5. **Learning experiences** : Suggesting suitable learning experiences is an essential component of making decisions about curruculum construction. They have a great role in deciding the quality of learning. It is not very difficult to develop learning experiences needed for cognitive domain. For instance, if acquisition of knowledge about the type of forest available in a rain-fed area is the concept, a visit to such a forest may solve the problem. Similar is the case with the learning experiences of psychomotor domain. In order to make the students draw a graph of the area covered by forests in our country, over a period oflast 50 years, it is enough if he can apply this concept to the already-known skill of drawing graphs. The crux of the problem lies in the selection of learning experiences for affective learning. Before we select the learning experiences for this domain it is necessary for us to realise that values, attitudes and interests which constitute the essence of learning in E E, are not achieved in a day or two. They are learnt over a period of months or years and the individual seems to pass through the four stages of affective learning suggested by Krathwohl etal before he becomes characterized by a value. It is for this reason that we need more time and a multiplicity of sources to influence. learning experiences that could be used for affective learning include puppetry and drama apart from the very influential skits on T V and the Radio. Field trips and public lectures, experience in living close to nature (immersion programmes) also are not to be undervalued. When I mention these expericence, I only mean that they also have to be added to the usual experiences, not to say that others are to be replaced.

6. **Methods and Media**: Since learning the content of E E should proceed concurrently with the development of suitable behaviour changes, the traditional classroom teaching methods havê a limited role. Though the lecture method has its own value even here,it is necessary at some stage to analyse the E E content for concepts, values and skills to be developed, the behavioural changes to be brought about and the method and the medium that could be used to realise the expected. Use of multi-media, project method, team teching, cooperative learning, organising E E fairs, participation in

debates and elocutions on E E are some of the methods and procedures we can explit to develop the much-needed involvement of the student in E E, the principle being:' he who does it, learns it'.

7. **Environment and legal provisions**: There are many occasions on which the present day status of environment in and aroaund India can be discussed.For instance, when we teach the use of minimum-maximum thermometer, we can show a graph of these two over a period of time. According to a report on the study published in *Mausam,* the quarterly research journal brought out by India Meteorological Dept. While the maximum temperatures showed a rise all over the country except in parts of East M.P., Bihar plateau and a tongue extending from Northwest Rajasthan to East U.P. through Punjab, Haryana and Himachal Pradesh, the minimum termperature showed a fall across the country, but for North coastal Andhra pradesh, South Orissa, Rayalaseema, interior Karnataka, parts of Gujarat, Madhya Maharashtra and Marathwada during the period. Similarly, the situtation about depletion of ozone layer when chlorofluoro carbons and ozone are discussed in chemistry.

Legal provisions available to protect the environnment need a special mention and these should form an important aspect of the students' knowlege in E E. They can also be integrated/correlated with the relataed topics. There are about 30 major enactments related to protection of environment now being administered by the central and state Governments. Prominent among the are wildlife (Protection) Act, 1972: The Forest (Conservation) Act, 1980: The water (Prevention and Control of pollution) Act, 1974: The Air (Prevention and Control of pollution) Act 1981; The water (prevention and control of pollution)Cess Act, 1977; The enviornment (Protection)Act, 1986; The public liability Insurance Act, 1991; The Motor vehicle Act 1938 as amended in 1988.

8. Role of Teacher, Student, Common Man, Industrialist and the Govvernemnt: In the process of protection of environment, the Government and the Industry have specified roles as per the Acts mentioned earlier. Submission of 'Enviornmental Impact Assessment Report' has been made compulsory for all industries, after 1978, to get clearance from the Government.

The responsibility of the teacher in E E is that of an animator, a director and a teacher. He will be publicizing the Govt. programmes in Environment protection, apart from his routine teaching duties, and takeas a lead in all Environment protection activities. The responsibility of the common man and the students would be to contribute to the success of these programmes by participating in the programmes and dveloping a positive attitude for the protection of enviornment. The teacher should bring it to the knowledge of the concerned about programmes like'Environmental Information System'initiated by the Ministery of Enviiornment and Forests to promote E E, and 'National Environment Month' from 19th November to 18th December every year wherein all resources are utilised to spread the message of Environment protection. A brigad called 'Parya Varana Vahini' has been launched during 1992-93 to create environmental awareness and to ensure active public participation by involving local people in activities relating to environmental protection. This 'vahini' plays a watch Dog role and reports instances of damage to environment to Collectors of the Districts. Students could be taken to the National Museum of Natural History set up in Delhi for an excursion. For teachers and all those interested, 'Environmental Inforamtion system' can provide the needed information on various aspects of environment. All these roles of the members cited above, if acted well, can certainly bring about a favourable attitude towards enviornment protection.

9. Evaluation : We are not used to the evaluaative measures other than written tests in our normal course. These may be enough to test the knowledge aspect of E.E. But to test his values, interests, attitudes and skills related to E E we have to resort to activity based and informal dignostic devices. Teacher's close observation of student activities is the key for this type of evaluation.

Having thought out the key issues in some detail, we should check a few points before we actually pass curricular changes for implementation.

* See whether the content we propose to include meets the criteria of learning across the curriculum in a particular class and learning over a period of years in a stage of education.

* No curriculum can be systematically implemented unless learning Units are prepared, implemented on a small target group, feed back

obtained, improvements made and evaluated after extensive field trials. Though the classroom teacher holds the key to the success of this curriculum, not everything can be left to his mercy. Before, it is implemented in the classroom, relevant teaching aids and teachers'handbooks, have to be prepared and supplied to the teachers. Also, organization of a well-planned orientation programme for the teachers is a necessity.

Friends! before I conclude my address, I would like to present, in brief, a few premises I assumed but never made them sufficiently explicit. They are;

1. In the development of curriculum for E E, I suggested correlation. But integration and subject organization are also possible. It is only my experience that has prompted me to put forth this idea.

2. Items of content quoted for E E were purely random. In fact, issues discussed could be from global to national to local and local isssues could get emphasis. A detiled curriculum for a stage in E E should be spelt out keeping the existing curriculum in view.

3. Structuring of curriculum could not be anything but topical as an E E topic related to the one available in the text had to be suggested. Spatial and temporal were not mentioned. But if such a structuring was available in any subject, it could be followed.

REFERENCES

1. Bose, A.C. The call of the Vedas. Trans. Bombay: Bharatiya Vidya Bhavan, 1988. P. 282-284.

2. Panneerselvam, A and Mohana Ramakrishna. Environmental Science Education. New Delhi: Sterling Publishers Pvt.Ltd., Rpt 1996. P.73

3. -------------- P. 57

4. Aggarwal, Anil and Sunita Narain "What will happen in Kyoto?" The Hindu Magazine, 2nd Novemebr 1977. P.1

5. Panneerselvam, A and Mohana Ramakrishna. Environmental science Education. New Delhi. Sterling Publishers Pvt.ltd., Rpt 1996, p.57

6. ----------- P.57

7. ------------- P.57

8. Aggarwal, Anil Sunita Narain. "What will happen in Kyoto?" The Hindu Magazine, 2nd November, 1977. P.1

9. Aggarwal, Anil and Sunita Narain."What will happen in Kyoto?" The Hindu Magazine, 2nd November, 1977. PP. I & II

10. Rao, V.K. and R.S.Reddy. Environmental Edcation. New Delhi; Commonwealth publishers, 1997. P.172

11. Panneerselvam, A and Mohana Ramakrishna. Environmental Science Education. New Delhi: Sterlilng Publishers Pvt.ltd, Rpt.1996.

12. Rao, V.K.and R.S.Reddy. Environmental Education. New Delhi; Commonwealth Publishers, 1997. P.P. 10-11

13. ----------- P.29

14. B.S. Padmanabhan. "A blow to anti-smoking campaign". The Hindu, 10th July 1997. P.10

15. Sunderarajan P. "Rainfall increasing in many cities. "The Hindu, 24th June 1997. P.16

22

ENVIRONMENTAL EDUCATION BEHAVIOURAL CONCERNS AND CURRICULUM DEVELOPMENT

A. Ramakrishna
Lecturer, IASE
Osmania University
Hyderabad- 7.

INTRODUCTION:

We are experiencing a hotter climate, holes in the protective ozone layer over the poles, toxic chemicals in ground water, ramines in Africa, food contaminated with pesticide residue, and extinction of untold numbers of species as forests recede before growing polulations. It is necessary to start taking the bold steps necessary to save the biosphere.

A 1987 report from the National Academy of Science argues that "It is not the lack of ecological information that leads to poor environmental planning, but simply the lack of its proper application." If we have the knowledge, why have we not already made the necessary changes? First, the knowledge and understanding is relatively recent. There has always been some lag time between the acquisition or information and the implementation of policy based on that information. Then there has been considerable progress, and changes are to a degree underway. But finally, scientific understanding is one thing; decision of what to do and when to do it are something else. Hoever, people also have many other values regarding such things as the use of materials and energy and the disposal or wastes. Many of these values are conflicting in ways that are not fully recognised, and conflicting values impede progress.

OBJECTIVES

In view of the foregoiong discussion the author proposes to-

1. Find the behaviours which enable a person to impress the community about environmental degradation & its implications andlive without altering the ecological balance; and

2. Stress on the development of these behaviours in children of classes I,II & III

It is to be noted that UNESCO/UNEP International Environmental Education programme (IEEP) began in 1975 has its impacts on primary and Secondary School and University levels. In 1977, the first inter-governmental conference on Environmental Education organised by UNESCO and UNEP was held in Tibilisi, USSR, The conference declared:

" Education Utilizing the indings of Science and Technology should play a leading role in creating an awareness and better understanding of environmental problems. Environmental education should be provided for all ages at all levels and in both formal and non-formal education."

The 5 - point framework of the Tiwari Committee report (Minimum National Programme, Department of Science & Technology, Government of India, 1980) emphasised the necessity of modification of educational curricula to promote environmental awareness amongst students.

Environmental education assumes great significance in education the people who are ignorant and indifferent to their environment. The NPE (1986) stessed the importance of this subject in school curriculum. Consequently, the entire science curriculum has been reoriented with activities pertaining to environmental problems from elementary school onwards. The subject acquires a lot of importance in the teacher education programe also.

Environmental education may be defined as curriculum encouraging understanding and appreciation of the environment through subjects like local history, ecology, pollution, etc. Environmental education is not confined to man-nature relationship alone; it also takes care of the relationship of man with his fellow human beings.

COMPONETNS TO CONSIDER IN DEVELOPING A CURRICULUM

Curricularists deal with content and curriculum (teaching and learning) experiences for developing a curriculum. The components considered include the following:

a. *Curriculum Content:* All curriculum content that is facts, concepts, generalisations and so on - should enable students to gain understanding and to apply that understanding to daily living present and anticipated.

b. *Organisation of Content:* A psychological organisation is a means to denote the way an individual might actually learn a subject. Content should be organised by going from the students' immediate environment to a more distant environment. Content, in other words, should be organised so that the concrete is experienced first, then the more abstract. This psychological factor is a key principle of sequencing content.

c. *Curriculum Experiences*: Curriculum experience involves the instructional component or the curriculum. It consists of teaching methods and activities that take place in the classroom for the purpose of attaining the schools'goals. There are a multitude of both teaching methods-such as inquiry, lecture, discussion & demonstration and educational activities - like film viewing, conduction experiments, viewing videos, interacting with computer programmes, taking field trips and listening to speakers. Both teaching methods and educational activities are integral parts of the curriculum and must be carefully considered in light of the content selected.

d. *Relationship of content and experiences:* Content and learning experiences always comprise curriculum unity. Students cannot just engage in learning,or in studying, without experiencing some activity and some content. Likewise, students cannot deal with content without being engaged in some experience of some activity.

ENVIRONMENTAL EDUCATION AT THE PRIMARY LEVEL

Environmental Education starts at home and in its immediate neighbourhood. Manipulative skills are developed through helping in the home and at play, regarding personal hygeine and prblems of food and water contamination. In rural areas it is easy to develop a sensitivity to the cycle of seasons and the elements of nature.

A child's perception of the environment develops into a hybrid consisting partly of formal schooling in nursery schools, temples, churches and other pre-primary institutions and partly of informal education at home.

In the past two decades some nursery andkindergarten schools equipped elements of social interaction, hygeine and nutrition and introduced it thorough organised play and co-operative activities.

Formal environmental education was introduced as a subject in primary school in India through National Museum of National history (NMNH) - Ministry of Education and Ministry of Environment, forest and wildlife. It was also introduced as an added component or existing subjects-hygiene, nature study and population education. Jain (1976) described the incorporation of social ethical and environmental values into Biology in India's elementary and secondary schools.

Likewise, a number of authorities grappled with the problems of developing curricula for primary schools and several studies took the module approach to introducing environmental collection into primary schools.

At the primary level, integrated general science curriculum is offered, and one of its variants covers, eleven themes, Houses, Land & people: Who live in them, Things we eat and drinks, 'Clothes we wear'. Things which help us work,'How we live and mix in communities', 'The world around us','Our school and its neighbourhoods'. ' The people who help us'. 'How we travel and communicate' Our earth and sky above it' and 'things we hear and see'; Moral education and religious education also find room in the primary school curricula in so far as they bear on the environment. In the primary schools, emphasis is placed on the gradual evaluation of values and behaviour favouring the portection and improvement of the environment. This is integrated with in-schools and out-school environment educational activities, making maximum use of the community school environment.

The role of the teacher among others, i.e. to (a) arouse the student's interest in their environment and to raise challenging problems in connection with it; and (b) discuss the approach to problems or topics. It is to be noted that the diversity of the environment required each for teacher to frame his teaching to suit local conditions.

The concept of "Self" is taken into consideration while listing the behaviours which enable a person to impress the community about environment degradation and its implications."Self" is described in terms of the mental processes that characterize the person and in terms of the meanings of the individual with favourable self concept is a contributing member of the community.

The behaviours enabling the person to impress the community are discussed below:

The reactions of the individuals during the curriculum experiences depend on their emotions. So, the various emotions which have a bearing either directly or indirectly were taken up. For example, anxiety is shown as *"sharing"* behaviour while curiosity is expressed as *"alertness"*. Affection continues as sharing things or ideas as he makes entry into school. The process or assimilating experience (gaining meaning) is speeded up tremendously when the child communicates with other persons. In middle childhood, reading permits him to share the experiences of persons who are not physically present.

Porents, usually do give thought to helping children develop personality traits that will lead to good social adjustments. They try to teach children to be unselfish *(altruistic)*. Good personal and social adjustements developed by the end of second year lead to the development of favourable self-concept. This will in turn makes child to take initiative and expressed as a leadership quality.

By the time child is 4-5 years of age the personality pattern gets established. The child who is developing an adequate personality has great store of positive perceptions of self which gives him the courage to function. For example, curiosity gives child a new perception of himself, increases his capacity to stand up to difficulty and enable him to handle a troublesome problem. In the older children curiosity is shown as "alertness"

The individual personalizes his/her reactions only when he/she makes decisions (or has decision making ability) permitted by him/her self.

An individual with favourable self-concept will be able to solve problems.as is own without relying on others *(independent thinking).* He is free of some of the forces which bear upon the child who feels inadequate.

Children are the most vulnerable section of the community. If they are unable to understand and *rationalize* the event, they may suffer from phobias, sleep disturbances, loss of interest in school work, and aggressive or undisciplined behaviour (the category most at risk are 8-12 years old). This is because the psycholgical processes involved in developing as a self include among others, reasoning.

The self-mediated, self-oriented processes continue to set new goals for experience, learning, role playing and inventing of creating and direct the behaviour of the individual towards their realization. He becomes dynamic and he initiates events to accomplish goals which he himself has set and leads others. Thus, when the child interacts with others, he may find himself organizing and directing group.

Thus, the behaviours which enable a person to discuss with community about environmental degradation & its implications and living without altering ecological balance are:

1. Adjustment 2. Alertness 3. Altruism 4. Decision making ability 5. Independent thinking 6. initiative 7. Sharing & 8. Rationalisation.

It should be clear that if our human system involving agriculture, industry, and so on is to be sustainable, it must be operataed in accordance with ecological laws and principles. Yet, we are, in large part, operating our human system according to notions and whims that bear little relationship to ecological natural laws.

The afore-said behaviours can be developed by incorporating the content specified (phrases) into activities at the primary school. This aspect is discussed below:

1. *Adjustement:* The ability of the individual to set right the things; regulating the things; and making suitable/convenient for use the things can be developed in Class 1, ii & iii through Science & Social Studies subjects. For example,

Class1	Science -	Keeping clean
Class 1	Social studies-	Keep everything in the proper place
Class II	Science -	Ventilators let out foul air
Class II	Social Studies -	Muncipality arranges to clean the surroundings, roads and markets
Class III	Science -	Collect glass pieces with thick cloth and put them carefully in dustbin
Class III	Social Studies -	Air-conditioning apparatus.

2. ***Alterness*** *:* Alertness is indicated by being watchful, vigilant and on the look-out against danger or mifrortune. These aspects have to be emphasised in classes 1, II & III through English, Telugu, Science and Social studies subjects. As an example.

Class I	English -	Watching
Class I	Telugu -	on the look-out against danger
Class I	Science -	Children watch plants grow
Class I	Social studies -	Watching the animals
Class II	English -	being ready, Columbus sat watching them
Class II	Telugu -	Carefully growing up the plants
Class II	Science -	Protect crop from grazaing animals
Class II	Social Studies -	People should be careful on roads
Class III	English -	"Wake" said the sunshine
Class III	Telugu -	Quickly run
Class III	Science -	good food at proper time should be given to animals
Class III	Social Studeis -	all were ready.

3. ***Altrusim*** : It is the aspect of "considering the well-being and happiness of others first, and also to be unselfish". It is included in the class I English, Class II English and Telugu, and Class III Telugu subjects as shown below:

Class I English -	If you are selfish, you will not have friends
Class II English -	We want all the Water
Class II Telugu -	harming others
Class III Telugu -	doing good to others.

4. ***Decision- making ablity:*** The ablity to decide and act accordingly is developed through English, Telugu & Science subjects of Classes, I, II & III. For example.

Class I English -	King decided to test his cleverness
Class I Telugu -	Riddles about coconut, onion, etc.
Class II English -	Finally decided to go in searach of water
Class II Telugu -	Problem of unity with bundle of sticks
Class II Science -	insecticides must be sprayed to kill insects
Class III English -	Problem of distingusihing the artificial from the natural flowers
Class III Telugu -	Unreached grapes are sour.

5. ***independent Thinking:*** The aspects of developing "not relying on others, action/thinking upon one's own lines, and unwilling to be under the obligation to others" is made through subjects English & Telugu in Class II and Social Studies of Class III as given below:

ClassII English -	let me think in the story of jackal, crow and deer
Class II Telugu -	don't deny elders
Class III Social Studies -	Wisdom dawned on Buddha

6. ***Initiative:*** The capacity to see what needs to be done and enterprise enough to do it, and without being prompted by others is developed

through English of Classes I, II & III and Social Studies and Telugu of Class II. As for example.

Class II English -	Alice's first adventure in wonderland
Class II Telugu -	Struck upon an idea
Class II Social Studies -	Sits on the first bench
Class III English-	Columbus discovered new islands

7. **Rationalisation**: The ability "to bring into conformity with reason or treat/explain in a rational manner" is achieved through Science Class III as stated below:

Class III Science -	What made the paper fan to rotate?

8. **Sharing**: The aspects of "gving away part of or enduring jointly with others" is most important from environmental concern-wise because it is due to lack of this behaviour each and everyone is causing harm to nature by being in one's own cocoon. This aspect of 'sharing' can be developed in the classes 1, II & III English & Mathematics subjects as a ground is already established. For example.

Class I English -	share what you have
Class I mathematics-	teacher shared 40 sweets between 8 students
Class II English -	I want to share my blessings, God.
Class II Mathematics -	60 mangoes are distributed among 8 boys equallly
Class III English -	Ant cannot give away her store of food
Class III Mathematics -	illustrates the distributive property in multiplication. [6(a+b)= 6a+6b]

CONCLUSION

Once these behaviours are instilled in the children, the concern for encironment will be great for them. They adjuct to the society where the needs are many but resources are few. They will be on the look-out against danger and alert the members of the community to save life and property in the wake of environmental impact/threats. This individual will be unselfish and does not hoard money/food grains which create resource crunch in the society. This person will be able to decide on his own what to do and how to do? The person trained in this manner will be able to think independently without depending on authority for overcoming the crisis situations. This child will have more initiative and does what his thought provokes (firm understanding). The rationalisation enables the individual to reason before taking any conclusions. The aspect of sharing is very much essential as the subject environmental education stresses on creating awareness of the environmental issues to all those concerned.

It could be summarised that the future citizens with these behaviours will be able to lessen environmental degradation by utilising alternative energy resources for their survival.

REFERENCES

1. Nebel B.J. (1990) : Environmental Science - The way The World Works, (3rd edition). Prentice Hall, Englewood Cliffs, New Jersey.

2. Radha Mohan (1995) : Innovative Science Teaching for Physical Science Teachers, Prentice Hall of India Private Limited, New Delhi.

3. Khanna G.N. (1993): Global Environmental Crisis and Management, ashish Publishing House, New Delhi.

4. Ornstein,A.C.(1988): Curriculum - Foundations, Principles and issues, Prentice Hall, Englewood Cliffs, New Jersey.

5. Frescott D.A.(1957): The Child in the Educative Process, Mc Graw Hill Book Inc. New York.

6. Jain S.C. "Value-oriented Edcation in Indian Schools Through Biology Teaching."Biology and Human affairs - 211 (2) 1976, P.10

7. Text books of all subjects from Sree Rama publishers, 15-1-513, Siddiamber Bazar, Hyderabad - 500 012.

23

TEACHING LEARNING STRATEGIES IN ENVIRONMENTAL EDUCATION

Dr. Digumarti Bhaskara Rao,
R.V. R. College of Education,
Guntur-522006

Dr. K.R.S.Sambasiva Rao
Department of Zoology
Nagarjuna University
Nagarjuna Nagar- 522 510
Guntur Dist, A.P.

Mr. N.Siva Ram Prasad
Department of Zoology
Junior College, Inkollu
Prakasam Dist, A.P.

Nuture is fascinating. The soft green leaf moving gently in the bird singing hidden in a mango groove, all are so enchanting so enthralling. No less is the child with its hazel eyes, silken hair, rose cheeks, toothless mouth and tender skin. Its father, the man, too is very handsome and is perhaps the most unique creation of nature, unique in the sense that it is man who has made the world so beautiful. But for him, nature would not have been so enjoyable as it is. He has converted wild forests into parks, gardens, orchards and cities, and deserves all praise for that. But in doing that and his attempts to make life more and more comfortable, he often—times destroyed forests thoughtllessly, polluted air, water and soil recklessly, spoiled nature ruthlessly. The inevitable consequence was an ominious deterioration of the environment. He did not stop even then, nor did he use that much caution and took those precautions which should have been taken. He, infact, jumped headlong towards himself and sober down, he is bound to find himself in an irreversible predicament, in an ecological catastrophe which will bring an end of the mankind on our lively planet. The answer to avert such a catastrophe is environmental education. The sudden increase in the activities for environmental education during the last two and half decades has resulted in the development of different kinds of curricula, out-of-school activities and literature. The purpose is to regenerate man's interest in preservation,conservation and imporvement of the environment before it is too latae and reaches the point of no return (R.C.Sharma).

ENVIRONMENTAL EDUCATION

Environmental education is a process to promote the awareness and understanding of the environment, its relationship with man and his activities, It is also aimed at developing responsible actions necessary for preservation, conservation and imporvement of the environment and its components. It is the education 'about' the environment 'from' the environment and 'for' the environment. Education about the environment' is acquired an understanding of the total environment. It is learning 'from the environment' when the environment is used as a vehicle for gathering concepts, knowledge and skills related to specific academic disciplines. The development of attitudes, skills and evaluation of abilities for the proper use and the develpment of the environment is 'education for the environment.

Environmental education is both a 'style' and 'subject matter' of educatiion. style of education means using environment as a teaching learning aid and as an approach to education. Subject matter or content means teaching about the components and constituents of environment. Teaching for environment here means controlling the environment, establishing proper ecological equilibrium and proper environmental planning.

These definitions of environmental education appear on first reaction to be simplistic and superficial, but actually it is comprehensive and deep: is a medium and process of education: is multi-disciplinary in character: is a life long process and is concerned with the whole biosphere.

The International Union for the Conservation of Nature and Natural Resources Commission of Education has remarked in the International working Meeting on Environmental Education in the School Curriculum held under the auspices of UNESCO in paris in 1970 as Environmental education is the process of recognising values and clarifying concepts in order to develop skills and attitudes necessary to understand and appreciate the interrelatedness among man, his culture and his biophysical surroundings. Environmental education also entails practice in decision-making and self-formulation of a code of behaviour about issues concerning environmental quality.

Thilsi Conference which was held at Georgia in the former Soviet Union in October 1977 under the auspices of the UNESCO and United Nations Environmental Programme resolved that Environmental Education should.

- Consider the environment in its totality-natural and built, teachinological and social (economic, Plitical, technological, cultural, historical, moral, austhetic).

- be a continuous, lifelong process, beginning at the preschool level and continuing through all formal and non-formal stages.

- be inter-disciplinary in its approach, drawing on the specific content of each discipline in making possible a holistic and balanced perspective.

- examine major environmental issues from the local, national, regional, international points of view so that students receive insight into environmental conditions in other geographical areas.

- focus on current and potential environmental situations while taking into account the historical perspectives.

- promote the values and necessity of local, national, and international cooperation in the prevention and solution of environmental problems.

- explicitly consider environmental aspects in plans for development and grwoth.

- enable learners to have a role in planning their learning experiences and provide an opportunity for making decisions and accepting their consequences.

- relate environmental sensitivity, knowledge, problem-solving skills and values-claraification to every age, but with special emphasis on environmental sensitivity to the learner's own community in early years.

- help learners discover the symptoms and real causes of environmental problems.

- emphasize the complexity of environmental problems and thus the need to develop critical thinking and problem solving skills.

- utilize diverse learning environments and a broad array of educational approaches to teaching/learning about and from the environment with due stress on practical activities and firsthand experience.

OBJECTIVES OF ENVIRONMENTAL EDUCATION

The objectives of environmental education are part of the general objectives of education. These objectives of environmental education can be subsumed in three domains viz., cognitive, affective and psychomotor. Let us list out the objectives of environmental education in all the three domains.

The cognitive domain includes those objectives which deal with the recall and recognition of knowledge and development of intellectual skills and abilities. The cognitive objectives of environmental education are;

1. To help acquire knowledge of the immediate environment.

2. To help acquire knowledge of the environment beyond the immediate environmnt including distant environment.

3. To help understand the interdependence of life at different trophic levels.

5. To help understand the effect of unchecked population growth or unplanned resource utilisation of the world of tomorrow.

6. To examine trends in the growth of population and interpret them for the socio-economic development of the country.

7. To evaluate the utilisation of physical and human resources and to suggest remedial measures.

8. To help dignose the different causes of environmental pollution and to suggest remedial measures.

9. To help diagnose the causes of social tensions and to suggest methods for avoiding them.

10. To help develop observational skill and notice usually not seen by an utrained eye.

11. To help develop skills required for making discriminations in form, shape, sound, touch, habits and habitats.

12. To help develop ability to draw unbiased inferences and conclusions.

13. To help develop ability to make meaningful suggestions.

The objectives of affective domain relate to creating interests, forming attitudes, fostering values, developing appreciations and making adjustmens. The affective domain objectives are :

1. To help acquire interest in the flora and fauna of the near and also distant environment.

2. To help evince interest in the people and problems of the community and society.

3. To show tolerance towards different castes, races religions and cultures.

4. To appreciate the gifts of nature.

5. To love the neighbours and value mankind as a whole.

6. To value equality, liberty, fraternity, truth and justice.

7. To value the cleanliness and purity of our nature.

Objectives of psychomotor domain are achieved through participation in environmental activities, excursions and camping programmes. The objectives of psychomotor domain are:

1. To participate in afforestation programmes.

2. To participate in programmes aimed at minimising air, water and noise pollution.

3. To participate in programmes aimed at preventing soil erosion.

4. To participate in programmes aimed at eliminating food contamination and adulteration.

5. To participate in urban and rural planning and execution programmes such as installations of gobar gas plants, solar heaters and lights, etc.

Comprehensiveness of the objectives of environmental education is ever essential for the successful formulation implementation and evaluation of its programmes.

TEACHING LEARNING STRATEGIES

In order to meet the challenge of environmental education and to accomplish its objectives the first think for the teachers will be to understand the teaching learning strategies very clearly.

Teaching methodologies or teaching learning strategies used in environmental education are as varied as objectives in various subjects. One of the major reasons for this seems to be the variation in environmental conditions, resources including material, money and personnel available, variety of environmental problems, and educational system. The teaching learning strategies such as class discussions, small group projects, field trips, outdoor studies, use of exhibits, simulation and games, material guides, debates, inquiry and guest lectures are useful in many occasions.

CLASS DISCUSSIONS

In class discussion, a problem or topic and its associated aspects will be discussed very clearly. Sometimes students are allowed to refer sources or read extensively to have a through idea about the problem and to discuss it in the classroom concretely. The class teacher also participates in the discussion in different phases of discussion to give additional information, to create new question, to extract opinions and views, to see the discussion move in a right way, ti gice suggestions, to involve all the class students in discussion etc. The advantages of all students, and it exposes the students to various phenomena of environmental education.

SMALL GROUP PROJECTS

In this strategy, the students have to take up certain projects. The total class is either divided into small group or work at a total unit depending on the nature of the project to be worked out. Sometimes the project is also divided into small units. Each students or small group of students is given a work for which the students or small group of work at a total unit depending on the nature of the project to be worked out. Sometimes the project is also divided into small units. Each students or small group of students is gicen a work for which the students take responsibility of completing it successfully. At the end of the project the activities of all the students or groups are presented to the total class in the from of reports and displays. They explain their experiences, data, conclusions and recommendations. If we take the problem of mosquitoes as a project, a small group will identify the causes of mosquitoes, another will map the ditches, another will look into the eradication techniques, and another group will apply the selected techniques to eradicate the mosquitoes. Field Trips

FIELD TRIPS

Field trips are very much educative and they create great curiosity in students and also bring out their creativity, Keown (1984) states that (1) those concepts that are integral part of the students environment are best learned in the outdoor environment(ii) the concepts have a better chance of being underst and retaining it, if parts of the concept can be relataed to students environment: (iii) critical thinking is enhanced in the outdoor environment: and (iv) investigations in the outdoor environment increase students desire for that environment. The selected places for field trip should be relative to environmental problem. Before the execution of a field trip, the teacher has to plan the trip, including the teaching learning strategies to be followed. It is better if the teacher visits the place earlier and plans the field trip according to the resources available at the place. After the successful completion of the trip, based on the experiences and observations the students may submit their work in the form of reports, drawings, stories, poems, etc. More field trips a teacher arranges, more awreness comes in the students towards environmental problems, Lucko et al. (1982) concluded, based on three studies, that field trip is an important and effective method for clear cut congnitive and affective gain in the eyes of teachers and educators. The choice of environment and its setting play an important role in the formation of right attitudes and behaviours.

OUTDOOR STUDIES

Students may study different aspects and objects of environment. They can study a village, a river, a lake, some specific problems of an area which include pollution aspects, inter-relationship of living beings, etc. The outdoor studeis also require a detailed planning like field trips, but these studies may be limited to the local environments. The study team has to plan the objectives of the study plan, execute and submit a report to take necessary action and for the benefit of the other students. Backmanand cromption (1984-85) feel that the effectiveness may be greatest if the outdoor experience is proceeded by an indoor experience which provides a cognitive framework into which pieces of information likely to be encountered outdoors can be fitted. Kirk (1980-81) felt that (i) the activities which focus the attention on the use of nature of study and field activities help the students to learn about countryside and conservation: (ii) the activities which develop skills and interest in regorous physical activities help in outdoor education (iii) the activities related to the study of man-made environment and social environment help students to learn urban traditions: and (iv) the activities related to the study of rural environment focus the attention of the students to learn about agriculture, horticlture, forestry and other forms of land managaement.

EXHIBITS

Exhibits also serve as an important media for environmental education. Exhibits or exhibitions can be arranged to show the project work of the students or to highlight the environmental problems in order to get suitable remedies. Different exhibits explaining various concepts of environmental education can be displayed in collaboration with various environmental organisations. Students will take part very actively in these exhibitions and show their abilities. They also explain the observers about the environmental problems and solutions.

SIMULATION AND GAMES

Simulation and games can be used to focus attention on both attitudes and content. The advantage of games and simulations, according to Troost and Altman (1972) is that they have intrinsic potential for motivation.

DEBATES

By arranging debates the teacher can make the students aware of environment. Its problems and the necessary feasible solutions.

READINGS

A teacher can ask the students to get further information through additional.readings. This will help to grow individually.

INQUIRY

On finding a problem or else by a student of any occasion a student can take up an inquiry to probe into it. Or a teacher can also assign inquiries into various aspects of environmental education. The teacher should develop Inquiry Guides for the benefit of the students.

GUEST LECTURES

Guest lectures given by eminent personalities will motivate the students in many ways and help the students to participate in environmental activities.

MATERIAL GUIDES

Many material guides are available on environmental education. They will enhance the teaching learning activities.

COMMUNITY RESOURCES

Community resources can also be used as effective means in environmental education.

OTHER STRATEGIES

Teacher can independently develop their own teaching learning strategies depending on the demand of each situation. They can also imbibe the concept of environmental education in their routine teaching.

WHAT DOES RESEARCH SPEAK?

Not many studies are available on the methodologies used for environmental education. Childress (1978) in a study found in U.S. that small group projets, class discussion and field trips are the strategies used often in the largest percentage of programmes and projects. Tewksbury and harris (1982) found that the most popular method is discussion used by 91% of teachers, and this is followed by audio-visual aids (74%), outdoor studies (64%), field trip and community resources (60%), and small group projets (60%). Nearly 40% techers use material guides and 29% guest lectures. Computer assisted instruction comes lowest with 2% teachers using it. Some other used methodologies such as camping (Jacobson and Beaver, 1984. Jacobson and Palonsky, 1976), use of zoo (Marshdoyle. 1982), excursion (Tripathi, 1983), Scwaab (1982-83) conducted to find out teachers (117 teachers) rating of the effectiveness of different methodologies and found that teacher led discussion (extent of use/mean effectiveness on 2-6 scale -92%/4.4) lecture (92%/3.9). Individual projects (87%/4.7). demonstrations (85%/4.3), individual reports *86%/4.1), readings (85%/4.3) group reports (74%/4.1) independent study (68%/4.7), cognitive skill development (68%/4.2), and debates (50%/4.5) have their relative effectiveness, Bhaskara Rao (1986) through discussions with teachers in the Mass Orientation Programmes organised by Government of India found that field trips projects demonstrations and use of audio-visual aids were effective teaching learning strategies.

CONCLUDING REMARKS

Studing the environment in the classroom itself is diffcult, unless issues are analysed dispassionately in terms of cause, effect and implications. The analysis of the problem starts with major environmental abuses. Now a teacher has to selct a suitable teaching learning strategy and insert the issues into the brains of the students. In continuation of it the students will try to solve the environmental problems and make the world beautiful.

24

ENVIRONMENTAL EDUCATION TRAINING A PRIMARY TEACHER

Dr. P.V.Seetha Rama Raju,
Lecturer in Social Studies,
D.N.R.College of Education
Bhimavaram - 534202.
Andhra Pradesh

It is obvious that the structure of Teacher Training Progaramme in any stage conveys some thing more than merely the acquisition of teaching skills, methodology etc., on setting time limits for teacher preparation at different levels of training starting from primary and ending with university. Each level of training has to be relevant to development stage of the pupils as well as teachers.

The course of training need to be formulated bearing in mind the capacity of the teacher, importance of the child, national ideas and goals, availability of physical and natural resources and their utilisation.

Teachers are the sacred trust of the future community and nation. Teachers are the valuable human resources on whose development depends the future of the nation.

Hence a special responsibility liies on us to ensure that every teacher in this country should grow into a responsible teacher by possessing a strong charecter and unique abilities and profound knowledge on our environment.

So the present teacher training should provide the practical knowledge to the teacher on his environment, as the mankind is totally associated with environment.

So it is high time to introduce the environmental Education in the primary teacher training programme to help the teacher in understanding the physical and social forces at work around them so that they could be able to prepare the children in dveloping the abilities and skills to cope with and manage their environment.

Environmental education helps the teacher trainee to learn about measures of protection of environment, knowledge on ecological balance, respoect towards nature, how the communities are formed and governed, how do they meet their needs,how the people use and misuse the resources on the earth, how to solve the social, physical environmental problems, so that the teacher trainee could be able to prepare the children to adjust themselves to the changing needs and expectations in the actual work field.

Ojectives in introducting Environmental Education in the primary Teacher Training Programme:-

1. To prepare the teacher to teach environmental Education.

2. To develop awareness about environmental aspects among teachers.

3. To prepare the teacher to develop his own curriculam basing on the local requirements.

The teacher plays an important role in teaching learning process and inturn the child is influenced by his teaching to meet the social and physical aspects of the environment. The teacher serves as a model for the child. The teacher should help the children to become aware of different aspects of the environment. So the teacher should first prepare himslef to teach about environment in an effective way. To make the teacher to prepare to teach environmental Education the programme is:-

1. Teaching of environmental Education should be introducted in the primary teacher training programme.

2. Conducting field trips, Local survery programmes, community service, visiting polluted and natural calamity areas etc.

3. Collection of data on present Environmental problems and their reasons.

4. Preparing the teacher trainess to participate in the natural calamity areas such as flood effected, cyclone effected, fire effected, earth quake effected areas etc.

5. Conducting citizenship training programmes including activites related to environment.

6. Arranging demonstrations with community workers.

7. Conducting debates and discussions on environmental problems and their solution.

8. Training in preparation of some activity project models.

In this way first we should prepare the teaacher trainee to feel the importance of Environmental Education.

To develop environmental awareness among teacher trainees knowledge on the following topics should be given.

1. Types of families and their advantages

2. **Community workers**: Doctor,Pliceman, Postman, lawyer, teacher, weaver, carpenter, milkman etc.

3. Community resoruces:

   Natural resources

   Manmade resources

4. Transportation facilities

5. Electricity

6. Communication

7. Panchayat, Mandal, Municipality, Z.P.

8. Nature and its importance

9. Natural calamities- protection.

10. Environmental balance-Maintainance of land- population,forests, rivers etc.

11. Types of pollution:

    Air, Sound, Water, food, Mind.

The teacher trainee should equip with the above fundamental knowledge.

Finally the teacher should be able to prepare himself to develop his own curriculam at the actual work field basing on the local requirements. For this three stages were suggested:

STAGE-I PREPARATION

1. Conducting sruvey of the community where he is working

2. Identification of environmental aspects.

3. Conducting meetings with parents and public to collect problems realted to the environment.

STAGE II PLANNING

1. He should organise the environmental aspects in a systamatic way.

2. He should allot appropriate time for the above aspects

3. He should prepare a plan of implimentation of the above aspects basing on the available resources.

STAGE -III IMPLINENTION

1. He should educate the public on the Government polices with available resources.

2. He should make the children to participate in the community activities.

3. He should work along with his children in the natural calamity areas.

4. He should conduct some environmental projects along with his children.

Thus the primary teacher can protect the environment by way of getting appropriate training on environmental Education in the primary teacher training programme.

The following suggession are made for the effective introduction of the environmental Education.

1. Specific and detailed training paackage should be developed basing on the above lines.

2. Environmental projects should be designed

3. Appropriate methods should be suggested which wll be conducive to the teacher trainee to learn the environmental Education.

4. Local curriculam models should be prepared

5. Detailed concepts on Environmental education should also be included along with existing syllabus

Finally it is concluded that well trained teacher on Environmental Education can only protect the environment with the help of the children.

REFERENCES

1. Ashok Kumar (1991), Current trends in Indian Education Ashish Publication house, New Delhi.

2. Ediger, Morular and Digumarti Bhaskara Rao (1997). *Science Curriculum*. Discovery Publishing House, New Delhi.

3. John Kurrien (1983), Elementary Education In India, Vikas Publishing house, Pvt, Ltd, Sahibabad, U.P.

4. Pankajam.G.(1994), Pre school Education(Philosophy & Practice, The Indian publications, Ambala cantt (India)

5. Sarma R.A. (1993), Teacher Education'(Theory, practive and Research), Loyal Book Depot, Meerut, U.P.

6. SCERT, 'Teachers hand book 'Environmental Education'(Telugu) Hyderbad, A.P.

25

WATER POLLUTION : STRATEGIES IN EDUCATION

Dr. T. Mrunalini
lecturer in Education I.A.S.E.
Osmania University
Hyderabad - 500007

INTRODUCTION

Everything origniated in the water and everything is sustained by water. Water is needed to fulfill diverse requirements in many different ways. Water is essential for day to day life activities, i.e.. right from quenching thrust to that of physiological system. It is essential for social life, for example, from small scale sanitary cleanliness to that of major industrial usage. It is vital to life. Besides temperature, water is an important factor that influences the global ecology. Water influences weather, climate and on any region involving its flora and fauna. Water is essential for agriculture. The indian agrarian economy largely depends on water. Therefore, without water there is no activity and without pure water rather life is impossible.

Unfortunately, it is often difficult to find uncontaminated water these days. The oceans, rivers, tanks and also lakes are polluted in various ways. Water contamination has been destroying the whole ecosystem. By and large, in all countris, dumping to toxic substances by way of effluents from factories and large industries inland waters is a common phenomenon. Untreated sewage is another important offender and excessive amounts of it can extingusih life. Run-off pollutants from agricultural lands in the form of rivers and lakes contaminate water for human consumption.

The indiscriminate use of detergents which use undissolved chemicals causes contamination of lakes and rivers. Pollution of sea water by oil slicks, dumping of radio-active wastes deep into the seas and conduction nuclear tests under the oceans are other causes of water pollution. Pollution of water is no more a local,but it is a global phenomenon.

Certain living examples of industrialization in the Indian context represents the alarming rate of water pollution at a global level. They are:

1. THE KABANI PAPER MILL IN KARNATAKA

This industry has polluted kabani river which is the lone source of drinking water and agriculture in the villages Kallchalli, Kathadipura, Chamalapura, etc.

2. INDUSTRIAL ESTATES AT PATANCHERU AND BOLLARUM IN A.P.

These industries are located at about 25-30 kms from the heart of the city of Hyderabad. Voltas factory is an industry spreading pollution into the rivers, like Nakka Vagu, where water has turned into crimson and purple. This river was a source for the prosperity for about 14 villages. But at present it used only for tanning leather. A sister river Chinna vagu has also became red in colour. Chinna vagu merges with Nakka vagu stream at the outskirts of the city carrying toxic water which ends up in the Manjira reservoir. The same reservoir supplies water to the twin cities of Hyderabad and Secunderabad. On Sept. 4th 1986 Nakka Vagu water was officially declared as dead. By recognising the seriousness of the pollution, Revenue Divisional Office at Sangareddy issued a notification that no person should utilize the water of the river any longer either for drinking or other purposes. What is important to note here is the dreadful impact of these polluted rivers on human life. One can see people with a number of health problems/disorders in the surrounding villages of these rivers.

3. THE TANNERIES OF NORTH ARCOT DISTRICT IN TAMIL NADU:

The tannery industries discharge on an averagae 500-600 million liters of untreated waste into the environment. The chemical chrome is find everywhere including in the breast milk of mothers in this area.

4. THE ORIENT PAPER MILLS (OPM) AMLAI, MADHYA PRADESH:

The OPM is located on the banks of river Sone in Madhya Pradesh OPM discharges about 16 million gallons of waste water into sone daily. This pollutes the river down stream to a distance of 40 Km and the water has become unfit for bathing and washing.

The above four cases are just a few examples of today to understand the causes behind environmental degradation. Neither the state nor the NGO's paid any attention on these issues. But Yamuna and Ganga river pollution issues are highly debated in political circles and they got high publicity.

According to India Today's Jan 15th, 1997, research report."From river to sewer" about the levels of pollution of Yamuna river found to be the pollutant material collected from 50,000 industries and sewage from 8 million people. India Today commissioned shriram Institute for industrial Research, to test the Yamuna water and particularly before it enters Delhi at Wazirabad. The biochemical analysis showed that, the californ count (reflection of bacteria mainly from human and animal waste- in the water), dissolved oxygen essential for aquatic life etc. are found less than the safe levels at Wazirabad, it is a clear reflection of the Yamuna river turning into sewage especially at Wazirabad.

The famous "Ganga Action Plan" (GAP) has turned into a 'Ganga inaction plan' where the country's largest clean-up operation is carried out with earmarked Rs. 17,000 crores. In this amount only Rs. 507 crores has been spent so far. In the next six years or so another Rs. 1.200 crores will have to be spent. Inspite of such large scale funding the Ganga remained polluted and it has become a source for diseases and health hazards. The major criticism about this plan is regarding the misuse of funds, overspending and tardy progress. Similary, the kanpur, clean-up schemes, with Rs. 60 crores,and patna toilets building schemes to stop people from defecating on river banks have become inaffective. Industries in Calcutta have been dumping affluents continuously into the river and no mechanism has been initiated to arrest this problem so far. At

Varanasi about 28,000 turtles were introduced into the Ganga to scavenge the dead bodies but they themselves have been poached, by the polluted water. Also dhobhi ghats constructed with huge amounts lies unused. At Allahabad efforts to treat sewage drains at the confluence of the Yamuna and Ganga have totally failed.

One can mention cases like above which show a grim state of our hopes of protecting our environment. Though there is a water (Prevention and control of water pollution) Act 1974, it is already two decades passed without any significant impact.

The alarming rates of water pollution are leaving an irreparable impact on human life. Especially people are affected by a number of health problems like, rickets, dental decay, lesion, on skin, other skin diseases, breathing problems, sterility (like: Patancheru case where mothers are not able bear a child, even if born they not survived), digestive tract diseases and gum diseases etc.

Hence, there is a need to arrest water pollution. And there is also a need to work out certain strategies from different directions and sectors.

The most important intervention can be thought from the field of education, especially school education. As the schools are the miniatures of the society and the teachers and students are the agents of social change, it is possible to work out certain strategies on water pollution at different levels of education.

STUDY OF WATER POLLUTION IN EDUCATION

The study of water and water pollution is introduced in the school curriculum to enable students to acquire knowledge about the complexities of water. But the methods of teaching water are mostly asocial. The topics about water are taught in isolation from social context. Like other topics in science, concepts of water are also discussed and repeated mechanically without giving any emphasis on the role of private industries, political decisions, legal aspects, etc. Generally the topic water is discussed with reference to its physical, chemical properties. No space is created in the curriculum to think critically about the implementation of the lopsided policies. Also not much emphasis is made in the classroom on the relationship between water, industry and human life.

The need of the hour is that, the teacher community being the largest and the most influential must directly take initiative in working out strategies to arrest the wataer pollution.

WATER POLLUTION: TEACHER EDUCATION

At present there is a great demand for teacher education in our country. A large number of students are getting training in the skills of teaching. It is a very potential area to catch the attention of youth and inturn influence the students at large. As a component in teacher training on current issues of soical relevance, student teachers can be encouraged to work on these areas and develop certain practical strategies from time to time.

First, the teacher educators must be made conscious of the sensitive issues and they should be provided with all the skills needed to develop awareness about the same in student teachers. Also the teacher educators should try to motivate them to participate in awareness camps. Every student teacher must be prepared in such a way that they should feel and show their concern about the problems of water pollution. They are expected to make their part of potential contribution for maintaining peace and harmony in life with pollution free environment.

In the light of the above discussion certain specific strategies have been identified. Some of these are discussed below:

ACTIVITIES AT PRE-SCHOOL LEVEL

The activities relevant to the children of two and half to five and half years age group are identified and presented below. Activities for this group of children be preferably informal and very simple to manipulate. These activities involve spontaneous activities of children and provide a space for habit formation.

ACTIVITY I: USING WATER BOTTLES

a) Objectives :

1. To develop awareness about water management on simple and unconscious ways.

2. To develop the concept of clean drinking water.
3. To develop the habit of using clean water
4. To make them aware about the health hazards of using dirty water.

b) Materials:

Water bottles, water (clean and dirty)

c) Procedure:

Children have to be encouraged in an informal way to use water which is clean and dirt free. They must also know how to use water more economically by using water bottles without spilling over water and making the surroundings dirty.

ACTIVITY II: USAGE TO TAP WATER:

a) Objectives:

1. To develop the habit of proper use of water
2. To make children to know about the importance of controlling waste/unwanted flow of wataer

b) Materials:

Water taps, simulated environment with water taps and water

c) Procedure:

Teachers have to train children to get habituated to close the taps immediately after using drinking water. They gradually learn that whenever they find the taps kept open and unnecessary flow of water, they have to close them.

ACTIVITY III: WASTE MATERIAL MANAGEMENT (AVOIDING WATER POLLUTION)

a) Objectives :

1. To develop awareness about waste material management
2. To make children conscious about fresh water and avoid garbage accumulation in water sources.

b) Material :

Pictures related to sources of water, models of sources of water, water, waste materials and dust bins etc.

c) Procedure:

Children should get exposed to the simulated conditons and they have to be involved in role playing to encourage them to throw garbage in the waste boxes, than in any other sources of water like small pools, lakes etc. Parents and teachers can practically involve them in using waste boxes.

ACTIVITIES AT PRIMARY LEVEL

Children of five and half (5½) to ten and half (10½) age group (ie.I-V standard) are included in this level. The project method, discussion method and experimental methods can be adopted at a micro-level. Children have to be motivated to take part in all the activities like awareness camps.

ACTIVITY I : STORED WATER AND HEALTH HAZARDS

a) Objectives:

1. To develop awareness about the consequences of long-time stored drinking water on health.
2. To make them know about presence of microbes in long-time stored water.
3. To make them know about wastage of excessive storage of water.

b) Materials:

Microscopes/transparent vessels, handlenses, water, storage vessels, photograph with diseased people and also real specimens etc.

c) Procedure:

Children are encouraged/activated to collect the information with regard to storage of water from different people in their locality. They can be informed by showing microbes and subsequent effects on health. Children will be able to develop awareness about problems of excessive storage of water in their community.

ACTIVITY 2: COMMUNITY WATER TAP MANAGEMENT

a) Objectives :

1. To know about the usefulness of community taps.
2. To realize the importance of drinking water.
3. To make children to observe/notice the leakages in cimmunity taps.
4. To make them conscious about wastage of water

b) Materials :

Community water taps, taps to damonstrate leakagaes, dust sheets etc.

c) Procedure:

Children could be encouraged to collect the information with regard to number of taps in their locality, hours of water supply in their locality, where children are made to develop awareness about the problems of wastage of water at mocro level.

ACTIVITY III: USAGE OF WATER FOR RESIDENTAIAL PURPOSE

a) Objectives:

1. To develop an insight about appropriate usage of water
2. To make children conscious about misuse of pure-water

b) Materials:

Pure-water, picture related to scarcity of water, and pictures of dried lakes and rivers.

c) Procedure:

Children must be motivated to observe and note carefully the appropriate usage of drinking water in their communities. They can also be encouraged to recognise misuse of water in residential localities and take necessary measures for arresting such misuses.

ACTIVITY IV: CLEAN AND SAFE DRINKING WATER

a) Objectives:

1. To develop the concept of clean water and its significance.
2. To make them know about microbes in dirty water.
3. To motivate them drink safe and clean water.

b) Materials:

Pure Water, dirty water with microbes, microscopes, transparent glass vessels, handlenses, pictures of sources of drinking water.

c) Procedure:

Children may be exposed to clean/fresh water and dirty water for physical discriminiation. Then in the next stage different orgnisms and microbes in the water has to be shown through microscopes. If microscopes are not available, it can be poured into transparent vessels for identification of the constituents of water seen through hand lenses.

ACTIVITY V: WATER AND ITS ALTERNATE USES

a) Objectives:

1. To develop awareness about reusing of water
2. To motivate children to realise the water management techniques.
3. To encourage children to reuse water for other purposes (like gardening, cleaning etc). b) Materials: Water, used water (water after cleaning rice, vegetable etc) vegetable, rice, vessels etc.

c) Procedure:

Children could be encouraged to use water more economically by reusing the water used already either for cleaning vegetables or any other such purposes) could be utiilzed for gardenting, sewage, etc.)

ACTIVITY VI : POLLUTED WATER AND POLLUTANTS COLLECTED FROM SOURCES OF DRINKING WATER

a) objectives:

1. To make them conscious about pollutantas in drinking water sources.
2. To find out the efflents present in water and their consequences on health.
3. To motivate them to manage such water appropriately for drinking washing and other such purposes.

b) Explanation:

Teachers may start giving training at a micro level by telling the children about the background of industrial polluted water. Then they can be exposed to polluted water collected from sources of water, where industrial wastes are dumped. Then the children may be able to distinguish between the two and realise the causes of water pollution.

ACTIVITIES AT SECONDARY LEVEL

Children belong to ten and half (10½) to fifteen and half (15½) years of age group are inclued in this level. These children compared to the last two groups, are matured enough to understand the importance of water in everyday life.

ACTIVITY I : FIELD VISITS TO INDUSTRIES

a) Objectives:

1. To make them conscious about the location of industries.
2. To make them know about the toxic effluents discharged from industries.
3. To involve them to observe the usage of water at different levels in the industries.
4. To make them critical about the existing practices in industries related to water.

b) Material:

Specimens of effluents collected from industries, literature reated to industrial practices.

c) Procedure:

Every school can adopt an industry (small or large in size) depending on the strength of the school. Children may be encouraged to visit them regularly (either bimonthly/quarterly/depending on the requirement). These field investigations should become an integral part of the secondary school curriculum. Government can take initiatives and create a space for harmonious interaction between schools and industries.

Activity II: Field trips to industrial 'areas:

a) Objectives:

1. To develop awareness about industrial effluents.
2. To make them know about the impact of water pollution on surrounding areas (on people's) health.
3. To make them know about effluents impact on land and environment.

b) Materials:

Samples of effluents collected from industrial areas from the sources water, disease causing microbes samples, disease affected people's photographs or people.

(c) Procedure: Teachers can motivate the children to visit the areas of industries. They may be motivated to observe the effluents discharged from the industries. Also they may be encouraged to develop and understand the effluents's impact on living and involve in planning the programmes to safefuard the environment from pollution through industrial effluents.

ACTIVITY III: AWARENESS CAMPS AND SENSITIZATION PROGRAMMES:

a) Objectives :

1. To develop understanding about water pollution.
2. To encourge children to take part in team work to plan for

controlling water pollution.

3. To motivate students to take part in sensitisation programmes.

b) Material:

Photographs, pictures, literature (related to water pollution), package (to train the children the to participate in sensitisation programmes) etc.

c) Procedure:

Initially children may be exposed to the industrial areas through visits. later on they may be encouraged made to participate in awareness camps. This will enable children to develop consciousness among people about water pollution, and these programmes influence them to take part individually in a variety of activities to control their environment from water pollution.

ACTIVITY IV: USAGE OF WATER

a) Objectives:

1. To develop awareness about community sources of drinking water.
2. To make conscious about leakages in public and other taps and their future consequences.
3. To make them know about excessive storage and excessive usage of drinking water

b) Materials :

Different taps, leakage bearing taps (for demonstration) pictures (related to future consequences)

C) Procedure:

Discussions can be initiated on negligance of overflowing of precious water from the public taps. Excessive use and excessive storage of drinking water and the future problems like scarcity of water can be discussed among the groups and also a space can be created for healthy exchange of ideas.

ACTIVITY V: GENERAL ACTIVITIES

Certain general activities with the following objectives can be developed on the theme water-pollution.

a) Objectives:

1. To develop awareness about water pollution.
2. To encourage them to participate in awareness programmes.
3. To develop awreness about industarial water into drinking water sources.

b) Material:

Introductory literature containing modules, instruction to participate in awareness programmes, industrial water, collected from sources of water where industrial pollutants mixes.

c) Procedure:

Teachers can train children to take part in programmes, where they get exposed to industries and the wastes which are dumped into water sources. By showing samples of different types of water and the factual information collected from their field investigations children are encouraged to take part in different activities like:literary, song, dance folk music and other competitions and activities and awareness programmes.

ACTIVITY VI: COMPETITIONS AT NATIONAL AND INTERNATIONAL LEVEL ON THE THEME WATER POLLUTION:

a) Objectives:

1. To make them conscious about pollution by taking part in competitions.
2. To make them involve and develop insight into the grave problems of water-pollution.
3. To enable them to know about the consequences of water pollution on human -life.

b) Materials:

Models, painting, clay, thermacol, cardboards, charts, play-cards, pictures of disease affected people, samples of polluted water from different sources, stationary llike papers, painting brushes and boxes etc.

c) Procedure:

Teachers, educationists, government and other concerned authorities may try to initiate the following competitions to develop consciousness about water polution.

COMPETITIONS

1. Exhibition displaying models of water pollution.
2. Paintings with the theme on water pollution.
3. Clay modeling with the theme on water pollution
4. Debates on water pollution.
5. Essay writing on water pollution
6. Futuristic models of rivers, sources of water etc. (depicting them w'th future consequences)
7. Display of charts and play-cards at public places.
8. Collection of water samples collected from all portable sources of water.
9. Collection of different types of industrial effluents (depicting their impact on health)
10. Exhibits on health hazards due to water pollution.

The above activities help us to reconstruct our curriculum activities and also to redefine the objectives of science education and the role of the teachers. Further, this discussion makes us realise that the topic 'Study of Water' can not be taught independently but it has to disscussed in the classroom context with a larger framework of understanding by bringing history, polity, sociology, culture, etc.

REFERENCES

1. Agnihotri, S.P. Environmental conservation for global development. Allahabad: Chugh Publications, 1995

2. Claude Alvares. Science development and violence: the revolt against, modernity, Bombay:Oxford University Press, 1994.

3. India Today, Jan, 1997

4. Panneer, Selwam A and Mohana RamaKrishnan. Environmental science education, New Delhi: sterling publishers, 1996.

5. Raj, R.K., Mohapatra, A.C., and Goel, N.P. Environmental management, physio-ecological facets, volume I. Jaipur:Rawat Publications, 1992.

6. Rathore, M.S. Environment and Development, Jaipur: Rawat Publications, 1996.

7. Singh, R.B. and Suresh Mishra. Environmental Law in India Issues and Rsponses. New Delhi: Concept publishing, 1996.

26

THE NEW GARDEN

Raavi Ranga Rao, Lecturer in Telugu,
A.J. College of Education,
Machilipatnam—521001, A.P.
(Translated by: Dr. Madiraju Rama Lingeswara Rao)

To create a new garden
Alas!
How much pains you have taken!!

You have uprooted all the greeny plants
And have planted the Croton ones!
Alright!
Why do you dye them with with green tint once!!

You have pinched the gragrant flowers
And have hung the plastic flowers!
O.K.!
Why do you sprinkle perfume on them!!

You have driven away the cool breeze
Converted the garden into a burning furnace!
But
Why do you fill it with air coolers!!

With the only ambition of
Keeping your corpse not decomposed
Furnishing the garden with air-conditioned
You die every minute
Till you get your dooms day!

You have demolished the natural garden!
Later on its grave

To give life to a plastic garden,
Tell me-

Why do you toil and boil yourself!!!
Why do you spoil our lives too !!!

27

HUMANISING EDUCATION THROUGH ENVIRONMENTAL ISSUES

Prof. J.S. Grewal
Regional Institute of Education
Shyamala Hills
Bhopal - 462013

INTRODUCTION: HISTORICAL PERSPECTIVE

Education has been influenced by numerous social, political economic and religious considerations in different cultures over the centuries. The period of early Christian education, during the first five centuries, viewed religious institutions as the 'products of tradions' which could mould human nature, make people humanic and, therefore, it was thought that these institutions must be retained. During 6th to 10th centuries there was decline of Greek-Roman culture which marked the onset of dark ages causing social, political,and economic instability to such an extent that all educational activity almost came to a standstill. The scholasticism of the medieval period (11th to 13th centureis) brought with it tremendous revical of learning where general education was based upon trivium (grammar, rhetoric and dialectic) and quadrivium (arithmetic, geometry, music, astronomy) and higher education was professionally oriented (law, medicine, theology).

During the Renaisance period (14th to 16th centuries) the educators longed for the study of classics as best means of cultivating the intellect. The classics, it was thought, should stand on their own merit, whether or not they were in harmony with the religious faith. They enabled man to rediscover himself as free being rather than as a child of church or the state. Thus there was shift in emphasis in higher schools from 'the study of the supernatural to the humanistic studies'. The humanistic curricula

(Philosophy, languages and literature) comprised the 'tool subjects (Latin, Greek, grammar, rhetoric, composition),,enabled the pupils to study the classics which included Cicero's Letters in Greek; Caeser, Ovid and Aesop's fables also in Greek; master works of Plato, Aristotle, Homer and others. Study of classics exemplified the 'loftiest style and beauty of written word'and led to the 'perfection of human intellect' It took the student seven years to complete the humanistic curricula-tool subjects and classics in five levels. The educators thus established their contact with the works of ancient world and viewed classic as the best way of cultivating intellect through humanistic studies. At the same time humanistic studies were meant for the intellectuallygifted. It was like Plato's ideal curriculum for future leaders (i.e. king Philosophers) and not for manual workers. It was believed that such a curriculum was the necessary foundation for all activities which are truly human. Verbal skills, rather than practical knowledge acquired with the training of the hand'. got higher priority. The humanistic content of education was thus completely verbal and intellectual although moral training some-how got integrated with the classical content.

The humanist tradition lasted upto 18th century when liberal influence took over. The past two centuries belong to the progressive era of science and technology which, it is thought, contributed to the very problems they purport to solve, hence the need for humanising education by cultivating values through 'a new educational order which is based on scientific and technological training, one of the essential components of scientific humanism'. (Edgar Faure et.al, 1973)

SCIENTIFIC HUMANISM

Scientific humanism of the 20th century rejects any preconceived, subjective or abstract idea of man. The kind of person it conceives is a concrete being for whom 'command of scientific thought and language' has become indispensable. In the modern civilization man can only participate in production if he is capable of understanding a certain number of scientific methods, rather than merely applying them. As a result of these perceptions,it is felt, science teaching should be based on a pragmatic search for solutions to problems arising out of environment. According to Edgar Faure (1978), 'The content of man's universe has changed. The individual is preecipitated into a world steeped in science. This applies as much to the indian peasant, caught up in the green revolution, as to the automated factory worker or the technician in a nuclear-physics laboratory".

HUMANIST PSYCHOLOGY

The emphasis of humanist psychologists is on the realisation of human potential through two approaches. One is propounded by B.F.Skinner, the well known psychologist. Skinner found that reward or positive reinforcement and not punishment is the most effective force for shaping human behaviour. According to Leonard (19684), "Every culture, and sub-culture, every school, every home has its own way-acknowledged or unacknowledged of using rewards and punishment."Too often people rely on punishment or its threat. Skinner's scientific and human impluses subsituted regarad for punishment and he increasingly relied on beautiful forms of positive reinformcement which, though mechanical, was a step towards humanising education by using environment. Two other prominent proponents, who advanced humanistic tradition, are Abraham Maslow and Carl Rogers. Maslow studied happy and successful people who were termed by him its 'self-actualising'people. They exist around us. Their capacity can be expanded with increased integration of their personality. Carl Rogers also possessed tremendous faith in human potential when he propounded his well known client-centred therapy where the client or student(not patient) defines and seeks his own goals and the therapist (or teacher) acts as a facilitaor.

INDIAN VIEWPOINT

In the Indian context, life philosphies of Gandhi, Tagore and Aurobindo are 'sibstantially humanistic'. Gandhi's humanism was throughly activitst and operational. Learning, according to him, comes through activity. It reflected his basic philosophy, that is, Kama Yoga. The out door field work approach is also use in creating awareness among the students about environmental issues. As for environment, Gandhi was conservationist of first order and was anti-consum erist. He wrote letters on the backs of used envelopes.Tagore, on the ohter hand, possessed a creative humanism whereby man consciously entered into community with his fellow beings, nature and the greater universe. This reflected Tagore's life philosophy, that is, Ananda-yoga. He established his school Shanti Niketan (abode of peace), amidst nature (trees, plants, flowers,birds, animals, small muddy huts) which have been established all over the world for educating children about environmental issues. Sri Aurobindo,on the other hand, was concerned with the total education of the man which is enunciated in transcendental humanism. Human personality is perfected through humanistic psychology. His life philosophy of purna-yoga (integral person) involved full human development taking palce in natureal setting amidst nature through psychic being.

ENVIRONMENTAL ISSUES

These are some of the important humanistic thoughts in educaton which have emerged over the centuries Recently, UNESCO's well known document on education, 'Learning to be', pointed out that the content of man's universe has changed. Therefore, one aim of education should be to help individual gain knowledge of the environment and the basic part which it plays in sustaining human life. Environmental education has three dimsions.knowlege aspect includes land, water, vegetation and soils which provide the resources that sustain all forms of life. Food, shelter, mobility, energy, goods and a number of other material things which contribute to the support of human life. Quality of life is known by human judgements based on values, beliefs, uses of envionmental resources and related aesthetic considerations. Environmental issues concern the students as future citizens who should be prepared to deal with the complexity of environmental issues which could be done by familiarising them with a number of concepts drawn from natural and social sciences. For example, man's adaptation of time to the changing environment and the resulting issues can be understood if we include the elements of ethnology (a study of culture and society in general)at some stage in education. Studies on man-environment' relations would enable pupils to understand that while some environment features or issues are generated by nature, others by human activity and many more by inter-action between nature and human activity. This makes a strong case for humanising the content and process of education through pressing environmental issues like explosion of population and resulting urbanization, pollution, congestion etc.

Science and technology have been pressed into service for finding solutions to these issues. But it is alleged by some that science and technology are contributing to the very problems they are trying to solve. Thus there is need to have the content of education woven around man, his needs, and the environmental issues vis-a-vis human activity. They are dealt with effectively through several inter-curricular areas representing history, geography, science and other subjects. The several familiar and unfamiliar issues have been identified by many environmentalists (Pachlke, 1986, Kwik, 1981). Through study of these issues the content of education can be humanised.

CREATING AWARENESS ABOUT ADVERSE EFFECTS OF POLLUTION

The adverse effects of pollution upon human body, buildings, forests and crops caused through, air, water and sound pollution may find place in science texts. For example, acid rain story is narrated to the children. They are told how pollution is poisonous to humans, animals and plants. It limits nature's ability to supply resources. Pollution causes climatic changes, disappearance of wild life, descertification, increased severity of smogs and forst fires.

KNOWING ABOUT EXTINCTION OF SPECIES

There is a deep impact of the extinction of various species of flora and fauna on humans. We are part of the natural world and as sepcies we are vulnerable. Human beings are the only species whose activities put at risk almost the whole of life we know of. This is done through nuclear war, toxic wastes andclimatic alteration caused by felling trees.

PROMOTING LONG-TERM SUSTAINABILITY

Industrial society must change the narure of its production process to new systems that are energy and materals efficient and, as such,more lasting,For example, the children are told:'forests must not be ruined, they must be harvested at a sustainable rate. Metals must be recycled and all metals production must be kept in relation to supply'.

AVOIDING WASTEFUL CONSUMPTION, CONSUMERISM

The children are made to understand that what is used by one person is naturally unavilable to others. Excessive and unnecessary use of goods not only appears'gluttony' in the face of global human hunger but leads to the exhaustion of non-renewable resources. Concrete examples are: excessive packaging of goods, non-returnable containers, printing of invitations and greeting cards on costly paper and use of gadgets which are not only avoidable but irritating to the human mind. Human life in affluent societies is becoming unduly materialistic in conception and quantitative in measure.

INCLUCATING LOVE OF SIMPLICITY

As oppsed to the classical humanistic education, contents of environmental education emphasize respect for craftsmanship through learning by doing' in field studies, growing kitchen garders,processing foods, undertaking nature walks in the woods, taking care of the elderly and sick in every day life.

PROMOTING ENVIRONMENTAL AESTHETICS

With population growth and increasing demand of goods, natural materials are being substituted by the synthetics. An important environmental issue is whether the substitutes (e.g.plastic tubes in place of iron pipes) are less costly in terms of the natural materials consumed. Again multi storeyed buildings with windows which never open for all season, climates and settings, whether they are in Nairobio, New York or Delhi. Such issues might find place in the curriculum of humanities and science subjects.

PROMOTING DECENTRALISM

Transportation of goods, agricultural products and transmission of energy not only leads to incresed costs but also depletion of resources. Self-reliance on local supply of solar energy, consumer goods and giving people more autonomy to manage their own affairs will encourage decentralization. Issues of self-management, self-reliance and autonomy represent a great challenge to the industrial society. Perhaps this is going back to the period when people in small village could meet almost all of their needs locally. Such issues should find place in our school texts.

BUILDING FUTURE-ORIENTED LONG-TERM PERSPECTIVES:

It is said that environmentalists are future oriented and think in terms of long-term needs and gains. This includes water, energy, food needs, disposal of wastes and potential long-term genetic effects. Energy planners, it is said, usually work on a 50-year time horizon but this is not the case in all sectors of development. Paehlke (1968) has rightly said, "Governments, alas, rarely see beyond the next elections".

DEVELOPING INTEREST IN NON-MATERIAL THINGS

Children have to be given an understanding that the present has evolved out of the past. For example, restoration of old and beautiful buildings 'like old forts, monuments, art pieces etc.are important. Recapturing of history' by the children through study of local specific situations is to be encouraged. Diaz (1987) has rightly suggested: "In each village children should have a history text book containing the history of their own people and their own locality".

DEVELOPING IDEA OF INTERDEPENDENCE:

Issues like human dependence on nature, adaptability of animals and humans to their environment, ecological sucession and eco-crisis should find place in curriculum. The students should know that living organisms interact with each other and their physical environments provide a sort of public service on which vivilizations depend. The nature is considered a type of genetic library from which the humanity with draws useful items. The rate of extinction of species is exceedingly alarming. Ehrlich (1987) has estimated that by the end of the century, perhaps 15 to 20% of the world's present complement of species will be lost.

AVOIDING CONFLICT BETWEEN DEVELOPMENT AND CONSERVATION

It would be unrealistic to hope that we can fully stop exploitation of renewable and non-renewable resources. People in the Third World need to progress so that 'they have minimum of comfort in order to develop their minds.' Perhaps there is need to guide and advise the eager governments or industrialists about the dangers of over use of the available resources.

PROJECTS HAVING BEARING ON ENVIRONMENTAL ISSUES

In India, several development projects in education have been undertaken during the past decade by the international, central and state level agencies namely, the nutrition, Health Education and Environmental Sanitation (NHEES) Project, Primary Education Curriculum Renewal (PECR) Project, Developmental Activities in Community Education and Participation(DACEP) Project, Comprehensive Access to Primary Education (CAPE) Project, Non-formal Education Project (NEEP) and National Adult Education Programme (NAEP). All these projects have a bearing on local specific environmental issues and problems where an effort has been made to relate education to human needs.

CONCLUSION

The content and process of education has undergone numerous changes over the centuries first starting with reigious bias to education, to classical studies (grammar, retoric, dialectic), to humanistic studies (philosophy, languages, literatures), to activity, nature and psychological oriented approaches of Gandhi, Tagore and Aurobindo and finally to science and technology in the modern era. Applications of science and technology have brought with them several alarming environmental issues like pollution, congestion, ecology and energy crisis which could be dealt with effectively with an alternative curricular approach as is suggested by Parfitt (1987) where 'pupils look at environmental issues within subject discipline but in which there has been an agreement and cooperation between (subject) departments in terms of objectives'.

Courtesy; Progressive Educational Herald

28

THE MAN INSIDE IS THE ENVIRONMENT OUTSIDE

Dr. Gogineri Aruna
Reader in Education,
St.Joseph's College of Education,
Guntur - 522 001

We, the human beings, live on the mother earth which is the only planet known so far to have life in the solar family. Universe is beyond man's perception in which solar family is one. Nature, the embodiment of the spirit of the creator is admired, adored and worshipped by poets, aesthetists, sages and seers since ages. The sournd of the breeze through the leaves, the song of the koel,the sunlight reflecting on the dew drops, the gragrance of flowers, the gentle touch of the breeze, the taste of the fruits what is not feasting?. The whole environment surrounding man is not only aesthetically enjoyable but also functionally useful. Nature has embedded in itself the beautiful, varied and living functions.

Since the appearance of man on the planet he has been trying to evolve newer ways of survival. As a result of fire, steam engine electricity-over a span of thousands of years brought about industrial revolution. The story of human progress is woven around his interaction with nature, more and intense use of raw materials and resources of the environment. His basic philosophy had been one of harmony with nature in sharp contrast to the present concept of conquest of nature. Once this planet was endowed with rich biological heritage. Various scriptures and books are full of vivid and beautiful accounts of wild life. Over thousands of Mammalian and avian species contribute to the richness of its wealth.

Man depended, depending and would depend on plants, animals and other natural resources for food, clothing, housing, medicines and what no! Having all the dependence on them too he is the most developed among a large variety in the existence. This unique creature not only interacts with his environment but is also seen as the vital factor in creating working relationships between various things of the environment.

Every where man learned to exploit ecological system for sustenance. Over population forced him to go for deforestation. Over cultivation, over grazing, human occupations leave little room for forests. As the soil conservation and forest conservation are neglected a large portion of the monsoon disappears into the sea as surface runs off. Though the English scientist and Writer Evelyn recognised the connection between air pollution and disease in 1961 itself we could not pay any heed to industrial smoke, pesticide evaporation, metallic dust and the radio active compunds polluting the atmosphere on global scale. Hence there is growing degradation in the immense power of people. In developing countries like India the major source of pollution(90 percent) in water bodies is domestic in origin, often feacal matter about which we are not educating each other. Besides the industrial wastes, dumping of sewage of big cities often in rivers, synthetic detergents are causing many communicable diseases, deficiencies and even death of water animals and plants.

Thus out of his greed, desperation, short sightedness, ignorance and selfishness he had been polluting the air, water, land and what not. Though he deserves praise for converting wild forests into parks, gardens, orchards and cities in his attempts to make life more and more comfortable. His thoughtless destruction of forests accelerated soil erosion, creeping deserts, increase of flooding and decline in soil fertility, air and water pollution increased death, hazardous respiratory, cancerous and heart diseases, albedominal and joint disorders, epilepsy, sterility, kidney damage and son on.

It is not feasible nor even desirable to halt the march of technology at this stage. A large quantity of produce both from crops and industries is necessary to our bourgeouing populations. At this juncture we can have an over all view of the development among different countries of the world screen. How is the life style of the people of progressed countries? How are the developing countries in their living patterns? some of the following observations can give us insights into the so-called progressive ways.

America, 5% of the world's population, is producing approximately 15% of Co_2. Whereas the 15% of world's population in India is producing approximately 1 percent of Co_2. If Co_2 rises at this rate mean global temperature could be raising by 4 ^{0} C by the next five decades. Likewise 15 (Fifteen) percent of American population is being treated by psychiathists for one form of anxiety or another. With these approximate data an intelligent and responsible man has to question as to what should be the measures of progress and development? Is it to acquire as much as possible or as little as one can to live happily? Whether to give priority to live happily? or to live lavishly? who is poor? Whether man living in a hut breething fresh air over the fields and living peacefully with the family or the man of crores assessing him against others and feeling inadequate? Is only the physical poverty a problem or mental poverty a serious factor?

More over in the background of growing violence, terrorism and rebellious fights in the society we can question who is civilized? Who protects with gun or who needs no protection? Who is cultured? The hypocrite who is after materialistic ends or the one caring human values?

Human relationships are turning unhygienic due to greed for materialistic possessions, ego maximisation, hypocricy and due to habitual responses of thinking and suggesting but not practising. As a result we find increase in violence, religious, linguistic, caste, political and communal conflicts along with the polluted air, water, atmosphere and polluted human minds. Pollution means excess of constituents which are harmful to the existing species.It is high time to think of the environmental health influencing man's well-being also. Man no doubt, is the source of environmental crisis. Solution also inevitably lies in the hands of man. hence time bound planning for environmental management is the urgent need. Environmental education plays a major role in this management.

Environmental education is education through environment about environment and for environment. Some sort of environmental education is carried out by poets, naturalists, ornithologists, town and country planners. Now the emphasis is shifted from individuals to specific groups, to national bodies like National Institute of Educational planning and Administration, New Delhi and to international bodies like UNESCO,

International Union for Conservation of Nature. If the minds are getting polluted who can take care of the minds. Each individual himself through right education only can care.

Environmental engineering is the immediate necessity. It refers to the study of man-environment relationships and modifications of environment for man's benefit to the extent that there is concern for man's environment as it relates to his health and well being. It includes freedom from illness, health maintenance, human efficacy, comfort and enjoyment of life, use of property and management of resources. It, as well, can include the study of human mind, its operations, consequences and related effects of his mind over the environment outside.

International work on environmental educatiion held at Belgrade in 1975 states that Environmental Education that is aware of and concerned about the environment and its associated problems. The present day human being thus needs a mind that is concerned not only with one's own problems but also that which is interested in the greater humanity.

Tiwari Committee Report (India) of 1980 mentions "India has now accepted the need to cultivate sound well organised interest in environment and incorporate environmental education at all levels as the country's progress depends upon the proper utilisation of environment. Environmental scientist Dr. T.N. Khashoo (1986) prepares the chief objective of Environmental Education as that individuals and social groups should acquire awareness and knowledge, develop attitudes, skills and abilities and participate in solving real life problems and preventing the new ones collectively. Environment could be met in three approaches:

1. Preservation of natural health of the environment.

2. Prevention of undesirable conditions like air pollution, water pollution, noise pollution, soil pollution, mind pollution.

3. Treatment of the polluted environment.

1. PRESERVATION

The great academician J.B.Florin advocated instruction in all subjects has to be under three classes. 1. Relation of man to nature. 2. Relation of man to himself and 3. Relation of man to other man.

Environment is a source of happiness to man and his happiness will be hightened if he learns to love and appreciate nature to see order in the various phenomena of nature and systematic functioning of various things contributing to the harmony in nature. The modern man needs a fresh and new mind to love and appreciate what is happening around him we don't need a new technique or a new philosophy or a new drug to see things of nature. One has to realise the values of nature and has to have clarity of understanding of his relationship to the biophysical surroundings. He has to develop right attitudes and skills to deal with environment rightly. Besides there is a grave necessity for self-formulation of a code of behaviour about issues concerning environmental quality. Hence its subject matter includes the components and constituents of environment, establishment of proper ecological equilibrium, conservation of resources and control of pollution through proper environmental planning, and also the sutdy of human mind disturbing the outside environment. This paper mainly focusses on certain, aspects of study of human mind.

UNDERSTANDING HUMAN MIND

Man can't solve any problem totally without understanding his vast complex mind. No doubt human brain is more evolved and his mental functioning is richer than other animals. Most of the human minds seem to be dull and insensitive due to problems of earning a livelihood, marriage, children and so on. Since decades the problem of population explosion and consequences have been informed. But he turned his deaf ears. As a result we see now in India 95 crores of population and will be reaching 102 crores by 2000 A.D. if it grows at the same rate. Earth does not grow neither the territory of India for the air surrounding earth, water resources too don't increase.

Why is modern man so much absorbed in his personal life and interests? Why is he so aggressive, quarrelsome and violent?

Is it because of his identification with and indulgence in his family or community or religion or race or nation?

Why is he so much identifying?

He wants to belong to a family or community or religion or nation with identification.

Why does he want to belong to?

He wants security in his family or religious group or racial group.

Does he have security by dividing and keeping him apart from other families and other religious groups?

By increasing conflicts and quarrels with other groups he is increasing his insecure feeling.

Why is this insecurity?

He has fears both conscious and unconscious.. He lived with fears from time immemorial. He has fear of death, fear of nature; fear of public opinion, fear of losing job, name & fame, fear of loneliness, fear of not fulfilling. Besides he also has much deeper unconscious layers of fears.

Out of the exhausting waves of fear he is turning hypocratic. He says one thing and does another, belives something and exercises quite the opposite of it. To support them he becomes an expert in arguing, justifying, condemning, complaining and is excellently finding fault with anybody and everybody. He turns aggresive with the slightest provocation and becomes a menace to society.

HUMAN RELATIONS

Modern man tends to pursue pleasure constantly the pleasure of possession, of domination, the pleasure of money which gives power. He is ambitious, proud of his belongings, his fame and achievements. He is turning angry at any kind of threat, envious and full of hatred at others success and anxious about his hopes. He acts egoistically narrowing the whole of this vast life into little 'me' and causing every sort of disorder. That is why he is less and less successful in maintaining relations with others and is becoming more mechanical in his living. In political social,familial, industrial and occupational spheres human relationships are very much disturbed. Jiddu Krishnamurti,the world renouned philosopher says that 'Life is a movement in relationship'. man can't live by himself. Humanity exists in relationship'. But man is failing in his relations. Why? If we looks into the nature of his relationships probably we can understand it, when we observe family relationships who has an image about husband, children and about herself. If thers do not behave as expected of them there is conflict. If others expect of her some particular pattern of behaviour and if she is unable to satisfy there is conflict. Husband has an image about himself, his wife and so on. Likewise each one has an image about the other, a picture about the other. These two images are in conflict with each other. Like that man has an image about everybody and everything build through his direct or indirect daily contact with people and things or out of information gathered from different sources. Images mean the symbol, the concept, the conclusion, the idea. However they develop these images which are in conflict. Man's relationships, thus, are existing between images but not between him and the other directly.

Man finds security in images whether false or sane. He has become an image worshipper neglecting direct relationship with people. But life is not an image. This habit of image making becomes stronger, longer, all demanding and insistant as man grows older. The more he acts and has his existence in that image the less he sees the beauty of life and feels joy at something beyond the little promptings of that image. As he lives in images he inevitably lives in illusions but not in reality.

Each one clings to his opinion or idea or conclusion. However intimate the relationship between such people may be there is always conflict. One dominates the other, one is jealous of the other. This is how the relationship between images of the people turns out to be. Human brain, the thought creates the image. As a result life of man has become so extraodinarily meaningless. Unless we understand these facts and let our images drop and relate directly to the beings and live in concern to them we fail in our relationships, in life, in preserving the healthy mental environment. If he goes insane his mental ill-health reflects on the environment outside him.

Man has many contradictory desires, so has conflicts. He is between the two approachable things or two avoidable things or between approachable and avoidable qualities of the samething. In the present day productive industries, the propaganda of the manufactured lots is adding to choose the best of them. Man is to choose among the flooding materials into market. Advertisement techniques are always forcing him to be in dilemma. Thus he is in a way habituated to entertain conflict and transfering the same spirit to his non-material life also. Thus the modern man is unable to live his life as it comes to him but tends to choose from various alternatives. In simple he is between what he is and what he wants to become. The conflict between these two states is not an image. It is a fact which is motivating him to become more greedy and restless. Due to this man is turning very aggressive, brutal, violent and causing chaos in society. This is the story of each one of us and hence the story of mankind. Wherever he is, he is part of that environment and society. When we turn to society it is full of injustice, corruption and immorality. Even nations talk of peace and prepare for war. No doubt man also is not personally at ease.

Modern man is lonely amidst the many. He is unable to share affection with a family due to his busy schedules or heavy work load. Dissatisfaction, helplessness and depression are becoming the common expressions. Desperation is enormously increasing in industrial countries. Suicides are common in North America. There is also increase of murders and chaotic states. Mankind itself is going through a great deal of anxiety due to constant striving for more and more. Hence he has indulgence in endless thoughts. Man does not seem to have unselfish ultimate goals in life which can make him responsible for the greater good of the society. Rather he is losing balance to deal with people and situations. Day by day there is an increase in the number of people walking into mental assylums.

Though his strong wish to become more than 'What he is' and others have is keeping him on the progressive track in the materialistic plane his health and well-being seem to be at its state. The whole inner mental environment is disturbed and reflects the same outside him. Besides the loss of the sensitive side of his life the polluted environment is disturbing nature the trees, the rivers, the squirrel, the tiger, the forest, the mountains and the whole environment.

What is the way out of the polluted inner and outer environment of man?

That is why environmental education has to be holistic in character, inter-disciplinary and integrated. It is to be imparted to the lay public in rural and urban areas, to slum dwellers, tribals, students, teachers of schools,colleges and universities, planners, decision makers, policy makers, administrators, managers. Every one is to be made responsible to understand how much his mind is polluted, which in turn is polluting the outer environment indescriminately. Each has to observe his own images, conflicts, greed, selfishness and be free of them. He can thus be factual and scientific first in his personal life. Then only he can spontaneously respond to the things happening around him in scientific and physical spheres of life on reailty level.

His routine mechanical life going to the office, repeating the same pattern,coming back home, sex, quarrels, ambition, vanity, superstition and so on cannot keep up, preserve his sensitivity to the nature and to resources. His introspection, his understanding of responsibility to the present day calamities and urgency to come out of them, his observation of his pollutants of his mind the contradictory desires, the conflicts exhausting his energy, the ideals, ambitions making him greedy, the images about others and about him turning him competitive, aggressive, uncertain and selfish, his blindness to the real facts, his false pursuits of security, his fragmenting approaches, his longing for pleasure and so on are to be part and parcel of formal and informal education.

Moreover ecologists plea to man to return to nature appears to be right. It is no more to remain a romantic ideation but an urgent necessity of the day. Nobody can denounce the civilisation but one must be cautious and observe its ill-effects so that evolution proceeds in a sane way. Nature has its own-intelligent plans, let us allow man to observe it and to return to it. His original nature is silence in which flowers equanimity, harmony and love in him.

But there is another great danger to nature observation that is indulgence of this generation in entertainment. Television, Cinema, Video Cassettes are making people to turn away from reality and distorting the opinions of people. The young and old are comparing themselves with cine stars or T.V. stars, the dream characters. George Williams and Rudolf Drussy in a book,'why we get sick-a new science of Darwinian Medicine' said about T.V. when compared-children, parents, wives, husbands-nobody is on par with those characters. Hence they are dissatisfied about them and their standards of life. Is there not a necessity to come out of that artificiality? Are not we to reeducate the people to be cautious of these effects and accept the reality? Besides these media are making people passive, dull and insensitive to things around. In place of such an entertainment can we encourage reading (general books) as an assignment for the short or long term vacation. Both parents and teachers can suggest even to children some good books to be read which can broaden their mental horizon, touch their hearts as realities. They can be guided to prepare, submit a gist of the book and discuss in the class during the reopening week.

Man has to learn ultimately to spend most of his time not in worry, anxiety, and understanding, fights, arguments and agony but to see the facts oflife including his mental facts, to be frank in relationship to himself and others and feel him as a part of nature. Likewise study of society, its organisation, working of its various institutions, interrelationships among men and their motives create a better understanding between different social groups, reveals the strength of oneness, arouses sympathy and leaves no place for prejudices.

The knowledge of oneself and others develops understanding of the magnitude and real cause of evils of society. Then the individual problems, social problems, national and global problems can be understood rightly without distorting them. Right perception results in right action which is always caring not merely the individual good but the common good.

REFERENCES

1. Bernard H.W. (1952) *Mental Hygiene for Class Room Teachers,* McGraw Hill Book Company, Inc., new York.
2. Dubey R.K. (1992). *Human Ecology and Environmental Education* (Vol. 1 and 2), Chugh publications, Allahabad.
3. Edgar Fanre, et al (1973). *Larning to be - The world of Education Today and Tomorrow,* sterling, Delhi,
4. Krishnamurti J.*Education and Significance of Life,* B.I.Pub., New Delhi, 1973.
5. Krishnamurti J. *Freedom from the Known,* New Delhi, B.I. Pub., 1969.
6. Prabhakarji. *On Business Management* Atak Bangalore.
7. Trivedi P.R. Gurdeep Raj (1992). *Encyclopaedia of Environmental Sciences* Vol. 1 to Vol.26), Akashdeep Publishing House, New Delhi.
8. Unanswered questions. *Misimi Writings Workshop* Misimi (- Telugu Monthly), Nov., 1995.

29

UN AND ENVIRONMENT PROTECTING THE GLOBAL ENVIRONMENT

Environmental degradation knows no national boundaraies. Sulphur emissions in one country cause acid rain in another downwind. Depletion of the ozone layer from CFCs use in one nation can lead to skin cancer on the opposite side of the world.

In an increasingly interdependent world, the United Nations has a crucial role to play in protecting the global environment and promoting sustainable dvelopment. The facts below show some of the UN's main achievements in this area over the past twenty-five years work that needs to be continued and expanded, for the sake of our planet and our future.

Earth Summit: At the Earth Summit the UN Conference on Environment and Development, held in Rio de Janeriro in 1992 Government leaders adopted Agenda 21, a global plan for sustainable development. It has since become the basis for many national plans, and thousands of cities and towns worldwide have created their own "local Agenda 21." The UN Commission on Sustainable Development meets annually to review progress and propose policy guidelines. A special session of the General Assembly in June 1997 (Earth Summit +5) will assess, at the five-year mark,how the Rio agreements are being carried out.

Climate Change: Under the UN Framwork Convention on Climate Change, opened for signing at the 1992 Earth Summit and now ratified by 164 nations, industriaized countries are commited to reducing their emissions of greenhouse gases to 1990 levels by the year 2000. Although few countries are on target to meet that goal, negotiations are under way to strengthen the agreement.

The Intergovernmental Panel on Climate Change (IPCC), coordinated by the UN Environment Programme (UNEP) and the World Meteorological Organization (a UN agency), issued its second assessment report in December 1995, finding "discernible human influence on the global climate". Based on the work of 2,000 leading scientists from 130 countries, the IPCC, set up in 1988, reviews scientific research on climate change.

Ozone Depletion: Industrialized countries have banned production of CFCs as of the beginning of 1996 under the amended 1987 Montreal Protocol, administered by UNEP. Developing countries have a 10 year grace period to comply. Schedules are in place to phase out other ozone-depleting substances.

Acid Rain: Acid Rain in Europe and North America has been significantly reduced under the landmark 1979 Convertion on Long-Range Transboundary Air Pollution, administered by the UN Economic Commission for Europe.

HAZARDOUS WASTES AND CHEMICALS

To regulate the 3 million tons of toxic waste that crosses national borders each year, in 1989 countries negotiated the Basel Convention on hazardous wastes, administered by UNEP and now ratified by 108 countries. In 1995 the treaty was strengthened to outlaw the export of toxic waste to developing countries, which often do not have the technology for safe disposal.

BIOLOGICAL DIVERSITY

The UN Convention on Biological Diversity, signed at the 1992 Earth Summit and since ratified by 161 nations, obligates countries to protect their plant and animal species through habitat preservation and other means. A protocol on safe use of biotechnology is under negotiation.

In 1995, UNEP launched the Global Biodiversity Assessment, the most comprehensive ever attempted. Based on the work of 1,500 scientists worldwide, the report found that the rate of species extinction and habitat loss, largely due to human activities, was unprecedented.

Protection of endangered species is also enfored under CITES- the 1973 Convention on International Trade in Endagered Speices -administered by UNEP. Countries meet periodically to update the list of which plant and animal species or products, such as ivory, should be protected by quotas or outright bans.

FISH AND MARINE RESOURCES

Global monitoring of fish stocks is carried out by the UN Food and Agriculture Organization (FAO),which estimates that 70 percent of commercial fishing grounds are depleted or recovering from overfishing.

A UN legal agreement to regulate fishing on the high seas, negotiated as an outgrowth of the Earth Summit, was adopted in December 1995. Nearly 60 countries have signed the agreement, which aims to prevent overfishing and ease international tensions over competition for dwindling fish stocks.

Marine Pollution: Oil Pollution from ships has been cut by 60 percent since 1981, after the adoption of a legal Convention negotiated by the Internation Maritime Organization, a UN agency. The treaty, which now applies to more than 85 percent of the world's merchant fleet, also sets strict controls for disposal of garbage by ships.

Governments have called for a legal agreement to regulate persistent organic pollutants, such as DDT, PCBs and dioxin, as part of a wide-ranging action plan adopted at a 1995 UNEP sponsored conference in Washington, DC on land-based sources of marine pollution.

Desertification: The UN Convention to Combat Desertification, called for at the Earth Summit, became legally binding in December 1996. Desertification, or the degradation of arid and semi-arid lands, is a problem that affects the livelihood and food supply of over 900 million people world wide, especially in Africa.

Forest: To combat deforestation globally, FAO monitors forest loss and trade in timber, and assists developing countries in managing forests. Some 15.4 million hectares of forest worldwide-an area the size of Peru and Ecuador combined - were lost during the 1980s, a rate that continues today.

The intergovernmental Panel of Forests, which met for two years under the UN Commission on sustainable Development, adopted over one hundred proposals for immediate action to implement Agenda 21 and the Forest Principles agreed at the Earth Summit.

Financing for the Environment: The Global Environment Facility (GEF) -jointly run by the World Bank, the UN Development Programme and UNEP -has become the main source of multilateral lending to developing countries for environmental projets. In 1994, the GEF was replenished by donor countries with over $2 billion

30

UNDP AND THE ENVIRONMENT

UNDP in India has been actively involved in the preparation of the Environment Action programme (EAP) and the national Forestry Action Plan (NFAP). These excercises, which contributed in a significant way to policy making, have taught important lessons. The EAP process established that india has institutions with the expertise and capabilities to contribute to policy formulation. The preparation of the statelevel plans as a pre-requisite to the NFAP, although complex and time consuming, has enriched both the process and the content of the national plan.

UNDP involvement in this sector has been largely in capacity building, and in strengthening of institutions. The Wildlife Institute of India and the indian Council of Forest Research and Edcation have been our partners in this process, and we expect to build on this substantially in our forthcoming programme, 1997-2001.

Given the environmental crisis in India today, the Environment programme within the GOI/UNDP Country Cooperaton Framework, 1997-2001, is considerably more ambitious, and seeks to address the problems of natural resource management and use through field level interventions and will facilitate informed decision making at all levels (information, research, networking, valuation, and risk assessments, etc). It also anticipates a more proactive and cooperative role for government as outlined in the Plan and other government statements. In accordance with the UNDP mandate of sustainable human development the thrust of the Environment programme is to change the orientation and level of decision making in such a way that larger numbers of people participate in processes controlling their lives.

UNDP's environment mission in India, as in other countries, is heightened by its role as joint implementing agency in the Global Environment Facility (GEF). and in managing the GEF Small Grants Programme (SGP). There are one completed and two operational projects, under the GEF, and an active pipeline of over ten projects 27 grants to Non-Governmental Organisations have been made under the GEF SGP, and the country Office prooses to widen the scale of this programme considerably in the forthcoming programme cycle. There are 4 completed and 14 operational projects supporting the Government's efforts to phase out the use of ozone depleting substances under the Montreal protocol, supported by UNDP and further implemented by UNDP and further 20 projects are currently under development.

Capacity 21 of UNDP places considerable emphasis on the need for sustainable development to be a central component of national development activities. This requires new approaches to development, the testing of new approaches,and willingness to adapt development processes in the light of experience. India's ongoing capacity 21 exercise in natural resource accunting, rooted in the Indira Gandhi Institute of Development Research, Mumbai, is a good example of the imaginative way in which capacity strengthening projects can be approached.

31

WHO HEALTH AND ENVIRONMENT ACTION

In 1993 the WHO Global Strategy for Health and Environment was endorsed by the World Health Assembly. The same year the Regional Strategic Plan for Health and Environment was also endosed. Action to promote the preparation of Country plans of actions to promote the prepration of Country plans of action for Health and Environment began in 1994 with Sri Lanka being identified as the first country chosen in this region (among 8 countries globally) to be included in the joint WHO/ UNDP Collaborative Initiative on Sustainable Development.

A regional workplan for promoting the Regional Health and Environment initiative was prepared by South-East Asia Regional Office (SEARO) in 1995; funds were sought from the Director-General's Development Funds to initiate action.

Health and Environment Initiative are currently taking place in seven countries of the Region. The proeces of consultation, preparations of national situational analysis of environmental concerns, setting up of coordinating committee for Health and Environment, and the conduct of intersectoral meetings to formulate H-E plans of action are taking place in all countries of the Region. These are at different stages of development.

1. In Nepal, the Nepal Environmental Health Initiative (NEHI) was undertaken parallel to the development and finalization of Nepal Environmental Policy and Action Plan (NEPAP) by National Planning Commission (NPC). As a result, most of the key programme areas and objectives of NEHI are reflected in NEPAP.NEHI was recently endorsed by the government as the national action plan for developing environmental health in Nepal.

2. In Sri Lanka, the report on the health and environment situation has been prepared by a national consultant and been reviewed by an intersectoral meeting held in Colombo in August 1996. The meeting identified a priority listing of input needed for preparing a national plan of action. The national consultant is now processing the information into a draft National Plan of Action for Health and Environment.

3. In Maldives, an intersectoral "brainstorming" meeting of senior officials from the various sectors and the planning ministry was held and preparation of the situational report as a collaborative effort among the Ministers of Health, Agriculture, and National Planning is also completed. The Inter-sectoral meeting to formulate a national PoA will be held soon.

4. In Thailand, the completed national situational analysis report was presented for review to an intersectoral meeting held in Pattaya in August 1996. The meeting identified concerns of overlps and redundancies among sctors in the implementation of these mandates. The multisectoral setting of the meeting helped generate concensus solutions towards collaborative efforts in the area of environmental planning, resurce sharing and capacity building.

5. Bangladesh has established a national working group for coordinating the formulation of the national plan of action for health and environment. The national situational analysis has been prepared by the national consultant and was submitted for review to an intersectoral workshop on health and environment, held in Dhaka in September 1996. A follow-up workshop was held in April 1997 to discuss the draft plan and agree on a plan of action, being prepared by a national consultant.

6. Indonesia is working on integrated health and environment concerns in developing the post-UNCED national capacity-building plan with UNDP assistance. Working groups were established to formulate programme recommendations for critical areas of Agenda 21, and the results were collated into a national programme SEARO financed 3 resource persons to assist in the work of 3 key groups.

7. In India activities have taken a different approach that has resulted

in facilitating formulation of a comprehensive national Programme of Sanitation and Environmental Hygience on the lines of Technology Mission involving different ministries, institutions and NGOs. Subsequently support was provided to the Ministry of Health and Family Welfare in preparing the following proposals:

(1) Strengthening of Environmental Health and Health Risk Assessment (HRA) in the country by establishing a Division of Environmental Health.
(2) Establishment of National Hospital Waste Management Programme
(3) Initiate Drinking Water Quality surveillance as a part of Disease Surveillance Programme.

8. In Bhutan and Myanmar, action to initiate preparation of situational analysis is in process.

HEALTHY CITIES IN THE REGION

The WHO South-East Asia Regional Strategic Plan for Health and Environment prepared in 1993 established urban environmental health management as one of four broad priority areas providing the lead for initiating health work in this important setting. The case on unbridled urbanization in the region is well documented and requires critical and immediate action. The Healthy Cities Programme provides the operational framework for the implementation of intersectoral health development actions in our cities and towns which can also be applied to other settings such as villages, islands, atolls and schools, market places, etc.

Efforts are being made at community participation to promote health in such gicven settings in this region. However, there is limited action in systematically applying the Healthy Cities approach in its technical and managerial aspects. Operating Healthy Cities programme are in place in Bangladesh (Chittagond, coza Bazar), in Thailand (Bangkok), Nepal (Kathmandu valley municipalities), and Sri lanka (Badulla). Sri Lanka has also initiated a healthy village programme with village of Welluvapitya being identified as an initiator. However, activities are under way in India (New Delhi Trans Yamuna settlement), Myanmar (Mandalay) and Indonesia. The promotion of Healthy Cities concept and practice on World Healthy Day 1996 has generated great interest in the programme concept and there has beeen substantial increase in the number of cities and towns inquiring after the methodology of HC process.

32

UNESCO AND ENVIRONMENT

UNESCO's involvement with environmental concerns and programmes in India dates back to 1950s. In 1959, UNESCO and UNDP, collaborated with the Indian Government in helping set up the Central Arid Zone Reserarch Institute (CAZRI) in Jodhpur. Since that time, CAZRI has developed into one of the world's leading scientific centres in respect to arid zone ecology and development,while contact with UNESCO include a continuing series of technical seminars and training activities.

UNESCO's programme activities in environment, in India, have largely been directed towards promoting interdisciplinary reserch relevant for policy-making, and to improve the scientific capacity of specialists through training programmes, and information transfer drawing on both natural and social sciences. The major thrust of both training and reserarch programmes has been bio-diversity conservation with emphasis on rehabilitation and traditional knowledge systems, practices and uses. UNESCO's encourages researchers to work with decision-makers, local populations, NGO's and the private sector in designing and implementing research projects, largely focusing upon portected areas. UNESCO's partners for training and research include key universities and scientific and research institutes such as Kerala Forest Research Institute, Peechi; G.B. Pant Institute of Himalayan Environment and Development, Almora; French Institute, Pondicherry; Wildlife Institute of India, Dehra Dun; indian Institute of Science, Bangalore; Indian Institute of Public Administration, New Delhi; and School of Environmental Sciences, Jawaharlal Nehru University New Delhi. This close co-opeation with key institutes has been instrumental in developing and building networks of researchers from different disciplines and sectors of society to address common environment and development problems.

UNESCO is presently implementing a major research project on biodiversity conservation and ecosystem rehabilitation emphasizing traditional knowledge systems. This three year project commenced in January 1996, to make a comparative analysis of the role of traditional knowledge on biodiversity conservation, and to develop management strategies for the rehablitation of degraded landscapes. The study sites under investigation are Chinnar Wildlife Sanctuary in kerala, investigated by the Kerala Forest Research Institute, Peechi, which includes 11 tribal settlements, inhabited by the Muthuvas and Hill Pulayas. These tribals depend on the biodiversity of the WLS, both natural and man-made. The second study site, under investigation by the G.B. Pant Institute of Himalayan Environment and Development, consists of 17 villages in the buffer zone of Nanda Devi Biosphere Reserve in the Central Himalayas and inhabited by two ethnic races- the Indo-Mongolian Botiya tribe and the Indo-Aryan Garhwalis and Kumaonis. While biodiversity and its management in these two sites, is considered in the context of people based conservation strategies, contrastingly, the Coorg-based study in the Western Ghats region, with the collaboration of the French Institute in Pondicherry, considers strongly human impacted eco-systems altered through coffee plantation-based economic activity, the objective being to understand landscape level processes influencing biodiversity.

Another important and evolving programme of UNESCO is to study the interrelationship between sacred sites, cultural integrity and biological conservation. Aim of this reserach study is to examine, analyze and document the sacred groves of Western Ghats, Rajasthan and Himalayas. This study will address the problems and prospects of conservation of sacred groves from the present-day socio-economic perspective of the locality. Until recently most of the sacred groves, which are hot spot areas of biodiversity, were well preserved because of taboos and religious faith associated with them. In recent years, however, weakening of social toboos and human interference are leading to the destruction of many of these groves. The preservation of these forests is important for conserving the germplasm that is otherwise under threat from human presure and could be used in a revegetation programme of damaged sites. The maintenance of these forests in a vastly desertified environment reminds the local people about the traditional value of nature conservation. Technical co-ordination is being provided by the School of Environmental Sciences, Jawaharlal Nehru University in New Delhi, to the World-Wildlife Fund (India), New Delhi; G.B. Pant Institute for Himalayan Environment and Development, Almora; Madurai Kamaraj University, Madurai; and Kerala Forest Research Institute, Peechi; for preparation of case studies.

A national meeting of experts will be held in new Delhi in June 1997 to examine the present status of some of the scared groves in India, Which will be followed by a regional meeting of experts in Peechi, Kerala, from 8-11 December 1997, in order to develop strategies for consrvation and management of sacred sites within the region and to develop a framework for a larger project in India.

Other planned activities of UNESCO include a regional training course on critical wetlands Habitat, to be held at the Keoladeo World Heritage Site, Rajasthan, from 24 November to 1 December 1997, and a planinng meeting for development of curricula, modules and other training materials in protected area management, to be held early next year. These two activities will be organized jointly with the Wildlife Institute of India, Dehra Dun.

UNESCO's environmental programmes are implemented both through the Man and the Biosphere Programme (MAB) and also through the World Heritage Centre. The major thrust of both the programmes is to promote the world's biological diversity. One of the major achievements of the MAB programme, launched in 1971, has been the establishment of an international network of biosphere reserves, which are protected areas representative of the world's major ecosystem types. The biosphere reserve concept is the most significant feature of UNESCO's contribution to the promotion of participatory approaches to the conservation and sustainable use of biodiversity conservation. Collectively these sites, currently numbering 324 in 82 countries, from an international network for information sharing. The significant feature of UNESCO's World Heritage Convention, adopted by UNESCO's General Conference in 1972, is to provide a legal framework for the protection of both cultural and natural heritage. The nominations which are submitted by the Governments must be of outstanding universal value, for inclusion in the World Heritage List. The following five natural heritage sites in India have been included in the World Heritage List: Nanda Devi National Park in Uttar Pradesh, Sunderbans national Park in Bengal, Manas Wildlife Sanctuary and Kaziranga National park in Assam, and Keoladeo Ghana National Park at Bharatpur in Rajasthan. During a recent meeting of World Heritage Site Managers in South Asia, held in new Delhi, from 16-1[illegible] anuary 1997, UNESCO agreed to provide US $ 2255,000 for the restoration of the Manas Tiger Reserve, emergency assistance. Which continues to be an endangered site. This assistance will be provided for a period of three years, commencing June 1997.

UNESCP's effors towards linking up ecological porcesses with social processes have continued towards arriving at policy level decisions for protected area management.

33

RIO DECLARATION ON ENVIRONMENT AND DEVELOPMENT

Having met at Rio de Janeiro from 3 to 14 June 1992,

Reaffirming the Declaration of the United Nations Conference on the Human Environment, adopted at Stockholm on 16 June 1972, and seeking to build upon it,

With the goal of establishing a new and equitable global partnership through the creation of new levels of cooperation among States, key sectors of societies and people,

Working towards international agreements which respect the interests of all and protect the integrity of the global environmental and development system,

Recognizing integral and interdependent nature of the Earth, our home,

Proclaims that:

PRINCIPLE 1

Human beings are at the centre of concerns for sustainable development. They are entitled to a healthy and productive life in harmony with nature.

PRINCIPLE 2

States have, in accordance with the Charter of the United Nations and the principles of international law, the sovereign right to exploit their own resources pursuant to their own environmental and developmental polices, and the responsibility to ensure that activities within their jurisdiction or control do not cause damage to the environment of other States or of areas beyond the limits of national jurisdiction.

PRINCIPLE 3

The right to development must be fulfilled so as to equitably meet developmental and environmental needs of present and future generations.

PRINCIPLE 4

In order to achieve sustainable development, environmental protection shall constitute an integral part of the development process and cannot be considered in isolation from it.

PRINCIPLE 5

All States and all people shall cooperate in the essential task of eradicating poverty as an indispensable requirement for sustainable development, in order to decrease the disparities in standards of living and better meet the needs of the majority of the people of the world.

PRINCIPLE 6

The special situation and needs of developing countries, particularly the least developed and those most environmentally vulnerable, shall be given special priority. International actions in the field of environment and development should also address the interests and needs of all countries.

PRINCIPLE 7

States shall cooperate in spirit of global partnership to conserve, protect and restore the health and integrity of the Earth's ecosystem. In view of the different contributions to global environmental degradation, States have common but differentiated responibility that they bear in the international pursuit of sustainable development in view of the pressures their societies place on the global environment and of the technologies and financial resources they command.

PRINCIPLE 8

To achieve sustainable development and a higher quality of life for all people, States should reduce and eliminate unsustainable patterns of production and consumption and promote appropriate demographic policies.

PRINCIPLES 9

States should cooperate to strengthen endogenous capacity-building for sustainable development by improving scientific understanding through exchanges of scientific and technological knowledge, and by enhancing the development, adaptation, diffusion and transfer of technologies, including new and innovative technologies.

PRINCIPLE 10

Environmental issues are best handled with the participation of all concerned citizens, at the relevant level. At the national level, each individual shall have appropriate access to information concerning the environment that is held by public authorities, including information on hazardous materials and activities in their communities, and the opportunity to participate in decision-making information widely available. Effective access to judicial and administrative proceedings, including redress and remedy, shall be provided.

PRINCIPLE 11

States shall enact effective environmental legislation. Environmental standards, management objectives and priorities should reflect the environmental and developmental context to which they apply. Standards applied by some countries may be inappropriate and of unwarranted economic and social cost to other countries, in particular developing countries.

PRINCIPLE 12

States should cooperate to promote a supportive and open international economic system that would lead to economic growth and sustainable development in all countries, to better address the problems of environmental degradation. Trade policy measures for environmental purposes should not constitute a means of arbitrary or unjustifiable discrimination or a disguised restriction on international trade. Unilateral actions to deal with environmental challenges outside the jurisdiction of the importing country should be avoided. Environmental measures addressing transboundary or global environmental problems should,as far as possible, be based on an international consensus.

PRINCIPLE 13

States shall develop national law regarding liability and compensation for the victims of pollution and other environmental damage. States shall also cooperate in an expeditious and more determined manner to develop further international law regarding liability and compensation for adverse effects of environmental damage caused by activities within their jurisdiction.

PRINCIPLE 14

States should effectively cooperate to discourage or prevent the relocation and transfer to other States of any activities and substances that cause severe environmental degradation or are found to be harmful to human health.

PRINCIPLE 15

In order to protect the environment, the precautionary approach shall be widely applied by States according to their capabilities. Where there are threats of serious or irreversible damage, lack of full scientific certainty shall not be used as a reason for postponing cost-effective measures to prevent environmental degradation.

PRINCIPLE 16

National authorities should endeavour to promote the internalization of environmental costs and the use of economic instruments, taking into account the approach that the polluter should, in principle, bear the cost of pollution, with due regard to the public interest and without distorting international trade and investment.

PRINCIPLE 17

Environmental impact assessment, as a national instrument shall be undertaken for proposed activities that are likely to have a significant adverse impact on the environment and are subject to a decision of a competent national authority.

PRINCIPLE 18

States shall immediately notify other states of any natural disasters or other emergencies that are likely to produce sudden harmful effects on the environment of those States. Every effort shall be made by the international community to help States so afflicted.

PRINCIPLE 19

States shall provide prior and timely notification and relevant information to potentially affected states on activities that may have a significant adverse transboundary environmental effect and shall consult with those states at an early stage and in good faith.

PRINCIPLE 20

Women have a vital role in environmental management and development. Their full participation is therfore essential to achieve sustainable development.

PRINCIPLE 21

The creativity, ideals and courage of the youth of the world should be mobilized to forge a global partnership in order to achieve sustainable development and ensure a better future for all.

PRINCIPLE 22

Indigenous people and their communities and other local communities have a vital role in environmental management and development because of their knowledge and traditional practices. States should recognize and duly support their identity, culture and interests and enable their effective participation in the achievement of sustainable development.

PRINCIPLE 23

The environment and natural resources of people under oppression, domination and occupation shall be protected.

PRINCIPLE 24

Warfare is inherently destructive of sustainable development. States shall therefore respect international law providing protection for the environment in times of armed conflict and cooperate in its further development, as necessary.

PRINCIPLE 25

Peace, development and environmental protection are interdependent and indivisible.

PRINCIPLE 26

States shall resolve all their environmental disputes peacefully and by appropriate means in accordance with the Charter of the United Nations.

PRINCIPLE 27

States and people shall cooperate in good faith and in a spirit of partnership in the fulfilment of the principles embodied in this Declaration and in the further deveopment of international law in the field of sustainable development .

Source : Earth summit, Agenda 21, The United Nations Programme of Action from Rio, The United Nations Conference on Environment and Development

Courtesy : United Nations

34

PROTECTION OF THE ATMOSPHERE

INTRODUCTION

1. Protection of the atmosphere is a broad and multidimensional endeavour involving various sectors of economic activity. The options and measures described in the present chapter are recommended for consideration and, as appropriate, implementation by Governments and other bodies in their efforts to protect the atmosphere.

2. It is recognized that many of the issues discussed in this chapter are also addressed in such international agreements as the 1985. Vienna Convention for the Protection of the Ozone Layer, the 1987 Montreal Protocol on Substances that Deplete the Ozone Layer as amended, the 1992 United natons Framework Convention on Climate Change and other international, including regional, instruments. In the case of activities covered by such agreements, it is understood that the recommendations contained in this chapter do not oblige any Government to take measures which exceed the provisions of these legal instruments. However, within the framework of this chapter, Governments are free to carry out additional measures which are consistent with those legal instruments.

3. It is also recognized that activities that may be undertaken in pursuit of the objectives of this chapter should be coordinated with social and economic development in an integrated manner with a view to avoiding adverse impacts on the latter, taking into full account the legitimate priority needs of developing countries for the achievement of sustained economic growth and the eradication of poverty.

4. In this context particular reference is also made to programme area A of chapter 2 of Agenda 21 (Promoting sustainable development through trade).

5. The present chapter includes the following four programme areas:

A) ADDRESSING THE UNCERTAINTIES : IMPROVING THE SCIENTIFIC BASIS FOR DECISION-MAKING,

B) PROMOTING SUSTAINABLE DEVELOPMENT:

(i) Energy development, efficiency and consumption;
(ii) Transportation;
(iii) Industrial development;
(iv) Terrestrial and marine resource development and land use;

C) PREVENTING STRATOSPHERIC OZONE DEPLETION;

D) TRANSBOUNDARY ATMOSPHERIC POLLUTION.

PROGRAMME AREAS

A) ADDRESSING THE UNCERTAINTIES: IMPROVING THE SCIENTIFIC BASIS FOR DECISION-MAKING

BASIS FOR ACTION

6. Concern about climate change and climate variability, air pollution and ozone depletion has created new demands for scientific, economic and social information to reduce the remaining uncertainties in these fields. Better understanding and prediction of the various properties of the atmosphere and of the affected ecosystems, as well as health impacts and their interactions with socio-economic factors, are needed.

OBJECTIVES

7. The basic objective of this programme area is to improve the understanding of processes that influence and are influenced by the Earth's atmosphere on a global, regional and local scale,including, inter alia,

physical, chemical, geological, biological, oceanic, hydrological, economic and social processes; to build capacity and enhance international cooperation; and to imporve understanding of the economic and social consequences of atmospheric changes and of mitigation and response measures addressing such changes.

ACTIVITIES

8. Governments at the appropriate level, with the cooperation of the relevant United Nations bodies and, as appropriate, intergovernmental and non-governmental organizations, and the private sector, should:

(a) Promote research related to the natural processes affecting and being affected by the atmosphere, as well as the critical linkages between sustainable development and atmospheric changes, including impacts on human health, ecosystems, economic sectors and society;

(b) Ensure a more balanced geographical coverage of the Global Climate Observing System and its components; including the Global Atmosphere Watch, by facilitating, inter alia, the establishment and operation of additional systematic observation stations, and by contributing to the development, utilization and accessibility of these databases;

(c) Promote cooperation in:

- (i) The development of early detection systems concerning changes and fluctuations in the atmosphere;
- (ii) The establishment and improvement of capabilities to predict such changes and fluctuations and to assess the resulting environmental and socio-economic impacts;

(d) Cooperate in research to develop methodologies and identify threshold leves of atmospheric pollutants, as well as atmospheric levels of greenhouse gas concertrations, that would cause dangerous anthropogenic interference with the climate system and the environment as a whole, and the associated rates of change that would not allow ecosystems to adapt naturally;

(e) Promote, and cooperate in the building of scientific capacities for, the exchange of scientific data and information, and the facilitation of the participation and training of experts and technical staff, particularly of developing countries, in the fields of research, data assembly, collection and assessment, and systematic observation related to the atmosphere.

B) PROMOTING SUSTAINABLE DEVELOPMENT

1) ENERGY DEVELOPMENT, EFFICIENCY AND CONSUMPTION

BASIS FOR ACTION

9. Energy is essential to economic and social development and imporved quality of life. Much of of the world's energy, however, is currently produced and consumed in ways that could not be sustained if technology were to remain constant and if overall quantities were to increase substantially. The need to control atmospheric emissions of greenhouse and other gases and substances will increasingly need to be based on efficiency in energy production, transmission, distribution and consumption, and on growing reliance on environmentally sound energy systems, particularly new and renewable sources of energy. All energy sources will need to be used in ways that respect the atmosphere, human health and the environment as a whole.

10. The existing constraints to increasing the environmentally sound energy supplies required for pursuing the path towards sustainable development, particularly in developing countries, need to be removed.

OBJECTIVES

11. The basic and ultimate objective of this programme area is to reduce adverse effects on the atmosphere from the energy sector by promoting policies or programmes, as appropriate, to increase the contribution of environmentally sound and cost-effective energy systems, particularly new and renewable ones, through less polluting and more efficient energy production, transmission, distribution and use. This objective should reflect the need for equity, adequate energy supplies and increasing energy consumption in developing countries,and should take

into consideration the situations of countries that are highly dependent on income generated from the production, processing and export, and / or consumption of fossil fuels and associated energy-intensive products and /or the use of fossil fuels for which countries have serious difficulties in switching to alternatives, and the situations of countries highly vulnerable to adverse effects of climate change.

ACTIVITIES

12. Governments at the appropriate level, with the cooperation of the relevant United Nations bodies and, as appropriate, intergocernmental and non-governmental organizations, and the private sector, should:

(a) Cooperate in identifying and developing economically viable, environmentally sound energy sources to promote the availability of increased energy supplies to support sustainable development efforts, in particular in developing countries;

(b) Promote the development at the national level of appropriate methodologies for making integrated energy, environment and economic policy descions for sustainable development, inter alia, through environmental impact assessments.

(c) Promote the research, development, transfer and use of improved energy-efficient technologies and practices, including endogenous technologies in all relevant sectors, giving special attention to the rehabilitation and modernization of power systems, with particular attention to developing countries;

(d) Promote the research, development, transfer and use of technologies and practices for environmentally sound energy systems, influding new and renewable energy system, with particular attention to developing counries;

(e) Promote the development of institutional, scientific, planning and management capacities, particularly in developing countries, to develop, produce and use increasingly efficient and less polluting forms of energy;

(f) Review current energy supply mixes to determine how the contribution of environmentally sound energy systems as a whole,particulary new and renewable energy systems, could be increased in an economically efficient manner, taking into account respective countries unique social,physical, economic and political characteristics, and examining and implementing, where appropriate, measures to overcome any barriers to thir development and use;

(g) Coordinate energy plans regionally and subregionally, where applicable, and study the feasibility of efficent distribution of environmentally sound energy from new and renewable energy efficiency;

(h) In accordance with national socio-economic development and environment and environment priorities, evaluate and, as appropriate, promote cost-effective polices or programmes, including administrative, social and economic measures, in order to improve energy efficiency;

(i) Build capacity for energy planning and programme management in energy efficiency, as well as for the development, introduction, and promotion of new and renewable sources of energy;

(j) Promote appropriate energy efficiency and emission standards or recommendations at the national level, aimed at the development and use of technologies that minimize adverse impacts on the environment;

(k) Encourage education and awareness-raising programmes at the local, national, subregional and regional levels concerning energy efficiency and environmentally sound energy systems;

(1) Establish or enhance, as appropriate, in cooperation with the private sector, labelling programmes for products to provide decision makers and consumers with information on opportunities for energy efficiency.

2) TRANSPORTAION

BASIS FOR ACTION

13. The transport sector has an essential and postive role to play in economic and social development, and transportation needs will undoubtedly increase. However, since the transport sector is also a source of atmospheric emissions, there is need for a review of existing transport systems and for more effective design and management of traffic and transport systems.

OBJECTIVES

14. The basic objective of this programme area is to develop and promote cost-effective policies or programmes, as approptiate, to limit, reduce or control, as appropriate, harmful emissions into the atmosphere and other adverse environmental effects of the transport sector, taking into account development priorities as well as the specific local and national circumstances and safety aspects.

ACTIVITIES

15. Governments at the appropriate level, with the cooperation of the relevant United Natons bodies and, as appropriate, intergovernmental and non-governmental orgnizations, and the private sector, should:

(a) Develop and promote, as appropriate, cost-effective, more efficient, less polluting and safer transport systems, particularly integrated rural and urban mass transit,as well as environmentally sound road networks, taking into accont the needs for sustainable social, economic and development priorities, particularly in developing countries;

(b) Facilitate at the international, regional, subregional and national levels access to and transfer of safe, efficient, including resource-efficient, and less polluting transport technologies, particularly to the developing counries, including the implementation of appropriate training programmes;

(c) Strengthen, as appropriate, their efforts at collecting, analyising and exchanging relevant information on the relation between environment and transport, with particular emphasis on the systematic observation of emissions and the development of a transport database;

(d) In accordance with national socio-economic development and environment priorites, evaluate and, as appropriate, promote cost-effective policies or programmes, including administrative, social and economic measures, in order to encourage use of transportation modes that minimize adverse impacts on the atmosphere;

(e) Develop or enhance, as appropriate, mechanisms to integrate transport planning strategies and urban and regional settlement planning strategies, with a view to reducing the environmental impact of transport;

(f) Study within the framework of the United Nations and its regional commissions, the feasibility of convening regional conferences on transport and the environment.

3) INDUSTRIAL DEVELOPMENT

BASIS FOR ACTION

16. Industry is essential for the production goods and services and is a major source of employment and income, and industrial development as such is essential for economic growth. At the same time, industry is a major resource and materials user and consequently industrial activities result in emissions into the atmosphere and the environment as a whole. Protection of the atmosphere can be enhanced, inter alia, by increasing resource and materials efficiency in industry, installing or improving pollution abataement technologies and replacing chlorofluorocarbons(CFCs) and other ozone-depleting substances with appropriate substitutes, as well as by reducing wastes and by-products.

OBJECTIVES

17. The basic objective of this programme area is to encourage industrial development in ways that minimize adverse impacts on the atmosphere by, inter alia, increasing efficiency in the producation and con-

sumption by industry of all resources and materials, by improving pollution-abatement technologies and by developing new, environmentally sound technologies.

ACTIVITIES

18. Governments at the appropriate level, with the cooperation of the relevant United Nations bodies and, as appropriate, intergovernmental and non-governmental organizations, and the private sector, should:

(a) In accordance with national socio-economic development and environment priorities, evaluate and, as appropriate, promote cost-effective policies or programmes, including administriative, social and economic measures, in order to minimize industrial pollution and adverse impacts on the atmosphere;

(b) Encourage industry to increase and strengthen its capacity to develop technologies, products and processes that are safe, are less polluting and make more efficient use of all resources and materials, including energy:

(c) Cooperate in the development and transfer of such industrial technologies and in the development of capacities to manage and use such technologies, particularly with respect to developing countries;

(d) Develop, improve and apply environmental impact assessments to foster sustainable industrial development;

(e) Promote efficient use of materials and resources, taking into account the life cycles of products, in order to realize the economic and environmental benefits of using resources more efficiently and producing fewer wastes;

(f) Support the promotion of less polluting and more efficient technologies and processes in industries, taking into account area-specific accessible potentials for energy, particularly safe and renewable sources of energy, with a view to limiting industrial pollution and adverse impacts on the atmosphere.

4) TERRESTRIAL AND MARINE RESOURCE DEVELOPMENT AND LAND USE

BASIS FOR ACTION

19. Land-use and resource policies will both affect and be affected by changes in the atmosphere. Certain practices related to terrestrial and marine resources and land use can decrease greenhouse gas sinks and increase atmospheric emissions. The loss of biological diversity may reduce the resilience of ecosystems to climatic variations and air pollution damage. Atmosheric changes can have important impacts on forests, biodiversity, and fresh water and marine ecosystems, as well as on economic activities, such as agriculture. Policy objectives in different sectors may often diverge and will need to be handled in an integrated manner.

OBJECTIVES

20 The objectives of this programme area are:

(a) To promote terrestrial and marine resource utilization and appropriate land-use practices that contribute to:

   (i) The reduction of atmospheric pollution and/or the limitation of anthropogenic emissions of greenhouse gases;
   (ii) The conservation, sustainable managaement and enhancement, where appropriate, of all sinks for greenhouse gases;
   (iii) The conservation and sustainable use of natural and environmental resources:

(b) To ensure that actual and potential atmospheric changes and their socio-economic and ecological impacts are fully taken into account in planning and implementing policies and programmes concerning terrestrial and marine resources utilization and land use practices.

ACTIVITIES

21. Governments at the appropriate level, with the cooperation of the relevant United Nations bodies and, as appropriate, intergovernmental and non-governmental organizations, and the private sector, should:

(a) In accordance with national socio-economic development andenvironment priorities, evaluate and, as appropriate, promote cost-efffective policies or programmes, including administrative, social and economic measures, in order to encourage environmentally sound land-use practices:

(b) Implement policies and programmes that will discourage inappropriate and polluting land-use practices and promote sustainable utilization of terrestrial and marine resources;

(c) Consider promoting the development and use of terrestrial and marine resources and land-use practices that will be more resilient to atmospheric changes and fluctuations;

(d) Promote sustainable management and cooperataion in the conservation and enhancement, as appropriate, of sinks and reservoirs of greenhouse gases, including biomass, forests and oceans, as well as other terrestrial, coastal and marine ecosystems.

c) Preventing Stratospheric ozone depletion

BASIS FOR ACTION

22. Analysis of recent scientific data has confirmed the growing concern about the continuing depletion of the Earth's stratospheric ozone layer by reactive chlorine and bromine from man-made EFCs, halons and related substances. While the 1985 Vienna Convention for the protection of the Ozone Layer and the 1987 Montreal Protocol on Substances that Deplete the Ozone Layer (as amended in London in 1990) were important steps in international action, the total chlorine loding of the atmosphere with ozone-depleting substances has continued to rise. This can be changed through compliance with the control measures identified with the Protocol.

OBJECTIVES

23. The objectives of this programme area are:

(a) To realize the objectives defined in the Vienna Convention and the Montreal protocol and its 1990 amendments, including the consideration in those instruments of the special needs and conditions of the developing countries and the availability to them of alternatives to substances that deplete the ozone layer. Technologies and natural products that reduce demand for these substances should be encouraged;

(b) To develop strategies aimed at mitigating the adverse effects of ultraviolet radiation reaching the Earth's surface as a consequence of depletion and modification of the stratospheric ozone layer.

ACTIVITIES

24. Governments at the appropriate level, with the cooperation of the relevant United Nations bodies and, as appropriate, intergocernmental and non-governmental orgnizations, and the private sector, should:

(a) Ratify, accept or approve the Montreal Protocol and its 1990 amendments; pay their contributions towards the Vienna/Montreal trust funds and the interim multilateral ozone fund promptly; and contribute, as appropriate, towards ongoing efforts under the Montreal Protocol and its implmenting mechanisms, including making avaiable substances and faciliating the transfer of the corresponding technologies to developing countries in order to enable them to comply with the obligations of the Protocol;

(b) Support further expansion of the Global Ozone Observing System by faciliating - through bilataeral and multilateral funding -the establishment and operation of additional systematic observation stations, especially in the tropical belt in the southern hemisphere;

(c) Participate actively in the continuous assessment of scientific information and the health and environmental effects, as well as of the technological/economic implications of stratospheric ozone depletion; and consider further actions that prove warranted and feasible on the basis of these assessments;

(d) Based on the results of research on the effects of the additonal ultraviolet radiation reaching the Earth's surface, consider taking appropriate remedial measures in the fields of human health, agriculture and marine environment;

(e) Replace CFCs and other ozone-depleting substances, consistent with the Montreal Protocal, recognizing that a replacement's suitability should be evaluated holistically and not simply based on its contribution to solving one atmospheric or environmental problem.

D) TRANSBOUNDARY ATMOSPHERIC POLLUTION

BASIS FOR ACTION

25. Transboundary air pollution has adverse health impacts on humans and other detrimental environmental impacts, such as tree and forest loss and the acidification of water bodies. The geographical distribution of atmospheric pollution monitoring networks in uneven, with the developing countries serverely underrepresented. The lack of reliable emissions data outside Europe and North America is a major constraint to measring transboundary air pollution. There is also insufficient information on the environmental and health effects of air pollution in other regions.

26.The 1979 Convention on Long-range Transboundary Air Pollution, and its protocols, have established a regional regime in Europe and North America, based on a review process and cooperative programmes for systematic observation of air pollution, assessement and information exchange. These programmes need to be continued and enhanced, and their experience needs to be shared with other regions of the world.

OBJECTIVES

27. The objectives of this programme area are:

(a) To develop and apply pollution control and measurement technologies for stationary and mobile sources of air pollution and to develop alternative environmentally sound technologies;

(b) To observe and assess systematically the sources and extent of transboundary air pollution resulting from natural processes and anthropogenic activities;

(c) To strengthen the capabilities, particularly of developing countries, to measure, model and assess the fate and impacts of transboundary air pollution, through, inter alia, exchange of information and training of experts;

(d) To develop capabilities to assess and mitigate transboundary air pollution resulting from industrial and nuclear accidents, natural disasters and the deliberate and/or accidental destruction of natural resources;

(e) To encourage the establishment of new and the implementation of existing regional agreements for limiting transboundary air pollution;

(f) To develop strategies aiming at the reduction of emissions causing transboundary air pollution and their effects.

ACTIVITIES

28. Governments at the appropriate level, with the cooperation of the relevant United Nations bodies and, as appropriatae, intergovernmental and non-governmental organizations, the private sector and financial institutions, should:

(a) Establish and /or strengthen regional agreements for transboundary air pollution control and cooperate, particularly with developing countries, in the areas of systematic observation and assessment,modelling and the development and exchange of emission control technologies for mobile and stationary sources of air pollution. In this context, greater emphasis should be put on addressing the extent, causes, health and socio-economic impacts of ultraviollet radiation, acidification of the environment and photo-oxidant damage to forests and other vegetation;

(b) Establilsh or strengthen early warning systems and response mechanisms for transboundary air pollution resulting from industrial accidents and natural disasters and the deliberate and/or accidental destruction of natural resources;

(c) Facilitate training opportunities and exchange of data, information and national and /or regional experiences;

(d) Cooperate on regional, multilateral and bilateral bases to assess transboundary air pollution, and elaborate and implement programmes identifying specific actions to reduce atmospheric emissions and to address their environmental, economic, social and other effects.

MEANS OF IMPLEMENTATION

International and rgional cooperation

29. Existing legal instruments have created institutional structures which relate to the purposes of these instruments, and relevant work should primarily continue in those contexts. Governements should continue to cooperate and enhance their cooperation at the regional and global levels, including cooperation within the United Nations system. In this context reference is made to the recommendations in chapter 38 of Agenda 21 (international institutional arraangements).

Capacity-building

30. Countries, in cooperation with the relevant United Nations bodies, international donors and non-governmental organizations, should mobilize technical and financial resources and facilitate technical cooperation with developing conutries to reinforce their technical, managerial, planning and administrative capacities to promote sustainable development and the protection of the atmosphere, in all relevant sectors.

HUMAN RESOURCE DEVELOPMENT

31. Education and awareness-raising programmes concerning the promotion of sustainable development and the protection of the atmosphere need to be introduced and strengthened at the local, national and international levels in all relevant sectors.

FINANCIAL AND COST EVALUATION

32. The Conference secretariat has estimated the averagae total annual cost (1993-2000) of implementing the activities under programme

area A to be about $640 million from the international community on grant or concessional terms. These are indicative and order-of magnitude estimates only and have not been reviewed by Governments. Actual costs and financial terms, including that are non-concessional, will depend upon, inter alia, the specific strategies and programmes Governments decide upon for implementation.

33. The conference secretariat has estimated the average total annual cost (1993-2000) of implementing the activities of the four-part programme under programme area B to be about $ 20 billion from the international community on grant or concessional terms. These are indicative and order-of-magnitude estimates only and have not been reviewed by Governments. Actual costs and financial terms, including any that are non-concessional, will depend upon, inter alia, the specific strategies and programmes Governments decide upon for implementation.

34. The Conference secretariat has estimated the average total annual cost(1993-2000) of implementing the activities under programme area C to be in the range of $ 160 million to $590 million on grant or concessional terms. These are indicative and order-of-magnitude estimates only and have not been reviewed by Governments. Actual costs and financial terms, including any that are specific strategies and programmes Governments decide upon for implementation.

35. The Conference secretariat has included costing for technical assistance and pilot programmes under paragraphs 32 and 33.

Source: Earth Summit - Agenda 21

Courtsy: United Nations

---

[1] New and renewable energy scources are solar thermal, solar photovoltaic, wind, hydro, boimass, geothermal, ocean, animal and human power, as referred to in the reports of the Committee on the Development and Utilization of New and Renewable Sources of Energy, prepared specifically for the Conference (see A/CONF.151/PC/119 and A/AC.218/1992/5).

[2] This includes standards or recommendations promoted by regional economic integration organizations.

35

PROMOTING EDUCATION, PUBLIC AWARENESS AND TRAINING

INTRODUCTION

1. Education, raising of public awarenes and training are linked to virtually all areas in Agenda 21, and even more closely to the ones on meeting basic needs, capacity-building, data and informtion, science, and the role of major groups. This chapter sets out broad proposals, while specific suggestions related to sectoral issues are contained in other chapters. The Declaration and Recommendations of the Tbilisi Intergocernmental Conference on Environmental Education, organized by UNESCO and UNEP and held in 1977, have provided the fundamental principles of the proposals in this document. 36.2 Programme areas described in the present chapter are:

(a) Reorienting education towards sustainable development;

(b) Increasing public awareness;

(c) Promoting training.

PROGRAMME AREAS

A) REORIENTING EDUCATION TOWARDS SUSTAINABLE DEVELOPMENT

BASIS FOR ACTION

3. Education, including formal education, public awareness and train-

ing, should be recognized as a process by which human beings and societies can reach their fullest potential. Education is critical for promoting sustainable development and improving the capacity of the people to address environment and development issues. While basic education provides the underpinning for any environmental and development education, the latter needs to be incorporated as an essential part of learning. Both formal education and non-formal education are indispensable to changing people's attitudes so that they have the capacity to assess and address their sustainable development concerns. It is also critical for achieving environmental and ethical awareness, values and attitudes, skills and behaviour consistent with sustainable development and for effective public participation in decision-making. To be effective, environment and development education should deal with the dynamics of both the physical/biological and socio-economic environment and human (which may include spiritual) development, should be integrated in all disciplines, and should employ formal and non-formal methods and effective means of communication.

OBJECTIVES

4. Recognizing that countries and, regional and international organizations will develop their own priorities and schedules for implementation in accordance with their needs, policies and programmes, the following objectives are proposed:

(a) To endorse the recommendations arising from the World Conference on Education for All: Meeting Basic Learning Needs[2] (jomtien, Thailand, 5-9 March 1990) and to strive to ensure universial access to basic education. and to achieve primary education for at least 80 percent of girls and 80 percent of boys of primary school age through formal schoolong or non-formal education and to reduce the adult illiteracy rate to at least half of its 1990 level. Efforts should focus on reducing the high illiteracy levels and redressing the lack of basic education among women and should bring their literacy levels into line with those of men;

(b) To achieve environmental and development awareness in all sectors of society on a world-wide scale as soon as possible;

(c) To strive to achieve the accessibility of environmental and development education, linked to social education, from primary school age through adulthood to all groups of people;

(d) To promote integration of environment and development concepts, including demography, in all educational programmes, in particular the analysis of the causes of major environment and development issues in a local context, drawing on the best available scientific evidence and other appropriate sources of knowledge, and giving special emphasis to the further training of decision makers at all levels.

ACTIVITIES

5. Recongnizing that countries and regional and international organizations will develop their own priorities and schedules for implementation in accordance with their needs, policies and programmes, the following activities proposed:

(a) All countries are encouraged to endorse the recommendations of the Jomtien Conference and strive to ensure its Framework for Action. This would encompass the preparation of national strategies and actions for meeting basic learning needs, universalizing access and promoting equity, broadening the means and scope of education, developing a supporting policy context, mobilizing resources and strengthening international cooperation to redress existing economic, social and gender disparities which interfere with these aims. Non-governmental organizations can make an important contribution in designing and implementing educational programmes and should be recognized;

(b) Governments should strive to update or prepare strategies aimed at integrating environment and development as a cross-cutting issue into education at all levels within the next three years. This should be done in cooperation with all sectors of society. The strategies should set out policies and activities, and identify needs, cost,means and schedules for their implementation, evaluation and review. A thorough review of curicula should be undertaken to ensure a multidisciplinary approach, with environment and development issues and their socio-cultural and demographic aspects and linkages. Due respect should be given to community-defined needs and diverse knowledge systems, including science, cultural and social sensitivities;

(c) Countries are encouraged to set up national advisory environmental education coordinating bodies or round tables representative of various environmental, developmental, educational, gender and other interests, including non-governmental organizations, to encourage partnerships, help mobilize resources, and provide a source of information and focal point for international ties. These bodies would help mobilize and facilitate different population groups and communities to assess their own needs and to develop the necessary skills to create and implement their own environment and development initiatives;

(d) Educational authorities, with the appropriate assistance from community groups or non-governmental organizations, are recommended to assist or set up pre-service and in-service training programmes for all teachers, administrators, and educational planners, as well as non-formal educators in all sectors, addressing the nature and methods of environmental and development education and making use of relevant experience of non-governmental organizations;

(e) Relevant authorities should ensure that every school is assisted in designing environmental activity work plans, with the participation of students and staff. Schools should involve school children in local and regional studies on environmental health, including safe drinking-water, sanitation and food and ecosystems, and in relevant activities, linking these studies with services and research in national parks, wildlife reserves, ecological heritage sites etc;

(f) Educational authorities should promote proven educational methods and the development of innovative teaching methods for educational settings. They should also recognize appropriate traditional education systems in local communities;

(g) Within two years the United nations system should undertake a comprehensive review of its educational programmes, encompassing training and public awareness, to reassess priorities and reallocate resources. The UNESCO/INEP Interantional Environmental Education Programme should, in cooperation with the appropriate bodies of the United Nations system, Governments, non-governmental organizations and others, establish a programme within two years to integrate the decisions of the Conference into the existing United

Nations framework adapted to the needs of educators at different levels and circumstances. Regional organizations and national authorities should be encouraged to elaborate similar parallel progaramme and opportunities by conducting analysis of how to mobilize different sectors of the population in order to assess and address their environmental and development education needs;

(h) There is a need to strengthen, within five years, information exchange by enhancing technologies and capacities necessary to promote environment and development education and public awareness. Countries should cooperate with each and with the various social sectors and population groups to prepare educational tools that include regional environment and development issues and initiatives, using learning materials and resources suited to their own requirements;

(i) Countries could support university and other tertiary activities and networks for environmental and development education. Cross-disciplinary courses could be made available to all students. Existing regional networks and activities and national university actions which promote research and common teaching approaches on sustainable development should be built upon, and new partnerships and bridges created with the business and other independent sectors, as well as with all countries, for technology, know-how, and knowledge exchange;

(j) Countries, assisted by international organizations, non-governmental organizations and other sectors, could strengthen or establish national or regional centres of excellence in interdisciplinary research and education in environmental and developmental sciences, law and the management of specific environmental problems. Such centres could be universities or existing networks in each country or region, promoting co-operative research and information sharing and dissemination. At the global level these functions should be performed by appropriate institutions;

(k) Countries should facilitate and promote non-formal education activities at the local, regional and national levels by co-operating with and supporting the efforts of non-formal educators and other community-based organizations. The appropriaate bodies of the

United Nations system in coperation with non-governmental organizations should encourage the development of an international network for the achievement of global educational aims. At the national and local levels, public and scholastic forums should discuss environmental and development issues,and suggest sustainable alternatives to policy makers;

(l) Educational authorities, with appropriate assistance of non-governmental organizations, including women's and indigenous peoples organizations, shuld promote all kinds of adult education programmes for continuing education in environmentand development, basing activities around elementary /secondary schools and local problems. These authorities and industry should encourage business, industrial and agriucltural schools to include such topics in their curricula. The corporate sector could include sustainable development in their education and training programmes. Programmes at a postgraduate level should include specific courses aiming at the further training of decision makers;

(m) Governments and educational authorities should foster opprotunities for women in non-traditional fields and eliminate gender stereotyping in curricula. This could be done by improving enrolment opportunities, including females in advanced programmes as students and instructors, reforming entrance and teacher staffing policies and providing incentives for establishing child-care facilities, as appropriate. Priority should be given to education of young females and to programmes promoting literacy among women;

(n) Governments should affirm the rights of indigenous peoples,by legislation if necessary, to use their experience and understanding of sustainable development to play a part in education and training.

(o) The United Nations could maintain a monitoring and evaluative role regarding decisions of the United Nations Conference on Environment and Development on education and awareness, through the relevant United nations agencies. With Governments and non-governmental organizations, as appropriate, it should present and disseminate decisions in a vriety of forms, and should ensure the continuous implementation and review of the educational implications of conference decisons, in particular through relevant events and conferences.

MENANS OF IMPLEMENTATION

FINANCING AND COST EVALUATION

6. The Conference sercretariat has estimated the average total annual cost(1993-2000) of implementing the activities of this programme to be about $8 billion to $9 billion, including about $ 3.5 billion to $ 4.5 billion for the international community on grant or concessional terms. These are indicative and order-of-magnitude estimates only and have not been reviewed by Governments. Actual costs and financial terms,including any that are non-concessional, will depend upon, interalia, the specific strategies and programmes Governments decide upon for implementation.

7. In the light of country-specific situations, more support for education, training and public awareness activities related to environment and development could be provided, in appropriate cases, through measures such as the following:

(a) Giving higher priority to those sectors in budget allocations, protecting them from structural cutting requirements;

(b) Shifting allocations within existing education budgets in favour of primary education, with focus on enviornment and development;

(c) Promoting conditions where a larger share of the cost is borne by local communities, with rich communities assisting poorer ones;

(d) Obtaining additional funds from private donors concentrating on the poorest countries, and those with rates of literacy below 40 percent;

(e) Encouraging debt for education swaps;

(f) Lifting restrictions on private schooling and increasing the flow of funds from and to non-governmental organizations, including small-scale grass-roots organizations;

(g) Promoting the effective use of existing facilities, for example, multiple school shifts, fuller development of open universities and other long-distance teching;

(h) Facilitating low-cost use of mass media for the purposes of education;

(i) Encouraging twinning of universities in developed and developing countries.

B) INCREASING PUBLIC AWARENESS

BASIS FOR ACTION

8. There is still a considerable lack of awareness of the interrelated nature of all human activities and the evironment, due to inaccurate or insufficient information. Developing countries in particular lack relevant technologies and expertise. There is a need to increase public sensitivity to environment and development problems and involvement in their solutions and foster a sense of personal environmental responsibility and greater motivation and commitment towards sustainable development.

OBJECTIVE

9. The objective is to promote broard public awareness as an essential part of a global education effort to strengthen attitudes, values and actions which are compatible with sustainable development. It is important to stress the principle of devolving authority, accountability and resources to the most appropriate level with preference given to local responsibility and control over awareness-building activities.

ACTIVITIES

10. Recongnizaing that countries and regional and international organizations will develop their own priorities and schedules for implementation in accordance with their needs, policies and programmes, the following activities are proposed:

(a) Countries should strengthen existing advisory bodies or establish new ones for public environment and development information, and should coordinate activities with, among others, the United Nations, non-governmental organizations and important media. They should encourage public participation in discussions of environmental policies and assessments. Governments should also facilitate and support national to local networking of information through existing networks;

(b) The United nations system should improve its outreach in the course of a review of its education and public awareness activities to promote greater involvement and coordination of all parts of the system, especially its information bodies and regional and country operations. Systematic surveys of the impact of awareness programmes should be conducted, recognizing the needs and contributions of specific community groups;

(c) Countires and regional organizations should be encouraged, as appropriate, to provide public environmental and development information services for raising the awareness of all groups, the private sector and particularly decision makers;

(d) Countries should stimulate educational establishments in all sectors, especially the tertiary sector, to contribute more to awareness building. Educational materials of all kinds and for all audiences should be based on the best available scientific information, including the natural, behavioural and social sciences, and taking into account aestetic and ethical dimensions;

(e) Countries and the United Nations system should promote a cooperative relationship with the media, popular theatre groups, and entertainment and advertising industries by initiating discussions to mobilize their experience in shaping public behaviour and consumption patterns and making wide use of their methods. Such cooperation would also increase the active public participation in the debate on the environment. UNICEF should make child-oriented material available to media as an educational tool, ensuring close cooperation between the curriculum, for the primary level. UNESCO,UNEP and universities should enrich pre-service curricula for journalists on environment and development topics;

(f) Countries, in cooperation with the scientific community, should establish ways of employing modern communication technologies for effective public outreach. National and local educatiaonal authorities and relevant United nations agencies should expand, as appropriate, the use of audio-visual methods, especially in rural areas in mobile units, by producing television and radio programmes for developing countries, involving local participation, employing interactive multimedia methods and integrating advanced methods with folk media;

(g) Countries should promote, as appropriate, environmentally sound leisure and tourism activities, building on The Hague declaration of Tourism (1989) and the current programmes of the World Tourism Organization and UNEP, making suitable use of museums, heritage sites, zoos, botanical gardens, national parks, and other protected areas;

(h) Countries should encourage non-governmental organizations to increase their involvement in environmental and development problems, through joint awareness initiatives and improved interchange with other constituencies in society;

(i) Countires and the United Nations system should increase their interaction with and include, as appropriate, indigenous people in the management, planning and development of their local environment, and should promote dissemination of traditional and socially learned knowledge through means based on local customs, especially in rural areas, integrating these efforts with the electronic media, whenever appropriate;

(j) UNICEF,UNESCO,UNDP and non-governmental organizations should develop support programmes to involve young people and children in environment and development issues, such as children's and youth hearings and building on decisions of the World Summit for Children (A/45/625,annex);

(k) Countires, the United Nations, and non-governmental organizations should encourage mobilization of both men and women in awareness campaigns, stressing the role of the family in environmental activities, women's contribution to transmission of knowledge and social values and the development of human resources;

(l) Public awareness should be heightened regarding the impacts of violence in society.

MEANS OF IMPLEMENTATION

FINANCING AND COST EVALUATION

11. The Conference secretariat has estimated the average total annual cost(1993-2000) of implementing the activities of this programme to be about $ 1.2 billion, including about $110 million from the international community on grant or concessional terms. These are indicative and order-of magnitude estimates only and have not been reviewed by Governments. Actual costs and financial terms, including any that are non-concessional, will depend upon, inter alia, the specific strategies and programmes Governments decide upon for implementation.

C) PROMOTING TRAINING

BASIS FOR ACTION

12. Training is one of the most important tools to develop human resources and facilitate the transition to a more sustainable world. It should have a job-specific focus, aimed at filling gaps in knowledge and skill that would help individuals find employment and be involved in environmental development work. At the same time, training ;programmes should promote a greater awareness of environment and development issues as a two-way learing process.

OBJECTIVES

13. The following objectives are proposed:

(a) To establish or strengthen vocational training programmes that meet the needs of environment and development with ensured access to training opprotunities, regardless of social status, agae, gender, race or religion;

(b) To promote a flexible and adaptable workforce of various ages equipped to meet growing environment and development problems and changes arising from the transition to a sustainable society;

(c) To strengthen national capacities, particularly in scientific education and training, to enable Governments, employers and workers to meet their environmental and development objectives and to facilitate the transfer and assimilation of new environmentally sound, socially acceptable and appropriate technology and know-how;

(d) To ensure that environmental and human ecological considerations are integratead at all managerial levels and in all functional management areas, such as marketing, production and finance.

ACTIVITIES

14. Countires with the support of the United Nations system should identify workforce training needs and assess measures to be taken to meet those needs. Areview of progress in this area could be undertaken by the United Nations system in 1995.

15. national professional associations are encouraged to develop and review their codes of ethics and conduct to strengthen environmental connection and commitment. The training and personal development components of programmes sponsored by p4rofessional bodies should ensure incorporation of skills and information on the implementation of sustainable development at all points of policy-and decision-makiing.

16. Countries and educational institutions should integrate environmental and developmental issues into existing training curricula and promote the exchange of their methodologies and evaluations.

17. Countries should encourage all sectors of society, such as industry, universities, government officials and employess, non-governmental organizations and community organizations, to include an environmental management component in all relevant training activities,with emphais on meeting immediate skill requirements through short-term formal and in-plant vocational and mangement training. Environmental management training capacities should be strengthened, and specialized to support training at the national and enterprise levels. New training approaches for existing environmentally sound practices should be developed that create employment opprotunities and make maximum use of local resource-based methods.

18. Countries should strengthen or establish practical training

programmes for graduates from vocational schools, high schools and universities, in all countries, to enable them to meet structural adjustments which have an impact on employment and skill qualifications.

19. Governments are encouraged to consult with people in isolated situations, whether geographically, culturally or socially, to ascertain their needs for training to enable them to contribute more fully to developing sustainable work practices and lifestyles.

20. Governments, industry, trade unions, and consumers should promote an underśtandig of the interrelationship between good environment and good business practices.

21. Countries should develop a service of locally trained and recruited environmental technicians able to provide local people and communities, particularly in deprived urban and rural areas, with the services they require, starting from primary environmental care.

22. Countries should enhance the ability to gain access to, analyse and effectively use information and knowledge available on environment and development. Existing or established special training programmes should be strengthened to support information needs of special groups. The impact of these programmes on productivity, health, safety and employment should be evaluated. National and regional environmental labourmarket information systems should be developed that would supply, on a continuing basis, data on environmental job and training opprotunities. Environment and development training resource-guides should be prepared and updated, with information on training programmes, curricula, methodologies and evaluation results at the local, national, regional and international levels.

23. Aid agencies should strengthen the training component in all development projects, emphasizing a multi-disciplinary approach, promoting awareness and providing the necessary skills for transition to a sustainable society. The environmental management guidelines of UNDP for operational activities of the United Nations system may contribute to this end.

24. Existing networks of employers' and workers'organizations, industry associations and non-governmental organizations should facili-

tate the exchange of experience concerning training and awareness programmes.

25. Governments, in coperation with relevant international organizations, should develop and implement strategies to deal with national, regional and local environmental threats and emergencies, emphasizing urgent practical training and awareness programmes for increasing public preparednesss.

26. The United Nations system, as appropriate, should extend its training programmes, particularly its environmental training and support activities for employers'and workers' organizations.

MEANS OF IMPLEMENTATION

FINANCING AND COST EVALUATION

27. The Conference secretariat has estimated the average total annual cost (1993-2000) of implementing the activities of this programme to be about $5 billion, including about $2 billion from the international community on grant or concessional terms. These are indicative and order-of-magnitude estimates only and have not been reviewed by Governments. Actual costs and financial terms, including any that are non-concessional, will depend upon, inter alia, the specific strategies and programmes Governments decide upon for implementation.

Meeting Basic Learning Needs, Jomtien, Thailand, 5—9 March 1990 (New York, Inter-Agency Commission (UNDP,UNESCO,UNICEF,World Bank) for the World Conference on Education for All, 1990).

Source : Earth Summit - Agenda 21

Courtsy : United Nations

---

[1]Intergovernmental Conference on Environmental Education: Final Report (Paris, UNESCO, 1978), chap.lll

[2] Final report of the World Conference on Education For All:

36

NON-LEGALLY BINDING AUTHORITATIVE STATEMENT OF PRINCIPLES FOR A GLOBAL CONSENSUS ON THE MANAGEMENT, CONSERVATION AND SUSTAINABLE DEVELOPMENT OF ALL TYPES OF FORESTS

PREAMBLE

(a) The subject of forests is related to the entire range of environmental and development issues and opportunities, including the right to socio-economic development on a sustainable basis.

(b) The guiding objective of these principles is to contribute to the management, conservation and sustainable development of forests and to provide for their multiple and complementary functions and uses.

(c) Forestry issues and opportunities should be examined in a holistic and balanced manner within the over all context of environment and development, taking into consideration the multiple function and use of forests, including traditional uses, and the likely economic and social stress when these uses are constrained or restricted, as well as the potential for development that sustainable forest management can offer.

(d) These principles reflect a first global consensus on forests. In committing themselves to the prompt implementation of these principles, countries also decide to keep them under assessment for their adequacy with regard to further international cooperation on forest issues.

(e) These Principles should apply to all types of forests, both natural and planted, in all geographical regions and climatic zones, including austral, boreal, subtemperate, termperate, subtropical and tropical.

(f) All types of forests embody complex and unique ecological processes which are the basis for their present and potential capacity to provide resources to satisfy human needs as well as environmental values, and as such their sound mangement and conservation are of concern to the Governmental values, and as such their sound mangement and conservation are of concern to the Governments of the countries to which they belong and are of value to local communities and to the environment as a whole.

(g) Forests are essential to economic development and the maintenance of all forms of life.

(h) Recognizing that the responsibility for forest management, conservation and sustainable development is in many states allocated among federal/national, state/provincial and local levels of government, each state, in accordance with its constitution and/or national legislation, should pursue these principles at the appropriate level of government.

PRINCIPLES/ELEMENTS

1. (a) States have, in accordance with the Chapter of the United Nations and the principles of international law, the sovereign right to exploit their own resources pursuant to their own environmental policies and have the responsibility to ensure that activities within their jurisdication or control do not cause damange to the limits of national jurisdiction.

(b) The agreed full incremental cost of achieving benefits associated with forest conservation and sustainable development requires increased international cooperation and should be equitably shared by the international community.

2. (a) States have the sovereign and inalienable right to utilize, manage and develop their forests in acordance with their development needs and level of socio-economic development and on the basis of national policies consistent with sustainable development and legislation, including the conversion of such areas for other uses within the overall socio-economic development plan and based on rational land-use policies.

(b) Forest resources and forest lands should be sustainably managed to meet the social, economic, ecological,cultural and spiritual needs of present and future generations. These needs are for forest products and services,such as wood and wood products, water, food, fodder, medicine, fuel, shelter, employment, recreation, habitats for wildlife, landscape diversity, carbon sinks and reservoirs, and for other forest products. Appropriate measures should be taken to protect forests against harmful effects of pollution, including airborne pollution, fires, pests and diseases, in order to maintain their full multiple value.

(c) The provision of timely; reliable and accurate information on forests and forest ecosystems is essential for public understanding and informed decision-making and should be ensured.

(d) Governments should promote and provide opportunities for the participaton of interested parties, including local communities and indigenous people, industries, labour, non-governmental organizations and individuals, forest dwellers and women, in the development, implementation and planning of national forest policies.

3.(a) National policies and strategies should provide a framework for increased efforts, including the development and strengthening of institutions and programmes for the management, conservation and sustainable development of forests and forest lands.

(b) International institutional arrangements, building on those organizations and mechanisms already in existence, as appropriate, should facilitate international cooperation in the field of forests.

(c) All aspects of environmental protection and social and economic development as they relate to forests and forest lands should be integrated and comprehensive.

4. The vital role of all types of forests in maintaining the ecological processes and balance at the local, national, regional and global levels through, *inter alia,* their role in protecting fragile ecosystems, watersheds and freshwater resources and as rich storehouses of biodiversity and biological resources and sources of genetic material for biotechnology products, as well as photosynthesis, should be recognized.

5. (a) National forest policies should recognize and duly support the indentity, culture and the rights of indigenous people, their communities and other communities and forest dwellers. Appropriate conditions should be promoted for these groups to enable them to have an economic stake in forest use, perform economic activities, and achieve and maintain cultural identity and social organization, as well as adequate levels of livelihood and well-being, through, *inter alia,* those land tenure arrangements which serve as incentives for the sustainable management of forests.

(b) the full participation of women in all aspects of the management, conservation and sustainable development of forests should be actively promoted.

6. (a) All types of forests play an important role in meeting energy requirements through the provision of a renewable source of bio-energy ,particularly in developing countries, and the demands for fuelwood for house hold and industrial needs should be met through sustainable forest management, afforestation and reforestation. To this end, the potential contribution of plantations of both indigenous and introduced species for the provision of both fuel and industrial wood shold be recognized.

(b) National polices and programmes should take into account the relationship, where it exists, between the conservation, management and sustainable development of forests and all aspects related to the production, consumption, recycling and /or final disposal of forest products.

(c) Decisions taken on the management, conservation and sustainable development of forest resoucrs should benefit, to the extent practicable, from a comprehensive assessment of economic and non-economic values of forest goods and services and of the environmental costs and benefits. The development and imporvement of methodologies for such evaluations should be promoted.

(d) The role of plante forests and permanent agricultural crops as sustainable and environmentally sound sources of renewable energy and industrial raw material should be recognized, enhanced and promoted. Their contribution to the maintenance of ecological processes, to offseting pressure on primary/old-growth forests and to providing regional employment and development with the adequate involvement of local inhabitants should be recognized and enhanced.

(e) Natural forests also constitute a source of goods and services, and their conservation,sustainable management and use should be promoted.

7. (a) Effors should be made to promote a supportive international economic climate conducive to sustained and environmentally sound development of forests in all countries, which include, *inter alia*, the promotion of sustainable patterns of production and consumption, the eradication of poverty and the promotion of food security.

(b) Specific financial resources should be provided to developing countries with significant forest areas which establish programmes for the conservation of forests including protected natural forest areas. These resources should be directed notably to economic sectors which would stimulate economic and social subsitution activities.

8. (a) Efforts shuould be undertaken towards the greening of the world. All countires, notably developed countires, should take positive and transparent action towards reforestation, afforestation and forest conservations, as appropriate.

(b) Efforts to maintain and increase forest cover and forest productivity should be undertaken in ecologically, economically and socially sound ways through the rehabilitation, reforestation and re-establishment of trees and forests on unproductive, degraded and deforested lands, as well as through the management of existing forest resources.

(c) The implementation of national policies and programmes aimed at forest management, conservation and sustainable development, particularly in developing countries, should be supported by international financial and technical cooperation, including through the private sector, where appropriate.

(d) Sustainable forest management and use should be carried out in accordance with national development policies and priorities and on the basis of environmentally sound national guidelines. In the formulation of such guidelines, account should be taken, as appropriate and if applicable, of relevant internationally agreed methodologies and criteria.

(e) Forest manangement should be integrated with management of adjacnt areas so as to maintain ecological balance and sustainable productivity.

(f) National policies and/or legislation aimed at management, conservation and sustainable development of forests should include the protection of ecologically viable representative or unique examples of forests, including primary/old-growth forests and other unique and valued forests of national, cultural, spiritual, historical and religious importance.

(g) Access to biological resources, including genetic material, shall be with due regard to the sovereign rights of the countries where the forests are located and to the sharing on mutually agreed terms of technology and profits from biotechnology products that are derived from these resources.

(h) National policies should ensure that environmental impact assessments should be carried out where actions are likely to have significant adverse impacts on important forest resources, and where such actions are subject to a decision of a competent national authority.

9. (a) The efforts of developing countries to strengthen the management, conservation and sustainable development of their forest resources should be supported by the international community, taking into account the importance of redressing external indebtedness, particularly where aggravated by the net transfer of resources to devel-

oped countries, as well as the problem of achieving at least the replacement value of forests through improved market access for forest products, especially processed products. In this respect, special attention should also be given to the countries undergoing the process of transition to market economies.

(b) The problems that hinder efforts to attain the conservation and sustainable use of forest resources and that stem form the lack of alternative options available to local communities, in particular the urban poor and poor rural populations who are economically and socially dependent on forests and forest resources, should be addressed by Governments and the international community.

(c) National policy formulation with respect to all types of forests should take account of the pressures and demands imposed on forest ecosystems and resources from influencing factors outside the forest sector,and intersectoral means of dealing with these pressures and demands should be sought.

10. New and additional financial resources should be provided to developing countires to enable them to sustainably managae, conserve and develop their forest resources, including through afforestation, reforestation and combating deforestation and forest and land degradation.

11. In order to enable, in particular, developing countries to enhance their endogenous capacity and to better manage, conserve and develop their forest resources,the access to and transfer of environmentally sound technologies and corresponding know-how on favourable terms, including on concessional and preferential terms, as mutually agreed, in accordance with the relevant provisions of Agenda 21, should be promoted, facilitated and financed, as appropriate.

12. (a) Scientific research, forest inventories and assessments carried out by national institutions which take into account, where relevant, biological, physical, social and economic variables, as well as technological development and its application in the field of sustainable forest management, conservation and development, should be strengthened through effective modalities,including international co-

operation. In this context, attention should also be given to researach and development of sustainably harvested non-wood products.

(b) National and, where appropriate, regional and international institutional capabilities in education, training, science, technology, economics, anthropology and social aspects of forests and forest managaement are essential to the conservation and sustainable development of forests and should be strengthened.

(c) International exchange of information on the results of forest and forest management research and development should be enhanced and broadened, as appropriate, making full use of education and training institutions, including those in the private sector.

(d) Appropriate indigenous capacity and local knowledge regarding the conservation and sustainable development of forests should, through institutional and financial support and in collaboration with the people in the local communities concerned, be recognized, respected, recorded, developed and, as appropriate, introduced in the implementation of programmes. Benefits arising from the utilization of indigenous knowledge should therefore be equitably shared with such people.

13. (a) Trade in forest products should be based on non-discriminatory and multilaterally agreed rules and procedures consistent with international trade in forest products should be facilitated.

(b) Reduction or removal of tariff and impediments to the provision of better market access and better prices for higher-value-added forest products and their local processing should be encouraged to enable producer countires to better conserve and manage their renewable forest resources.

(c) Incorporation of environmental costs and benefits into market forces and mechanisms, in order to achieve forest conservation and sustainable development, should be encouraged both domestically and internationally.

(d) Forest conservation and sistainable development polices should be integrated with economic, trade and other relevant policies.

(e) Fiscal, trade, industrial, transportation and other policies and; practices that may lead to forest degradation should be avoided. Adequate policies, aimed at management, conservation and sustainable development of forests, including, where appropriate, incentives, should be encouraged.

14. Unilateral measures, incompatible with international obligations or agreements, to restrict and/or ban international trade in timber or ther forest products should be removed or avoided, in order to attain longoterm sustainable forest management.

15. Pollutants, particularly airborne pollutants, including those responsible for acidic deposition, that are harmful to the health of forest ecosystems at the local, national, regional and global should be controlled.

Source : Earth Summit - Agenda 21

Courtsy : United Nations

37

EARTH SUMMIT + 5

INTRODUCTION

Some 70 Heads of State or Government are expected to attend a special session of the United Nations General Assembly in New York from 23 to 27 June to assess progress on sustainable development since the 1992 Earth Summit.

The session, called Earth Summit +5, aims to review action taken in the five years since the United nations Conference on Environment and Development met in Rio de janeriro, and to set priorities into the 21st century. Talks in March and April 1997 to negotiate a platform that world leaders will adopt have led to some decisions on key issues, but have left until June many unresolved differences, especially on financing questions, between industrialized and developing countries.

Mostafa Tolba of Egypt, current Chairman of the UN commision on Sustainable Development, acknowledged at their conslusion that the negotiations had been "very difficult," but he was confident that an agreement would be reached in June. In the talks so far, important steps forward have been taken on international co-operation to conserve and protect freshwater supplies, encourage greater energy efficiency and ensure better management of oceans and coastal areas. The question of whether to begin negotiations for a legal convention on forests has not yet been decided.

In these areas, the talks have aimed to build and expand on Agend 21, the blueprint for sustainable development adopted at the Earth Summit. But on most finance issues, Governments have not been able to get beyond the fundamental North-South differences that dominated the debate in Rio.

Deteriorating Environment: Assessing progress since Rio, Governments have noted in the draft agreement that some global trends appear positive. Growth in world population is slowing, food production is still rising, and the majority of people are living longer and healthier lives.

But overall, the state of the global environment has continued to deteriorate, with rising levels of toxic pollution, greenhouse gas emissions and solid waste. Renewable resources, particularly freshwataer, forests, topsoil and marine fish stocks, continue to be used at rates that are clearly unsustainable.

Accelerated globalization of the world economy has benefitted some developing countries, but many, especially in Africa, continue to be marginalized. The number of people living in poverty has increased, and gaps between rich and poor have grown, both within and between countries. Few Specific Targets:

Few Specific Target: Some 60 ministers of environment, forests, agriculture and development and other seniour officials attended the three-day high-level segment of the April session of the Commission on sustainable Development, to give political impetus to the talks. Many ministers noted the urgent need for concrete proposals for action, together with targets and timetables for reaching them, but when negotiations began, few specific recommendations were made or agreed.

Environment and development groups participating in the Commission session saw the lack of concrete commitments as a serious setback. Speaking for the non-governmental organizations (NGOs) at a UN-sponsored press conference, Clif Curtis of Greenpeace International said that "we feel we are going backward, not forward, in addressing sustainable development." Considering the urgency of the situation, far too little was being. Issues unresolved at April talks will be negotiated in an Ad HocCommittee of the Whole that will meet during the june special session, while Heads of State and other high-level representatives speak in the main General Assembly Plenary.

A draft political statement, intended to be a popular-style preamble to the final document in which Heads of State would reaffirm the commitments pledged at Rio, was circulated by the Commission Chairman at the close of the session, based on informal consultations. By the text, which has still to be formally negotiated, Heads of State would declare that implementation of Agenda 21 is "more urgent now than ever" and that "we decide to more now from words to deeds. "Saying that "We must reverse the trend of deterioration of the environment," Government leaders would express their intention to reduce by half, by the year 2015, the proportion of people living in absolute poverty and reaffirm their commitment to the target of 0.7% of GNP for official development assistance (ODA) or developing countries.

Financing Contentious: On financing, the "Group of 77," representing 132 developing countries, is urging donor countries to honour commitments taken in Rio to make available "new and additional" resources beyond existing levels of ODA- and environmental technologies at concessional prices. Although the Rio agreements and the draft document for adoption in June continue to affirm the target of 0.7% of GNP for ODA, the draft text also notes that ODA has "drastically declined" since Rio, from an average 0.34% of GNP in 1992 to 0.27% in 1995.

Indicative of deep divisions, northern and southern countries disagree on basic wording as to whether provisions on finance and technolgy transfer in Agenda 21 are "commitments" or "objectives". They have, however, agreed to call for studies on the root causes of this decline and on policy approaches to reverse it. Some donor countries have stressed that larger flows of private foreign direct investment(FDI) have compensated for lower ODA. Developing countries have noted that FDI benefits only a few countries and does not necessarily encourage sustainable development. The draft agreement for June calls for studies and policies to attract private foreign capital and ensure that it promotes long-term sustainable productivity. It also calls for further work on domestic resource mobilization in developing countires. Governments have agreed to urge donor countries to provide new and additional resources through a "satisfactory replenishment" of the Global Environment Facility(GEF), the fund established just prior to Rio that channels grants to projects tackling certain environmental problems. Some NGOs had called for a commitment to double GEF funding from the current $ 2billion covering a three-year period, but this did not gain support. Although compromise positions have been reached on these and other longstanding international economic issues, such as the impact on countires of external debt, the open split between indistrialized and developing countries has dimmed the "Rio spirit" of partnership. "The situation is very much like the situation right before Rio," commented Ms.Joke Waller-hunter, Director of the UN Division for Sustainable Development, which provides substantive support to the Commission."All negotiations (are) related to a decision on finance." Mr. Tolba has commented that what some perceive as a deadlock are merely firm positions taken as negotiating tactics by Governments, and he fully expects an agreement to be reached.

Among new initiatives, the European Union has tabled a proposal for a tax on aviation fuel to provide funds for sustainable development,and the draft document calls for further studies by the UN system on innovative financing mechanisms. Some countries and NGOs have expressed support for a new Intergovernmental Panel on Finance to spearhead negotiations, and for a proposal by Norway that Heads of State hold a special meeting on finance issues at the June session, with the heads of major financial institutions.

Progress on Sectoral Issues: In an important step, Governments have urged in the draft final document that the highest priority be given to the serious problems of scarcity and pollution of freshwater supplies facing many regions. Among other recommendations, the draft calls for talks, at next year's Commission session, on a global strategy to address the impending crisis. A recent UN assessment study has shown that two-thirds of humanity will suffer from shortages of clean freshwater within thrity years unless action is taken. On oceans, the draft document goes a step beyond Agenda 21 to state that there is an urgent need for Governments to prevent or eliminate overfishing, excess fishing capacity and wasteful fishing practices, and to consider the impact of government subsidies.

This refects a growing international consensus, in light of FAO reports that 70% of commercial fisheries are overfished or depleted. Regarding forests, Governments have left pending until June whether to begin negotiations for a legally binding instrument on forests, or to establish an Intergovernmental Forum on Forests to continue talks exploring this option and to monitor action on over 100 recommendations for sustainable forest management made by an intergovernmental panel in February 1997, after two years of work.

Among countries with large forest reserves, Canada, Malaysia and Russia favour a legal convention, Brazil wants to consider this question later, while the United States is opposed. Most environment groups oppose a new treaty because they feel that the several years of negotiation required would delay action needed immediately and existing agreements such as the Biodiversity Convention offer adequate protection for forests. Studies show that, worldwide, forests continue to be cut and burned at alarming rates. On climate change, in setting the stage for the meeting of the parties to the UN climate change treaty in Kyoto, Japan, this December, Governments have not agreed on action needed. The European Union has proposed a 15% reduction in emissions of greenhouse gases below 1990 levels by the year 2010. The Alliance of Small Island States, concerned by the threat of rising sea levels, has called for commitments to a 20% reducation in carbon dioxide emissions below 1990 levels by the 2005. The United States prefers wording urging Governments to adopt "the strongest possible agreement," including legally binding tragets at this time. A menu of options has been forwarded to the June session for futher negotiation.

The draft document also calls for strenthening the Montreal Protocol for protection of the ozone layer and replensihing the fund to assist developing countires to shift to ozone-frendly technologies. Concerning energy, many countries have raised the need for more sustainable patterns of production, distribution and sonsumption. Among other actions, the European Union has proposed that Governments and the private sector be encouraged to adopt energy pricing better reflection economic and environmental costs and benefits, and to reduce and gradually eliminate subsidies, but the "Group of 77" developing countires, the United States and some others have opposed this. Proposals for intensive discussion on energy issues at a future Commission session or in an expert group have not been resolved. On transport policy, proposals as yet unresolved have called for accelerating the phase-out of leaded gosoline and for promoting guidelines for eco-friendly transport and reduced vehicle emissions, preferably within the next ten years.

How to improve eco-efficiency in energy and materials produced and consumed has been a major theme of the talks. A proposal by the European union to consider "Factor 10," a goal of ten-fold impovement in productivity in the long term, with perhaps an intermediate goal of "Factor 4," a four-fold improvement with the next two or three decades, has been left unresolved until June. Also, the need for policies that promote sustainable tourism has been raised higher on the internation at agenda for study at future sessions.

Next Review in 2002: On institutional issues, Governments have called for an enhanced role and adequate funding for a revitalized UN Environment programme. The work programme for the Commission on Sustainable Development through the year 2002 has been disussed but not completely resolved. It was agreed that the next review of the implementation of the action plan adopted at the 1994 Barbados Conference on small island developing states be held at a two-day special session of the Assembly in September 1999. To provide input from the major civil society groups involved in sustainable development, dialogue sessions were held during the April talks with representatives of business and industry, women, children and youth, farmers, trade unions, indigenous people, NGOs, sceientists and local authorities such as mayors. Each group's recommendations have been forwarded to the Commission.

Action at All Levels: Although the Government review of trends in sustainable development since 1992 shows mixed results, it also recognizes the wide-ranging activity generated by the Earth Summit process.

Internationally, legal conventions on climate change, biodiversity and desertification have entered into force, and a legal agreement on high-seas fishing has been signed. New Programmes of action have been negotiated for small island developing states and for the protection of the marnine environment from land-based activities. Considerable progress has been made towards sustainable management of all types of forests and towards a legally binding regime on chemical saftey. At the national level, some 150 countries have established commissions or similar bodies to coordinate sustainable development policies, often including representatives from business, envirionment groups and other areas of civil society. Over 1,800 local Agenda 21 plans have been adopted by cities and towns worldwide. Many civil society groups have been actively working to promote sustainable development, and major initiatives have been put forward by farmers, scientists, youth and women's groups.

UN SECRETARY-GENERAL'S ADDRESS

(The text of the address by Secretary-General Kofi Annan to the special session of the General Assembly to review implementation of Agenda 21, in New York 23 June, 1997)

"A very warm welcome to you all. I am delighted to see so many Heads of State and of Government, and so many senior officials, in this great hall today.

Your presence here is a welcome demonstration of political will. You have come because you are determined that the process begun five years ago at Rio djanerio should not falter. You are convinced that more must be done to safeguard life on our planet, today and for the generations to come.

Our task at this special session, therefore, is to turn that political will into deeds and actions. We must aim this week to set a sure course for the world community into the new millennium, on this most urgent and vital global issue. Our task is to build on what has been achieved. Our foundation, the United Nations conference on Environment and Development (UNCED) and the Rio process, is a firm foundation.

The UNCED was a landmark in the new global diplomacy. It brought together governments, non-governmental organizations and concerned individuals as never before. Its objectives, scope and focus were loftier than any previous conference, its basis of support broader and its implementing partners more varied.

The UNCED marked a conceptual breakthrough, too. It gave practical effect to the relationship between environment and development in the new concept of "sustainable development." The concept embraces the human and social dimension of sustainable development. It generated new hope that poverty and deprivation cab be attacked with greater clarity and coherence. As we review progress since UNCED, we see some signs of progress. Many countries have reported to the Commission on Sustainable Development that they have established national coordinating mechanisms for sustainable development and the implementation of Agenda 21.

All three of the Conventions- on climate change, biodiversity and combating desertification- entered into force a very short time after they were opened for signature.

This year marks the tenth anniversary of the Montreal Protocol on substances that deplete the ozone layer. Phasing out chlorofluorocarbons-CFCs- is almost complete in the industrial countries. This is an impressive achievement.

There has been notable progress in switching to renewable energy sources, such as geothermal, windpower and photovoltaic systems. The number of people with access to safe water increased by 472 million between 1990 and 1994.

But the balance sheet also has a negative side.

The United Nations Development Programme (UNDP) Human Development Report 1997 shows that more than a quarter of the developing world's people still live in absolute poverty.

There is concern that there has been virtually no progress in following up UNCED commitments for the transfer of concessional finance and environmentally sound technology to developing countries to assist them in implementing Agenda 21.

Carbon dioxide emissions continue to rise. World-wide fossil fuel consumption increased from 7,5000 million tons of oil equivalent in 1992 to 8,000 tons in 1996.

The rate of depletion of natural forests is, at last, solwing, but total forest loss continues at an unacceptable rate.

While more people have access to safe water, one third of the world's population lives in conuntries facing moderate to servere stress on water resources. Experts have calculated that, unless there are new efforts to manage global water resources, there will be a global water crisis by the year 2025.

In the world's oceans, the majority of species subject to fishing are now fully exploited, or over-exploited. We are now at, or nearing, the critical point at which overall fishing stocks- not simply single species -begin to decline.

It is vital that the Convention to Combat Desertificiation be implemented as soon as possible. Halting and reversing the march of deserts, especially in Africa, remains an urgent necessity.

The world is hoping for serious progress at December's third session of the Conference of the parties of the United Nations Framework Convention on Climate Change, to be held at Kyoto.

At stake this week is the capacity of the international system of States to act decisively in the global interest.

The United Nations Secretariat, funds and programmes, and the specialized agencies, have worked together to put new ideas, programmes and ways of work into global efforts for sustainable development. My programmes of reform in the United Nations will usher in a broader process of renewal in the United Nations. But we must go even further.

Governments and the United Nations must join with the private sector, civil society and non-governmental organizations in a new partnership. Such a partnership, based on a recognition of mutal interest and a readiness to share responsibilities, would link all global environment stakeholders in an alliance for action. Agenda 21 was unprecedented. We must act in unprecedented ways to implement it.

Failure to act now could damage our planet irreversibly, unleashing a spiral of increased hunger, deprivation, disease and squalour. Ultimately, we could face the destabilizing effects of conflict over vital natural resources.

But if we raise our sights to the well being of our planet, and of all those on it, today and in generations to come, we will not fail. We must not fail."

PROCEEDINGS OF THE SESSION

FIRST DAY

Opening the session, President of the General Assembly Ambassardor Razali Ismail of Malaysia urged delegates to strip themselves of the old excuses for not tackling effectively enough the driving forces of environmental degradation and underdevelopment.

"This special session will certainly have failed in the eyes of the world if it produces noting more than stirring rhetoric that seizes the headlines and exhortations to continue to do more,"said Mr. Razali."I challenge governments North and South to tackle the real obstacles to implementing Agenda 21."

United States: Vice President Al Gore of the United States, who welcomed the delegates on behalf of President Clinton and the American people, said that sustainable development must become a guiding principle in the 21st Century. Appealing to the international community to "roll up our sleeves," he said that the forum's task in the coming days was to chart the course for the years to come.

Brazil: President of Brazil Fernando Henrique Cardoso called on the special session to identify, objectively, the areas in which no progress had been made and recongnize that today's challenges are even greater than those of five years ago when the UN Conference on Environment and Development had convened.

"We have moved forward in the consideration of critical issues, such as climate change, biodiversity, forests,and desertification,. Progress, however,has been hindered by a lack of efficient means of implementation and financing," he noted.

Zimbabwe: Zimbabwe's president Robert Mugabe urged developed countries to honour their commitments made at Rio, noting that if financial resources were forthcoming, Africa would refrain from cuting down trees for energy and polluting water resources for lack of appropriate technologies.

"There could be no preservation of the environment amidst the massive and pandemic prevalence of poverty, ignorance and disease, "stressed President Mugabe" and these could not be eradicated in the absence of sustainable development. This organic link between environment and development was what had been woefully ignored since the Earth Summit in Rio," said President Mugabe.

Japan: In his address to the session, Prime Minister Ryutaro Hashimoto of Japan announced serveral new initiatives aimed at enhancing international cooperation in the field of sustainable development. The Comprehensive Strategy for the prvention of Global

Warming,or Green Initiative, he said, was designed to promote the efforts of developed countires in the development of energy conservation technologies, the introduction of non-fossil energy sources, the development of innovative energy and environmental technologies and worldwide preservation of forests.

As for a second initiative, Prime Minister Hashimoto said that japan would promote, for developing countries, a new plan entitled Initiatives for Sustainable Developing countries, a new plan entitled Initiatives for Sustainable Development Towards the 21st Century (ISD). The plan contains a series of measures on air and water pollution, global warming, water issues, the preservation of the natural environment and the promotion of environmental education.

Tanzania: President of Tanzania, Benjamin William Mkapa, speaking on behalf of the "Group of 77" developing countires and China, stressed that developing countries were ready and willing to implement the commitments undertaken five years ago at Rio. But he said that developed countires should reciprocate, by worlds and deeds, for the sake of their common destiny.

This Special Session should mark the beginning of a renewed spirit of global and practical partnership for sustainable development and poverty reduction measures, said the Tanzanian President. The goal could be achieved through increased official development assistance (ODA) and foreign direct investment(FDI) for financing capacity building as well as preferential and unrestricted access to the markets of the developed countries.

Netherlands: The netherlands, speaking on behalf of the European Union and associated States, called on the industrialised world to conclude a legally binding commitment in reducing the emissions of greenhouse gases. Prime Minister Wim Kok said the European Union had agreed to a phased reduction of the emissions of greenhouse gases of 15 percent below the 1990 level by the year 2010.

"We are in danger of passing thresholds beyond which serious damage will occur, some of it irreversible. And even if part of the damage would be reparable, it would be against an unnecessarily, or even unaffordably, high price. To safeguard future generations from this danger and burden, it is our duty to act now,"the Prime Minister said.

United Kingdom: Prime Minister Tony Blair on Monday said that by the year 2010 Britain would be ready to reduce carbon dioxide emissions by 20 percent below its 1990 level. in his address at Earth Summit + 5, he also said that Britain intended to share its long experience of the public and private management of forests with other countires. "Today I can announce that we intend to adopt a new Forest Standard to provide a benchmark for the regeneration of forests. It may help to provide a model for other countires. So I can also announce that Britain will be increasing its development assistance for forestry management to countries wanting to share our experience," said the Prime Minister.

Stressing that industrialized countries must work with developing nations to help combat climate change, Prime Minister blair proposed to enhance the United Kingdom's parternship with key developing countries in energy efficiency and climate change research and conservation.

Germany: Leaders of Germany, brazil, Singapore and South Africa have launched a joint initiative to protect the environment, Chancellor Helmut Kohl of the Federal Republic of Germany announced in his speech at the special session. The initiative, he said, was designed to demonstrate that the North and South could take joint action to protect the environment.

Chancellor Kohl warned that conflicts over natural resources would become ever more likely if no urgent action was taken to protect those resources.

The German leader pointed out, however, that there were also developments that gave hope, such as the use of solar power and other forms of energy. Chancellor Kohl proposed that industrialized countries should adopt the position of the Europen Union to cut the levels of the main greenhouse gases by 15 percent by the year 2010.

France: Stressing that to "attack nature is to attack mankind," President Jacques Chirac of France said that the sense of responsibility was an absolute requirement for protecting the planet. In his address to the special session he said it was presumptuous to claim that Man, through his inteligence, would always be able to repair the damage wrought in the name of progress. No one knew how to reconstitute the ozone layer, and no one knew how to correct the global warming caused by the greenhouse effect, the French President added.

Stressing the importance of water as a source of life, President Chirac said that France, with the support of the European Union, had submitted proposals to the Commission on Sustainable Development which he hoped would lead to concrete programmes and to a partnership on a world-wide scale. "let us together decide that in ten years' time, every village in the Third World, in Africa in particular, must have its own well or access to drinking water," he said, The French President also urged an early start of negotiations for the convention on forests and said that the commitments regarding the conventions on biological diversity and the fight against desertification should be finally defined.

SECOND DAY

Despite some progress over the past five years, environmental conditions at the global level are still deteriorating rapidly, the General Assembly heard on 24 June as it met for a second day of its special session to review the implementation of Agenda 21 adopted at the 1992 Earth Summit in Rio de janerio. Many speakers highlighted the decline in official development assistance (ODA) and underscored that eradication of poverty and preservantion of the environment must be the concern of all nations. There was general consent that environmental degradation of any member of the international community was a threat to all. There were also repeated calls for a re-awakening of the Rio spirit.

Ukraine: Ukraian President Leonid Kuchma called for the drafting of a universal internationl legal instrument aimed at guaranteeing global ecological security. President Kuchma said that such an instrument was needed to establish the norms of permissible ecological behaviour in the interests of the survival and prosperity of civilization in the 21st century.

Outlining various measures his Government had undertaken to harmonize national and international legislation in the sphere of ecology, President Kuchma said the implementation of such measures had been complicated by a number of factors, including the problem of Chernobyl. He said the Chernobyl disaster continued to be a substantial obstacle to attaining sustainable development in Ukraine.

Canada: Prime minister Jean Chretien of Canada told the Assembly that there was a growing global consensus that the environmental harm caused by some was a threat to all. Drawing attention to the problems of forests, Prime Minister Chretien noted that the forests of the world continued to decline at an alarming rate.

The Prime Minister said sustainable forest management was a high Canadian priority and Canada was convinced that the Special session presented a unique opportunity to achieve an international forest convention, through the creation of an intergovernmental negotiation committee. He said his government believed that a strong, legally binding agreement was the best way to ensure the international will needed to reverse the tide of deforestation.

New Zealand: New Zealand's Minister of Environment Simon Upton said there was a need to distinguish between problems that occurred globally, and problems that demanded global solutions. He told the Assembly that if environmental damage was not contained within national borders,and if national institutions would be undermined by noncompliance of others, then global solutions made sense.

Stating that the release of greenhouse gases and ozone depleting substances, marine pollution and the unsustainable exploitation of migratory fish stocks posed obvious challenges to the sustainabiity of the global commons, the Environment Minister called for legal instruments with truly global reach. "But success will be dependent upon tightly focused achievable goals," he said.

Jamaica: The effects of global warming were likely to be felt more directly by small island states, Jamaica's Minister of Environment Easton Douglas told the Assembly. He identified areas of vulnerability such as coastal areas becoming submerged; protective coral reefs being threatened, and the region being subject to more frequent and stronger hurricanes.

The sustaniable development of small island developing states was of global importance, the Environment Minister said, adding that it was more than climate change and natural disasters. "It is about the existence and survical of a particular group of States, and requires the forging of effective partnerships between peoples and governments and between developed and developing countries," he said.

Mozambique: Poverty is perhaps the single most important barrier to sustainable development, Mozambique's Minister for Coordination of Environmental Affairs Bernardo Pedro Ferraz told at the special session on 24 June. He said that the burden of external debt on poor economies of developing countries hindered their development , resulting in a vicious cycle of poverty which threatened the very continuity of life on the planet. "Poverty and environmental degradation are reciprocal. Poverty is absolutely incompatible with sound environmental protection on management," said Mr. Ferraz.

Mr. Ferraz said that Mozambique was being very successful in putting sustainability on paper in the form of policies and legislation, and in establishing appropriate institutions. He pointed out, however, that the country needed human and financial resources, means and tools for local capacity building and community empowerment in order to consolidate achievements in breaking" the vicious circle of absolute poverty." Mr. Ferrazjoined other speakers in appealing to the international community for a more effective assistance to the process of sustainable economic growth and development.

India: Saifuddin Soz, Minister of Environment and Forest, India: In Rio, the international community recognized that meeting the environmental objectives in Agenda 21 would place onerous burdents on developing countires, at considerable cost to themselves, have since inplemented local versions of Agenda 21. In India, a legislative framework is in place to implement the commitments undertaken at Rio. At the international level, progress has been less encouraging. The intergovernmental panel of forests has done commendable work, and while a convention would be premature, the panel's recommendations should be enhance. India endorses the sound management of chemicals. It is imperative that access to relevant technologies on preferential terms, as well as capacity-building, be built into any international action.

The major issue at this special session is the failure of industrialized countries to fulfil their international commitments to assist developing countires. There is an effort to erode the framework for partnership built at Rio, notably the principle of common but differentiated responsibilities, by prescribing equal obligations and liabilities on unequal players.

India will not accept a renegotiation of Agenda 21 through introduction of new issues. Some of these issues, such as labour standards or the relationship between trade and the environment, do not enjoy international consensus. It is a matter of grave concern that this forum is being used to distort the mandate of bodies such as the World Trade Organization by seeking to use environmental considerations as trade barriers. The task is to review and accelerate implementation of Agenda 21. Emphasis must be placed on time-bound commitments by industrialized countires for resource and technology transfer on non-commercial terms.

As world leaders spoke in plenary meetings of the special session, intensive debates went on in a General Assembly committee which has the task of completing the negotiations of the draft final outcome of Earth Summit + 5. That outcome would now be called the draft programme of action for further implementation of Agenda 21, according to Mustafa Tolba, the Chariman of the Ad Hoc Committee of the Whole.

The Committee of the whole, which held its first meeting on 23 June, continued to hear from observers, heads of secretariats of the various organizations dealilng with conventions related to sustainable development, representatives of United Nations programmes and organizations, international financial institutions and regional organizations.

THIRD DAY

On the thrid day of debates (25 June) the Assembly heard repeated calls for concerted international cooperation without which plans for action, no matter how far-reaching, were bound to fail. It was said that official development assistance (ODA) was declining at a time when developing countries were struggling to implement remediation programmes of afforestation, coastal zone and fisheries management, poverty alleviation and education.

Environmental restoration would require a fundamental rethinking of economic activity, the Assembly was told. Least developed countries were destroying the environment with poverty. In developed countires, where 25 percent of the world's population produced 95 percent of waste, the destruction was caused through over consumption.

The world Bank: President of the World Bank james Wolfensohn unveiled a five-point environmental plan of action, committing his institution to do "all it can to forge a global partnership to promote equitable approaches to environmental issues. "As an institution dedicated to reducing poverty, we at the Bank are more aware then ever of the continuing link between the degrading environment and the poverty afflicting so many of the world's people"; he told the special session. Outlining the five-point plan, Mr. Wolfensohn said it provided for the World Bank's contribution in the areas of climate change, biodiversity, ozone depletion, desertification and the water crisis. In all of these areas, he said, the World Bank would work in partership with others.

FOURTH DAY

All social sectors must cooperate to implement Agenda 21, speakers told the General Assembly on 26 June as it continued its debate on implementation of the recommendations of the 1992 Rio Conference on environment and development. Several speakers noted that world wide foreign investment had replaced overseas development assistance in amount and frequency. Yet foreign investment was not an appropriate replacement for overseas development assistance. Speakers also called for the institutional setting for sustainable development and global environment to be strengthened.

United States: President William Clinton of the United States has applauded the European Union for its strong focus on the issue of reducing contribution to global climate change. Addressing the special session of the Assembly, President Clinton said "we must all do out part" - industrial nations that emitted the largest quantities of greenhouse gases and developing nations whose emissions were growing rapidly. As for the United States, he said it was first necessary to convince the American people and the Congress that the climate change problem was real and imminent.

Outlining several initiatives his government had undertaken to deal with climate change and to advance sustainable development, president Clinton announced that in order to help developing nations reduce greenhouse gas emissions, the United States would provide them with $1 billion in assistance over the next five years. Those funds, he said, would, among other things, go to programmes that supported energy efficiency and the development of alternative energy sources. He also announced that the United States would continue to encourage private investment that met environmental standards, adding that "at home we must unleash more of the creative power of our people to meet the challenge of climate change."

Nigeria: Nigeria's Minister of State for Works and Housing Alhaji Abdullah Adamu stressed that appreciable efforts had been made at the national level to implement Agenda 21 in some developing countires. However, he said, for the majority of the countries, the current trend towards globaization of the world economy marginalized developing countiries in terms of performance of their respective economies. "We believe the that the issues of trade and environment, access to the markets of the developed countires, direct foreign investment, access to environmentally sound technologies on concessional and preferential terms, as well as official development assistançe, require concerted action by the international community," he said.

Malaysia: Malaysia's minister of Science, Technology and the Environmental law, Hieng Ding told the special session that the rapid globalization process threatened to overwhelm both environment and developmental goals. Noting that unbridled liberalization and globailization could have negative impacts on sustainable development, the Minister said the goal should be to devise stratgies to direct globalization towards economic, social and environmental sustainability. He said that developing countries expected that industrial countries as a whole would adhere to fixed targets of greenhouse gas emission reduction according to a time bound schedule, adding that the credibility of the Climate Change Convention had been diluted by the lack of commitment by some countries.

UNDP: Progress in the implementation of Agenda 21 has not been as rapid, or as far-reaching as had been hoped, the Administor of the UN Development Programme(UNDP) James Gustav Speth told the special session of the Assembly. He said that while there had been gains since the 1992 Rio Earth Summit, " We've also failed in many undertakings."

The head of the UN development agency said the continuing deterioration of the environment and the expanding demands to address environmental issues on an international basis under scored the need for a strong international body to facilitate the work of the national environmental authorities at the regional and global levels. He expressed the hope that UNDP's sister agency, the United Nations Environment Programme (UNEP), could be strengthened, to meet these urgent needs.

Global Environment Facility: Mohamed El-Ashry, Chairman, GEF, said that the Facility represents the first and most significant financial commitment arising from the Rio Summit. With its restructuring in 1994, the Facility now ensures universality in membership, flexibility in operations, transparency and democracy in governance, predictability in funding, as well as accessibility and non-conditionality. It has 161 participating nations and through its implementing agencies - UNDP,UNEP and the World Bank - it is at work in more than 110 countires, a clear sign of a sucessful strategic alliance between the United Nations and the Bretton Woods institutions for the purpose of global environmental management.

38

A RECESSION OF SPIRIT

Nirmala Lakshman

Five years ago, a blueprint to halt environmental decline and usher in a new era of sustainable development, was evolved at the Earth Summit in Rio de Janeiro. A few weeks ago, the United Nations special/ression of the General Assembly reviewed the progress since Rio. The 170 nations who met, felt that there has been a lot down in terms of the promises and commitment made at Rio. Poverty, environmental degradation, high resource consumption, intense social and economic inequities have driven deeper wedges between the developed and developing world.

In El Salvador, the most dangerious thing a child can do is breathe. Respiratory disease from air pollution is today the leading cause of death among children in that country. In Uganda, when forests are cleared, often with funding from the developed, would, people are shot or hurt to death in their hoes. In India in the name of development villages and valleys are submerged and thousands of people are frequently rendered homeless. In New York's manhattan, a couple of weeks ago, not far from where the heads of government were debating the earth's future, a young couple haddled together in a street corner begging for small change and food from passers by. The woman's body riddled with kaposi's sarcoma was little more than a bag of bones and the man feebly held up a placard which announced that they were both dying of AIDS. This is the age of a new globalisation. A time when viruses. Pollution, the devastation of natural resources and the spectre of unrelenting povery criss-cross diverse national boundaries. A universal sense of urgency to deal with these colossal challenges confronting an already overburdened and fragile planet forced the world's nations to come up with a plan of action at Rio de Janerio five years ago. But today there is an overwhelming sense of disappointment especially among the nations of the developing world, that there has been a let-down in terms of the promises and commitments made at the Earth Summit in Rio. The situation in terms of environmental degradation and resource consumption in most parts of the world is worse than ever before.

The review session at the United Nations General Assembly in New Yoork at the end of June called Rio Plus Five, ended in shambles with countires trading charges in terms of issues of environmental responsibility and revealing a complete inability to arrive at a consensus document or a political stament that could take the world further. With the scale and nature of environmental degradation accelerating at an alarming pace, the failure to face up to these challenges has to be laid at the door of every nation and community that continues to consume scarce resources, mindlessly adopts unsustainable developmental and economic goals and thereby contributes to the entrenchment of poverty. The threat is not only to human life but to the viability of the planet itself. Since the Earth Summit, as a World Watch document shows, human numbers have grown by roughly 450 million. An estimated 1.3 billion people are so poor that they cannot manage their basic needs and the earth's biological resources have been rapidly and irreversibly diminished.

The Earth Summit's main achievement in 1992 was that it clearly established the inextricable links between unsustainable growth patterns, environmental degradation and deepending povery.

Countries committed themselves to implementing two legally binding conventions. One to protect biological diversity and the other to deal with climate change. Conventions on desertification and high-seas fishing were also drafted. Agenda 21, the blueprint for sustainable development, was also adopted and this became the basis for many national and local plans for environmental protection. A Global Environmental Facility was set up and the developed world made a commitment of 0.7 percent of ODA in terms of assistance to the developing world for sustainable environmental projects. All these promises seemed to herald the emergence of a new transnational ethic where nations would work together to ensure sustainability for future generations. Unforunately, as the last five years have demonstrated, it did not quite work that way.

However, it must be pointed out that one of the triumphs of the Rio Earth Summit was that it brought to centre-stage the whole issue of environment and sustainable development. Before this, it was largely viewed as the esoteric concern of a privileged few and its critical links to poverty and the quality of human life were neither clearly pursued nor understood. The world-wide attention and debate that was generated at Rio in 1992 did much to change all this. The consequences of unsustainable growth and resource-diminishing consumption patterns adopted by a small minority of the world's population in contrast to the needs and predicament of a vast number were made abundantly clear.

The Rio enthusiasm translated into international agreements that chalked in impressive goals, but little of this became actual public policy within nations, and much less could be transferred to the realms of international policy especially in areas such as aid and trade. Further, there are countries like the United States which not only refused to ratify the Biodiversity Convention, but also failed to meet their commitments with regard to critical issues like energy saving and consumption. The parochialiism that has crept into the developed world's perceptions over recent years has had a nagative impact on issues like funding, resources and technology transfer. This has also been fuelled by a growing dominance of the private sectors in those countires many of whom are making business forays into the developing world. There is therefore little interest or inclination in keeping long term sustainability or environmental costs in the planning and implementation of economic activities both globally and sometimes even within countries, although a discernible watchdog element has emerged recently in some communities when local projects are planned or executed.

In the last five years in spite of the efforts of the Rio Summit, the big picture has not changed much and what is worrying is that there has been a deterioraton in some critical spheres. For instance, 20 percent of the world's population still consume 80 percent of its resources, and higher consumption lifestyles are also obviously growing in many developing countries. United Nations statistics reveal that although food production is increasing, acute poverty is also intense and more than 800 million people suffer from hunger and malnutrition. Further, the use of pesticides and poor farming methods have caused the degradation of 300 million hectares of farmland worldwide and one quarter of the earth's surface has been affected by desertificaation. In the area of biodiversity, species extinction and habitat loss are growing alarmingly and continue is spite of various post-Rio efforts. More than 50,000plant and animal species are expected to be lost each year. Global emissions of carbon dioxide and other greenhouse gases are rising and polluting fuel emissions are also on the increase. The U.S. is a notable polluter in this regard. Energy consumption is also expected to more than double over the next few decades, and the transfer of environmentally firendly technology to the developing world has been minimal or market driven.

A clearly negative trend commented upon by almost every speaker at the Rio Plus Five summit, was the fact that official development assistance has declined considerably since 1992, from 0.34 percent of donor GNP in that year to 0.27 percent which is a farcry from the 0.7 percent committed at Rio. Rising debt amd trade terms which are far from eqitable add to the crisis with gloabal business moving on its own momentum, and private investors looking for new pastures in the developing world entirely on their own terms. It is not merely a question of industries and businesses that degrade local environments but also those that are positively hazardous and polluting in terms of their often disastrous impact on communities. The most pernicious of all as Prof. M.S.Swaminathan, eminent scientist and environmentalist points out, is the tobacco industry which faced with growing regulatory pressures from multi-million dollar class action law suits and stagnating markets in countreis like the U.S. are aggressively moving to capture markets in Estern Europe and in the developing world.

Therefore what the Rio Plus Five meet witnessed was in effect what the conference president Razali Ismail described as a "major recession-not economic but a recession of spirit" as the 170 countries failed to generate the political will at the level of international co-operation to carry forward in concrete terms the enthusiasm and commitment of five years ago. Although extremely sobering, there are perhaps several lessions in this. One is the realisation that international agrements on issues relating to sustainability and environmental degradation are tied up in an increasingly complex way with issues like international aid and trade. As martin Khor of the Third World Network pointed out in a dialougue at one of the NGO sessions, there is now a new kind of globalisation with the U.N.'s role being steadily eroded by free trade and trade walls. "The World Bank and the WTO are taking decisions within nations and new conditionalities are likely to occur" he said, emphasing that the rules of world trade have become so harsh that they dominate the globalisation process. He felt however that the Bank has now realised that structural adjustment policies have had a deleterious impact on societies and is currently re-examining its approach and strategies. Market forces have become so powerful that the feeling among serveral NGO group was that the State cannot ignore its responsibilities, especially in the case of societies which have large groups of the disadvantaged and the marginalised.

Secondly, it is clear that environmental issues at many local and national levels are bound up with issues of poverty, sustainable livelihoods, economic growth, questions of equity, and community participation. The lack of horizontal linkages in planning and implementing of programmes in these areas is a tremendous problem in a country like India, says Prof. M.S.Swaminathan." India is data and resource rich but poor in terms of action" he said in a conversation with *The Hindu* before the Rio Plus Five meeting. He stressed for the need to develop "sustainable options" and promote an "ecology of hope" that would take into account the special vulnerabilities of local communities such as those in the North East for example, where the sense of injustice and inequity is palpable.

The difficulties of putting together a consensus document or political statement at the end of the meeting in many ways represented a far more honest approach to the complex problems of countires implementing their environmental agendas in the current international context.

At a press conference at the end of the meeting, the president of the Session Razali Ismail conceded that the sense of being aggrieved among many developing nations, as well as the sharp divisions within the developed world on issues of environmental responsibilities including finance, technology transfer and binding targets for emissions were the road-blocks to cobbling a consensus. As Ismail put it: "Let us call a spade a spade. When over five years there obviously have not been enough things done, then in that context the impasse that came out of the political statement reflected that. "While the final statement that emerged after protracted negotiations merely reaffirmed the Rio principles most specially Agenda 21, it also embodied much more realistic assessment of what has been achieved and what could still be possible.North-South divide remined as sharp as ever especially in terms of prioritising issues such as poverty, technology transfer, finance, forests and carbon dioxide emissions.

The pro-poor environmental rhetoric was spouted fiathfully not only by the developing nations but by the developed world in their plenary statements but with little evidence of specific national or international strategies in this regard. With perhaps the exception of the U.K. and one or two other European governments that made specific statements about increasing aid to the poorest nations as an essential part of their commitment to global sustainability, the essential preoccupation with a northern environmental agenda was very obvious. For instance, climate change, global warming and the Kyoto Conference in December this year where it is hoped that legally binding targets for emissions will be set, generated a lot more debate than the fact of the deepening divide between the rich world and the poor.

Interestingly, the meeting also revealed a certain ennui with rhetoric and phraseology. The need for specifics in terms of finance and other pollution targets was reiterated by many governments. The Europen challenge to U.S.the world's biggest polluter, was most potently evident in the British Prime Minister Tony Blair's address to the plenary where he called for a backing of the EU's proposal to cut carbond dioxide and other greenhouse gas emissions by 15 percent below 1990 levels with a deadline of the 2010. The German Chancellor Helmut Kohl also made a strong plea for an action plan at the end of the summit to "achieve concrete progress on key issues" and joined hands with three other nations-Brazil, Singapore and South Africa in a new environmental partnership.

India's statement at the plenary delivered by the Environment Minister Saifuddin Soz underlined its "non-presence" at the summit. Beyond issuing a stern warning on the "non-negotiability" of Agenda 21, Mr.Soz said that India had taken major steps to meet its environmental commitments, unlike many other industrialised countries. The bland and completely lacklustre approch to the crucial environment and development issues confronting the country typified what environmentalists Anil Agarwal and Sunita Narain have described as "the governmentalisation of the green agenda". In a international arena where certain very specific northern environmental priorities such as the issue of climate change or forests are pushed with specious arguments, the Indian contingent's failure to tackle the challenges of environmental priorities in the global context keeping in view the enormous complexity of the problem within the country, bodes ill for the future of sustainable development in India. The Worldwatch Institute lists India as one of the eight environmental heavyweights who shape global trends in terms of certain parameters such as economic strength, material consumption, population, rapid economic develpment, natural resources as well as in terms of pollution. These countries are expected to have the greatest impact on the sustainable future of the planet.

The way forward in a country like India is perhaps to move out of the existing bureaucratisation of critical environmental and development issues to what leading environmentalist professor Madhav Gadgil calls "a new paradigm". The growing number of local initiatives at the grassroots that have challenged imbalances and inequities is perhaps a movement in the right direction.

Writing in *The Hindu* recently, Prof. Gadgil said that positive decision on environmental issues at the local level can only emerge through a process of "informed decision making". He said "easy availability of information is now empowering people to demand their due share of involvement in the decision making process.. We must once and for all abandon the bureaucratic culture of control and command and embrace a new democratic culture of share and inform. Only then can we hope to vanquish the forces of environmental destruction that have been gathering strength over these 50 years.."

Nine environmental heavyweights

Country	Share of World population 1996 (Percent)	Share of Gross World Product 1994 (Percent)	Share of World Carbon Emissions 1995 (Percent)	Share of World Forest Area 1990 (Precent)	Share of World Flowering Plant Species, 1990 (Percent)
China	21.1	2.4	13.3	3.9	12
India	16.5	1.1	3.8	1.9	6
USA	4.6	26.1	22.9	6.1	8
Indonesia	3.5	0.7	0.9	3.4	8
Brazil	2.8	2.1	1.0	16.4	22
Russia	2.6	1.5	7.2	21.9	9
Japan	2.2	16.8	5.0	0.7	2
Germany	1.4	8.1	3.8	0.3	1
South Africa	0.8	0.5	1.5	0.2	1
E-9Total	55.4	59.3	59.4	54.8	--

Source: State of the World 1997

It is also perhaps the momentum of these kind of small initiatives and local environmental activism in india and in other parts of the world that will ultimately create the new transnational ecological ethic. The Rio Plus Five summit in many ways reflected sharply the ground realities which the global community has to deal with. While political consensus at the international level could not be forged, there was evidence of the partnership of civil societies where the media, the NGO and other democratic forces including marginalised groups such as poor women could play a crucial role. Perhaps this is where the real hope for the earth's sustainable future lies.

39

YET ANOTHER ENVIRONMENT DAY

Kalpana Sharma

Environment days, weeks and years will come and go but in the long-term, only a combination of pressure from below and a demonstrable political will at the top can give any meaning to the environmental rhetoric generated at Rio.

June is environmentally important. It not only heralds the onset of monsoon, there by determining health of the economy for the rest of the year but it is also the month when the ritual of paying obeisance to environmental concerns is routinely observed. The critical word is "rountine". for june 5 World Environment Day seems to be gradually losing any meaning.

This became particularly apparent this June as the World community plans to observe another anniversary five years since the Earth Summit held at Rio de Janeiro, Brazil,in 1992. At this U.N. Conference on Environment and Development (UNCED), the nations of the world met and acknowledged that economic develpment without factoring in environmental concerns was unsustainable.

An extensive programme of action,in the form of Agenda 21, was drawn up after a protracted debate over every word and comma. Two important conventions, on biodiversity and on climate change, were signed by the majority of the countries present. These two documents accepted the need to conserve biological diversity in all its forms for the sake of the future of the planet and also agreed that lifestyles needed to change in many parts of the world to restrict the releases of greenhouse gases and global warming.

Where do all these concerns stand five years hence? For the last few months, meetings have been held to prepare the documentation for a special session of the U.N.General Assembly scheduled for June 23-27. It will assess the five years after Rio and suggest what more should be done to continue on the path set out at that conference.

But well before the session begins, there is already a sense of pessimism. What is termed Rio Plus Five in international jargon has already been called Rio Minus Five by some, Non-government organisations argue that far from moving ahead, the world seems to have regressed in terms of environmental consciousness in the post-Rio period.

Much of this has to do with the nature of economic change taking place in rich and poor countires. With the market mantra, privatisation, liberaisation and globalisation becoming the catch phrases among economic planners in most of the developing world, words of caution about the speed or type of development are considered obstructionist. Our own former Prime Minister, Mr. H.D.Deve Gowda, reflected this attitude when he chided environmentalists for blocking development. Hearing his remarks, one could not help but wonder whether he was aware that India had supported the concept of "sustainable development". at Rio.

Another reason the Rio Plus Five fails to generate much interest, unlike as the Earth Summit,is the growing disillusionment in the world community with the U.N. system. In the last five years, the U.N. has faced one of its most serious crises. In the post-Rio follow-up, this was reflected in the low-key and undynamic performance of the Commission for Sustainable Development (CSD), set up to see through the implementation of Agenda 21. The CSD suffered for lack of funds and backing and has essentially limped along in thelast five years without making any memorable intervention.

These five years have also been marked by donor fatigue. The funds that the U.N. hoped would be generated to implement the provisions of Agenda 21 are just not there. Bilateral and multilateral donors have spread their funding over various areas and environmental programmes are not receiving as much as was expected.

Another shift that has taken place in the last years and wich is only just being acknoledged is the increasing role that private investors are playing in developing infrastructure in many poorer countires. Five years ago at Rio, the private sector did not receive so much attention. The large environmental movements were focussed on projects funded by the World Bank of other multilateral funding agencies.

Today, the strongest environmental movements in many countries are focussed on projects where the private sector is the major player. Just last week, women protesting against the patern of development of the Konkan region,including the location of the Enron power plant and the expanding chemical belt, were beaten up by local police in Raigad district, Maharashtra, Ms. Medha patkar of the Narmada Bachao Andolan (NBA) took the opportunity of the Prime Minister, Mr.I.K. Gujral's visit to Mumbai to p4ersonally register her concern at the attitude of the authorities to peaceful demonstrations of this kind.

Will the Governments of developing countries, anxious to attract foreign private investment, be willing to lay down strict environmental conditions? Given the performance of the governments including ours, in recent years, it is unlikely. The question in this post-Rio follow-up is whether the world community can put some pressure on the private sector as it increasingly moves out from the industrialised world to the developing world. Will Governments in the north be willing to publish their own industries for polluting other parts of the world with the same determination as they are anxious to punish poor countires for cutting down forests or using child labour?

The Rio conference drew attention to the fact that the profligate lifestyle of industrialised countries had done more to harm the global environment than the destruction of the natural environment in poor countries to make way for infrastructure and other needs. After considerable and predictable resistance, this point was incorporated in many of the documents. But in just the area of climate change and restricting the release of greenhouse gases, it is evident that not enough is being done in the North to effect a change in lifestyles.

Although a commitment was made to restrict the emission of carbon dioxide (Co_2), one of the greenhouse gases, to the 1990 levels by the year 2000, CO_2 emission levels have increased by five percent in the industrialised countries and will continue to rise till the year 2000. In sum, the debates at the U.N.General Assembly's special session are unlikely to be differnt from what occureed at Rio. While the poorer countires will confinue to demand funds and also a change in the North's lifestyle, the latter will press for punitive measures to restrict the poor countries from depleting their natural resources.

While on international fora countries such as India are perfectly justified in drawing attention to lifestyle issues in the North, these five years have shown that domestically, we need to also look at the wasteful use of resources by the "North" within our country. Even the pretence of encouraging alternative lifestyles, energy conserving methods, water conservation and less energy-intensive building styles has been abandoned as urban India heads full-scale into the same pattern of resource use that has landed the planet in the current dilemma. Whatever happened to solar cookers, solar heaters, wind power and recycling water for saving energy? Read the newspapers, look at the advertisements or speak to people in the building industry not even a passing thought is being given to these concepts.

In the globalised consumer economy that we have so wholehertedly embraced, such ideas will never be accepted until they come back to us from the North, for instance, the Indian tiffin-box, made from aluminium or stainless steel, is begining to find favour with parents in the U.K. who are environmentally conscious and want to discourage the use of plastic. But in India, millions of school-children are abandoning this practical and sturdy invention for flimsy, though colourful, plastic models.

The one positive difference visible in the last five years is the recognition by the U.N.that non-government organistions and civil society have an important role in ensuring that international agreements and conventions are followed. At the Earth Summit, although the NGOs did have a presence, they could not intervene directly and had a sideshow. Today, they are participating directly in the process although some of them have argued that this is a waste of their time and resources and is deflecting attention from more radical actions that they ought to be taking.

Regardless of the difference of opinion, it is evident that what little has been achieved in areas such as conservation or women's rights or human rights is because of this kind of pressure generated from below on individual governments and on international organistions such as the U.N. Environment days, weeks and years will come and go but in the long-term only a combination of such pressure from below and a demonstrable political will at the top can give any meaning to the environmental rhetoric generated at Rio.

40

ENVIRONMENTAL CITIZENSHIP

The concept of Environmental Citizenship encapsultes many strands of how UNEP and other information outlets have been engaging the public in the organization's work.

The essence of environmental citizenship is mobilization of civil society, through education in the broadest sense of the word. Public education and information activities are an important instrument for improving general environmental literacy and a means to unleashing energy and creativity of people in their communities around the world.

The global environmental citizenship programme seeks to assert the ethical obligations of different sectors of society needed to protect life on Earth. One of the fundamental prerequisties for the achievement of sustainable development is broad public participation in decision-making. This commitment and genuine involvement of all social groups advocated in Agenda 21 can only be assured with the careful targeting of different satakeholders in society so that they consciously try to live sustainably in their daily, normal existance. In this regard, therefore, environmental citizenship is simply the idea that people and their organizations have a responsibility to conserve the environment.

The tools for inculcating environmental citizenship include special information packages, features, news releases, exhibits, publications and regular contact with the media and governments. Special compaigns like the Clean Up the World Campaign, special events like the World Environment Day, awards like the Global 500 prize, audio-visual productions and photographic competions, conferences and workshops, manuals, booklets and magazines aim at alerting people to environmental issues and to stimulate community and non-governmental action.

The cornerstone of UNEP's environmental citizenship programme is partnerships with international, regional, national, local and community-based organizations. These organizations non-governmental organizations, women's,youth, religious and consumer groups and service clubs, to name a few- have a great multiplier effect as they communicate with their memberships and constituencies on a regular basis. The role of these partners is, in addition to serving as effective channels for communicating with their constituencies, to shape UNEP's output and to make it relevant and responsive to real needs and requirements of users.

Behaviour change is the ultimate goal of UNEP's global environmental citizenship programme. We will achieve this through an alliance of partners including consumers organization and especially the media to work towarads UNEP's mission as the world's body for catalytic environmental action.

PURPOSE OF STRATEGY

An Environmental Information and Communication Strategy for Asia Pacific (1995-2000) was first mooted in November, 1994. It aimed to provide a framework for UNEP and its partners inthe region to build an integrated, proactive, responsive and longterm environmental communications system in the Asia Pacific region to;

* Assess, investigate, disseminate and exchange information with and amongst its main user groups

* Educate and raise awareness about the four critical environmental issues of:

  1. Sustainable management and use of natural resources
  2. Sustainable production and consumption
  3. Improved environmental health and human well-being
  4. Global economic trends and the environment.

* Enhance collaboration and cooperation on multi-sectoral projects (efforts);

* Influence the adoption of the principle of Agenda 21 in policy making by governments, organizations and peoples throughout the region.

By first analysing the information needs of its main user groups, then matching these to UNEP-ROAP's and other existing services and current capabilities, the Strategy has indentified opportunities for refocusing, strengthening and expanding UNEP's information products and services in the region with the assistance of its partenrs. The Strategy is also designed to be a fund-raising tool for financing environmental projects and a source book for Governments, NGO's and the media to develop their own ideas for environmental action.

These communication and information opportunities form the basis for the Action Plans which are the Strategys main outcomes and which will enable UNEP to fulfill its role as the catalyst for responsible environmentaal citizenship in the Asia-Pacific region in the coming years.

PARTNERS AND THEIR NEEDS

The target groups for the Environmental Information and Communication Strategy for Asia-Pacific (1995-2000) are the prime users of environmental information in the Asia-Pacific region:

Subgroups: Federal, State, Local, IGOs Development Banks, Information Focal Points

Needs: Accurate, accessible environmental information and materials, Technical advice and expertise, Clear understanding about UNEP/ROAP's services

Subgroups: UNEP HEADQUARTERS, HABITAT, ESCAP, UNDP, UNESCO, UNICEF, FAO, UNEP, ILO, ETC.

Needs: Accessible, accurate, current information on the environment and projects, Timely, technical environmental information to support their programmes Information exchange on coordinated public awareness activities Regular updates on UNEP's programmes Guidelines for joint projets

Subgroups: Environment Liasion Centre Internation (ELCI), NGOs dealing with the Environment Sustainable Development Community and social Development

Needs: Imporved information access and delivery, Traiing and researach, Information dealing causes and solutions not only effects, Interactive communication, Support for MEDIA collaboration, Support to education communication activities to create awareness among various target groups, Promotion of inter-organizational collaboration among NGOs dealing with environment and sustainable development, Promotion of transnational cooperation among children and youth of South East Asian countries through appropriate education and communication projects

Subgroups: Multinationals, Large Corporations, small Corporations, Universities/MBA programmes, manufacturers associations, chambers of commerce and industry

Needs: User guidelines for cleaner producation and sustainable business practices Expertise in implementing guidelines Economic data linking short-terms cost of producation to long-term cost to environment User friendly, easily accessed information from UNEP/ROAP environment data-bank.

Subgroups: Newspapers Journalists, National and community Radio Stations, TV stations,. cable channels, Film, Coomercial producers, Print, Radio, billboard Advertising.

Needs: Accessible, accurate, timely environmental information Access to a directory,database, and updated information Categorization of information by subject and source for maximum user friendliness Information center and focus point in each country Clipping service, media watch (or access to current clipping service) Training and education.

Subgroups: Students (school and University),Academicians, Scientists, Ordinary citizens interested in acquiring UNEP/ROAP's environmental information.

Needs: User friendly access to environmental information Proactive approach in mobilising environmental projects Support for organizations institutions with direct access to target groups undertaking green projects.

Subgroups: Staff as providers and users of environmental information such as seminars, etc.

Needs: Awareness and knowledge of all the organization's products and services Skills for accessing and disseminating this information Clear procedures for referring enquries

UNEP'S CURRENT CAPABILITIES

RESPONDING TO GOVERNMENT AND IGOS

Strengths

- Regular contact with government focal points through mail, faxes, and meetings
- Technical assistance
- Cooperation on public awareness events - World Environment Day, Clean up the World, etc.
- Workshops to meet and train national Focal Points
- Ability to network
- Ability to provide governments with environmental information on request
- Government needs assessment programme underway.

Needs

- More effective method of dealing with government information 'gate-keepers'
- Improved Government response to environmental activities
- Better avenues to reach local gocernment level
- More information officers in sub-regions

- Additional funding needed to achieve these goals
- Multi-sectoral training programmes in all aspects of environmental communication-presentation, skills; media relations, writing and publishing know-how
- Encouragement of environment-related career development and opportunities

RESPONDING TO UN AGENCIES

Strengths

- Regular meetings to coordinate UN environmental activities
- Joint programming exercises
- Joint information campaigns -World Water Day, Biodiversity Day, UN 50th Anniversary
- News letters
- Close working relationship with Department of Public Information, UN, New York and United Nations Information Centres (UNICs) in the region

Needs

- Guidelines for cooperative projects - "Working together for a United World"
- Expanded involvement of other agaencies in environmental activities such as World Environment Day
- Closer links with Nairobi Information Centre, and UNEP'S Regional Office about information activities "to eliminate duplication and provide more effective collaboration"
- Compilation of successful (case) studies on environment sourced from regional and global services

RESPONDING TO NGOS

Strengths

- Working through Environment Liaison Centre Internationl (ELCI) to disseminate NGO information
- Youth advisors inform UNEP about the regional concerns of young people saperate link Infoterra service
- Collaboration with NGOs on community development

projects/programmes
- Global 500 Roll of Honour for Environmental Achievement
- UNEP Sasakawa Environment Prize
- Free Publication and Television Trust for the Environment (TVE) films upon request (user supplies blank tape)
- Clean and green Earth manual (UNEP Publication for NGOs)
- Joint UNEP-NGO Projects in environmental education and communication
- Networks

Needs

- More user-friendly distribution and delivery of information
- Improved contacts with NGOs through their umbrella organizations to focus information on causes and solutions rather then only on effects and emergencies
- Improved relationships with information gets through to NGOs and the public
- More funding to support worthwhile NGO Projects
- More systematic, accurate procedure for answering NGO enquiries
- Expanded library products and services
- Wider disseminiation of practical infomation to reach children, youth and indigenous people through NGO and related programmes
- Larger youth network and more youth representation in UNEP process
- An NGO desk in local resource centers

RESPONDING TO THE PRIVATE SECTOR

Strengths

- Access to services of Paris-based UNEP's Industry Environemnt Office(IEO) including cleaner production guidelines, eco-tourism guidelines, Awareness Preparedness for Emergencies at Local Level (APPELL) service and publications
- Public awareness workshops
- Global 500 Award system includes environmentally sen-

sitive business people and industrialists
- mechanisms for handling or directing specific enquiries on environmental impacts
- Networking system with internation Chambers of Commerce

Needs

- Clear messages from UNEP to industry with data cor relating long-term profitability with environmental responsibility
- Corporate economic data to highlight need to cost environmental impact in production process (including successful studies)
- More collaboration and joint sponsorship on programmes of awareness and action
- Mechanisms to reach mid-level and smaller companies
- Collaboration with business schools on curricula for corporate environmental responsibility
- Training programmes on the role of environmental responsibility in corporate decision-making
- Dissemination of information on low-cost environmental equipment and technology

RESPONDING TO MEDIA

Strengths

- Media information products and on-line services such as Infoterra
- Press releases and features on UNEP regional international meeting and key issues
- Dissemination of UN Department of Public Information (UN/DPI) information products and services
- Educational teaching aid packages like Outreach (covers over 100 environmental topics)
- Educational radio spots and programmes, TVE programmes
- Journalists training workshops
- Fellowships for young Journalists
- Environment and Media Handbook
- Writing contests on issues like eco-tourism

- Extensive library and materials, including reports and sourcebooks
- UNEP Information Centre in Nairobi
- United Nations information Service, UN/ESCAP
- Free English-language radio/TV spots
- Query Response Service
- Newsletters on programmes services
- Backgrounders to issues

Needs

- More training and education of journalists on investigative and responsible environmental reporting
- More radio programmes
- Efficient electronic information linkages -full installation UNEPNET and UNEP on line facilities
- Additional and more user-friendly library services/products (both literature and on line information) directed to media
- Subject-categorized material and solution-base information
- Utilise more innovative ways of communicating environmental issues such as TV, radio, video, billboard and cumputer graphics rather than only print
- Proactive assessment and dissemination of information on environmental trends
- Translation into UN languages for radio/TV spots TV talk shows
- Environmental action lines on TV/Radio
- Environmental Columns/Feature corners in print media
- NGO/Media Directory (completed)
- "Media Environment Watch"
- Jouralists'exchange programme
- Establishment of a Center for Science and Environmental Journalism
- A commercial environment magazine (run by Asia Pacific Forum for Environment Journalists (AFEJ and suppoted by UNEP)

RESPONDING TO CITIZENS

Strengths

- Mass media, NGO and government channels to reach the ordinary citizen
- Public enquiry service (environmental information centres)
- Infoterra network and source registration
- Network for Environmental Training at Tertiary Level in Asia-Pacific Newsletter(NETTLAP)
- Focus on Your World photo exhibition and competion open to citizens worldwide
- Clean and Green Earth Manual
- Agreement with International Olympic Council (IOC) to promote sportas and environment

Needs

- Accurate, systematic way of answering enquiries
- Proactive approach to involve citizens in environmental projects
- Improved awareness and use of infoterra service and Environmental Assessment Programme for Asia and the Pacific
- Public seminars and wrokshops on initiating environmental action in the home and the community
- Promote sports and environment in Regional events

RESPONDING TO AND ENHANCING EFFECTIVENESS OF STAFF

Strengths

- Hardworking, knowledgeable staff
- Staff access to existing library and materials
- Program-oriented approach shifting to results-focus

Needs

- Expanded information skills training
- Input from daily environmental clippings
- More strategic versus institutional approach to communications to optimise responsiveness
- More partnership projects to share responsibilities

CAPABILITY ANALYSIS AND CONCLUSIONS

UNEP's Regional Office for Asia and the Pacific (ROAP) current capabilities present clear opprotunities for refocusing, strengthening and expanding its role as the prime resource and service for accurate and credible environmental information to guide decision making throughout the Asia-Pacific region in the coming decade. Here is a look at what its services are.

CURRENT INFORMATION PRODUCTS AND SERVICES

UNEP—ROAP programmes and areas of focus:

* NIEM (Network for Industrial Management) Deals specifically with pulp and paper industry, ozone depletion, acciednt prevention and cleaner production in Asia-Pacific

* The Project on Assistance Concerning CFC Use and Its Control in Developing Countries Helps developing countries eliminate substances which deplete the ozone layer

* Safe Handling and Use of Pesticides and Household Chemicals Workshops to train leaders of women's groups on the effects and dangers of pesticides and chemicals. Promotes organic farming and user of organic (bio-base) fertilizers and products NETTLAP (Network for Environmental Training at Tertiary level in the Asia-Pacific Region) Empowers tertiary institutions in the region with environmental iformation on such subjects as: toxic chemicals and hazardous waste management, environmental economics, and coastal zone management

* RCU/EAS (Regional Coordinating Unit for East Asian Seas) Serves as the implementing arm for the East Asian Seas Actions Planfor the portection and sustainable development of the marine environment and coastal areas of Asia and the Pacific

* UNEP/EAP-AP (Environmental Assessement Programme for Asia and the Pacific) Provides institutional capacity building and servicing, information management, data harmonization and dissemination, and assessment at the regional and sectoral levels

* Law Provides legal and institutional advice, information and material for development and implementation of environmental agreements, national legislation for sustainable development and further strengthening the teaching of environmental law in universities and other institutions

* Habitat (the United Nations Center for Human Settlements/UNCHS) Serves as an outreach facility for urban development and shelter support programmes in Asia-Pacific.

UNEP/HABITAT INFORMATION SERVICES ROAP PUBLICATIONS

* Economic and social Commission for Asia and pacific (ESCAP)-UNEP Asia Pacific Environment Newsletter

* Towards Environmental Citizenship -UNEP/ROAP Profile

* Access Newsletter on Environment and Media for UNEP's journalism trainees

* Asian Mass Communication Bulletin (AMCB) - six UNEP supplements annually

* Periodic Press Releases and Information backgrounders

* Technical reports

* NETTLAP, NIEM and OZONET Newsletters

* Environment and Media Handbook

* The Environment is Your Business Too-information Services pamphlet

* UN Asia Pacific newsletter

* Technical and meeting reports

* Habitat's newsletters, press releases

* Youth newsletter

* UN Information Services and

* UN information Centres help

* UNEP disseminate environment news

* Let's Protect Our Seas-Guidelines for Youth Participation and Action (East Asian Seas Regional Coordinating Unit)

* Taking Action, an Environmental Guide for you and Your Community

SOON TO BE PUBLISHED

* Asia-Pacific Water problem and Solution Handbook. Joint Programme between UNEP and AMIC (Asian Mass Communication and Research Institute)

* Tourism Backgrounder (AFEJ-UNEP)

UNEP/ROAP'S AUDIOVISUAL MATERIALS

* Environmental videos produced by UNEP through TVE

* Radio scripts

* Radio tapes

DATABASES AND NETWORKS

* INFOTERRA - One of the most comprehensive environmental resource network systems available which facilitates the exchange of scientific and technical information. Links over 6.800 national and international institutions, NGOs, industrial and commercial enter-

prises, academics, and experts from around the world. Can be accessed from any personal computer through the INTERNET

* NETTLAP- refer to programmes

* EAP - refer to programmes UNEPNET (TES)- Telecommunications and Electronic Services. Aims to be established by the year 2000 to link all UNEP offices by satellite communications, allow for retrieval of large graphic files, provide sphisticated uploading down loading facilities, set up nodes in all regional offices, provide UNEP information in all its libraries (by Unit and subject), and provide teleconferencing, dial-out and fax facilities

* Mediascan - In-house, on-line environmental clipping service

* UNEP/EAP-AP -refer to programmmes

WORKSHOPS AND TRAINING COURSES

* UNEP Workshop/Attachment Programme for Government Officials to learn about UNEP's programmes and services

* Training/Attachment Programme for indigenous journalists in five Asia-Pacific countires (Joint programme with Inter-press Service)

* Traning Fellowships for young journalists (Joint programme with the Asia-Pacific Forum for Environmental Journalists and Worldview Foundation International)

* Workshops for Government Information Officers to test UNEP Communication and Information Strategy

* Oneday media workshops (Organized in 1995 - Bejijing, Kathmandu, New Delhi and Colombo)

* Support for training in Journalism

FELLOWSHIPS AND GRANTS

* Fellowships and Grants for young environmental journalists

MEDIA COLLABORATION PARTNERS AND PROJECTS

* AMIC and AFEJ joint projects
* Worldview International Foundation (Thailand) - environmental radio spots and programmes
* South Asia Cooperative Environment Programme (Sri Lanka) joint publications, children's books
* Asia Pacific Institute for Broadcasting Development (AIBD)-collaboration on radio training in desertification, environment and health
* Video Resource Centres for effective distribution of films

SPECIAL EVENTS

* World Environment Day (June 5)
* Clean-Up the World Campaign (September)
* Focus On Your World Photo Exhibition -for exhibitions throughout the region
* Global 500 Forum Conferences
* Global Youth Forum
* G-500 Youth Awards
* International Children's Conference

* Biodiversity, Water Day
* Press Club Seminars
* Journalists conferences (local, regional, internation)
* Talk shows

CONTESTS

Eco-Tourism Writing Competition

Focus On *Your World Photo* Competition -open to citizens world-wide

Viceroy Environment programme and Writing Competition

Painting Competition

UNEP'S FOCUS ON TELECOMMUNICATIONS

Contribution to the development and installation of MERCURE and the UNEPnet.

UNEPnet

The UNEP international environmental internet (the "green global lane")

Developed by UNEP

Using cost-effective modern data communications

Designed to better meet the needs of developing countries for timely and comprehensive environmental information

UNEPNET-OBJECTIVES

The backbone of UNEPnet is a satellite-based communications system called MERCURE. The MARCURE Project will result in an initial array of sixteen gound antenna stations around the world, communicating through "intelsat" satellites located over the Indian and Atlantic Oceans. This will allow UNEP Headquarters and Regional Offices, national environment agencies and scientific partners to exchange documents, environmental data, image and messages economically, rapidly, easily and reliably, The MERCURE system will provide long-term flexibility by servicing users in hundreds fo countries. MERCURE is donated to UNEP by member states of the European Space Agency (ESA).

UNEP/GRID-Arendal is acting as the technical coordinator in the implementation of this unique environmental internet network which will be operational in 1996. As shown below, one of the 7.3 m parabola antennas will be located at UNEP/GRID-arendal. This antenna has been funded by the Norwegian Ministry of Environment and UNEP/GRID-Arendal.

The objective of this unique environmental internet network is to enhance access to environmental information products from UNEP and other sources. This will give national and international policy-makers and the public access to the most up-to-date environmental information. Research institutions, involved in a range of environmental issues, will now be able to link together through UNEPnet.

ACTION PLANS

The following section "Action Plan" for various sectors is based on the UNEP's internal communication strategy and it is used here as an example to illustrate how projects, outreach efforts may be planned.

ACTION PLAN FOR NGOs

GOAL

To provide NGOs with timely, accurate and user-friendly environmental information

Key action areas:

1. Establish an effective system for proactively supplying NGOs with critical information and responding to their requests

2. Identify fund-rasing opportunities to support NGO projects

3. Offer information in both solution-based and message format

4. Develop effective projects for youth using UNEP's Youth Advisors in the region

DESIRED RESULTS

Short-term

* Stock and organize library with materials offering solution-based information related to needs of indigenous people in Asia Pacific children and the environment

* Expand outreach with NGOs, community, and service organizations

Long-term

* Establish information focal point networks

* Contact UNEP-ROAP for all environmental materials Plan larger projects with NGOs

ACTION PLAN FOR MEDIA

GOAL

To provide current, accurate and accessible environmental information and training to media

Key action areas:

1. Provide timely, accurate and investigative information on environmental problems with emphasis on actions and solutions

2. Utilise new and innovative ways of working with the media to draw public attention to environmental issues

3. Identify media partners in each major city

DESIRED RESULTS

Short-term

* Stock library with solution-based information and all UNEP publications

* Publicise environmentally-sound innovative technology or method the organization has implemented

Long-term

* Develop a programme of innovative communications sponsored by and in collaboration with media or advertising agencies

* Media Directory of Environmental Specialists

ACTION PLAN FOR CITIZENS

GOAL

To encourage environmental citizenship among the people of Asia and the Pacific.

Key action areas

1. Organize competitions (i.e.art,photo,etc.)with the environment as the theme

2. Organize joint environment programmes with communities, schools and other institutions

3. Recognize, award and communicate environmental achievements of individuals-especially studetns and communities

DESIRED RESULTS

Short term

* Joint project with a school promoting the environment

* A Competition (i.e.art, photo, writing, etc.) promoting the environemt.

Long term

* Sponsorship for a long-term project such as environmental "road shows"

* Award scheme established/extended

UNEP: CHANGE AND CHALLENGE

The United Nations Environment Programme (UNEP) came into being in 1972 after the Stockholm Conference. Its purpose was to raise environmental awareness and action at all levels of society world-wide.

Twenty years after its inception, UNEP's role, as perceived by those attending the 1992 United Nations Conference on Environment, and Development (UNCED) in Rio de Janeiro, Brazil,was ripe for change. Out of the meeting came an ambitious plan of action -Agenda 21. is document, which acknowledged a whole new direction in environmental thinking was endorsed by world leaders.The emphasis was on sustainable development, highlighting the link between environment Agenda 21 reinforced UNEP's catalytic and coordinating role and assigned it responsibilities.

UNEP has reassessed its role and reoriented its work to take into account the development perspective, socio-economic dimensions of natural resource use and the role of major groups in society. The organization's priority is to ensure its effectiveness and responsiveness in providing a sound basis for policy making.

UNEP has adopted a mission statement to reflect its new direction. The mission statement describes what UNEP does, how it does it and why. In essence, UNEP is there to provide leadership and encourage partnership in caring for the environment by inspiring, informing and enabling nations and peoples to improve their quality of life without compromising that of future generations.

UNEP's broadly defined strategy is neither sectoral not structural and each activity area is underpinned by the interdepndence of the application of sound science, the mobilization of social consensus and the development of effective public policy. There will be a focus on; achieving results, being responsive, nurturing partnership, regional delivery and the integration of environment and development.

The focus today is on achieving results rather than on accomplishing tasks. The priority is on the best use of our resources towards getting things done, whether it be reducing pollution, promoting the sound use of natural resources or integrating environmental considerations in economic activities.

Being responsive means heeding the needs of governments and stake hodlers for a clean environment, natural resource security and sustainable development. Partnerships will be nurtured, not only within the United Nations sytem but also with scientists, industry and non-governmental organizations. As trustee for the environment, UNEP will play a distinctive and strategic role in the Global Environment Facility.

Agenda 21 also recognized that within the framework for global action. UNEP should enhance its capability at the regional level. Regional delivery and programme integration are the two most crucial pillars of UNEPs current strategy. This will lead to more timely and accountable programme design and delivery, greater cost effectiveness and a more realistic assessment of needs.

Cluster areas have been identified to assist in the push towards more effective results and programme delivery.

* International Consensus Building - UNEP has already demonstrated that it is good 'broker' as far as regional and international agreements are concerned. A number of conventions have been developed, signed and ratified under UNEP's auspices and it continues to manage several of their secretariats. As natural resources become scarce due to popuation growth, consumption and increased economic activities, the need to negotiate better management of those resources in a holistic way becomes ever more pressing. UNEP's role will be to facilitate and assist countries in this regard.

* National Environmental Management Support - Capacity building is much more than the provision of training or equipment, it involves everything from the design of laws and institutions to the mobilization of funds and the education of a wider audience. UNEP's ability to convene meetings world-wide and its access to governments, other organizations, scientific institutions and technical expertise will be harnessed more effectively.

* Environmental Assessment, Information for Decision-making and Disaster Prevention, Preparedness and Response -UNEP has the capacity to compile, analyse and disseminate timely information in usable terms, whether it be in reasonse to an environmental emergency or for the long-term assessment of the use of natural resources and their degradation. Requests may be very specific, sectoral or geographical in nature or they could be about general public awareness. UNEP realizes that environmental management if it is accurate, accessible and relevant. Core -Policy development, internal information..public and technical information, communication, awareness building, out reach, resource information resource mobilization and conference services support all the programmes of UNEP.

UNEP has its headquarters in Nairobi, Kenya and is led by Executive Director and governed by a council comprising members of 58 governments. It is represented around the world by six regional and six outlying offices.

Source: Strategies for Environmental Citizenship UNEP, Courtsy: UNEP.